Vicente Aleixandre's Stream
of Lyric Consciousness

Vicente Aleixandre's Stream of Lyric Consciousness

Daniel Murphy

Lewisburg
Bucknell University Press
London: Associated University Presses

Associated University Presses
440 Forsgate Drive
Cranbury, NJ 08512

Associated University Presses
16 Barter Street
London WC1A 2AH, England

Associated University Presses
P.O. Box 338, Port Credit
Mississuaga, Ontario
Canada L5G 4L8

The paper used in this publication meets the requirements of the American National Standard for Permanence of Paper for Printed Library Materials Z39.48–1984.

Library of Congress Cataloging-in-Publication Data

Murphy, Daniel, 1949–
    Vicente Aleixandre's stream of lyric consciousness / Daniel Murphy.
        p.   cm.
    ISBN 0-8387-5464-3 (alk. paper)
    1. Aleixandre, Vicente, 1898– destruccíon o el amor.   2. Aleixandre, Vicente, 1898—Criticism and interpretation.   3. Poetics.

PQ6601.L26 D436 2001
861'.62—dc21   00-034281

A ti

Contents

Preface

Vicente Aleixandre and His Contemporaries: An Overview

At the time Vicente Aleixandre (1898–1984) was awarded the Nobel Prize for Literature in the fall of 1977, his poetry was so little known outside of Spain that commentators in American journals were vexed. *Saturday Review* (10 December 1977) carried a thirteen-line squib that began, "The Nobel people have again outdone themselves in the matter of obscurity." Although from a Hispanist's perspective such ignorance may be deplorable, it really should not have surprised us, because those who do not read Spanish had been offered scant opportunity to acquaint themselves with Aleixandre's work, despite the esteem he had long merited in his own country. Until one year prior to the prize award, he was represented in the United States by a few scattered translations of individual poems, mostly in the little magazines. In 1976–77, with remarkable prescience, two bilingual volumes of his poetry were published, and nine poems appeared in Hardie St. Martin's *Roots and Wings* (New York: Harper & Row, 1976), a bilingual anthology of modern Spanish poetry. Yet the three 1976–77 books provided English-speaking readers with a total of only forty-two poems from Aleixandre's immense production—duplications taken into account. It was a beginning that was later to be supplemented, though insufficiently, the Nobel having provided the impetus. In his anthology's introduction, St. Martin, writing of Aleixandre's generation, claimed, "There probably have never been in recent times so many great and distinguished poets living and working in the same place, at the same time, each one different from the others, as there were in Spain in the 20s" (7). It is easy to agree with him; Aleixandre was a worthy recipient of the Nobel Prize, whether one views the award entirely as a response to his work, or partially as recognition of his poetic group, the Generation of 1927, or even as due in some measure to his extraordinary and continuing influence as poetic genius and guiding friend among the poets who followed him. José Luis Cano's *Homenaje a Vicente Aleixandre* (Madrid: Insula 1968) contains poems

9

by eighty Spanish poets who in the proffered verses take the master
himself and his work as poetic subject. The previous recipient of the
Nobel in Spain (1956) had been Juan Ramón Jiménez, who had
played that same role for Aleixandre's own generation. J. M. Cohen,
who visited and spoke with the poet in the last weeks of his life, tells
us that "Aleixandre saw himself less as an individual creator than as
a link in the poetic chain of evolutionary creation. Hence his stimu-
lation of the young poets who were to follow him, not as a master but
merely as a precursor. The chain must not be broken: that was the
purpose of his endeavour" (*Linden Lane Magazine,* 4:1, January/March
1985, 4). Daniel Murphy, in the chapters that follow this preface, has
new and fascinating things to tell us about the "chain of poetry" in
Aleixandre's work.

The Generation of '27 includes an unusually large number of
excellent poets. Centered in Madrid (though not native to it), of
similar ages, and moreover, personal friends each with the others,
they form an exceedingly impressive group, and their collective production is one of the enduring glories of Spanish literature. They
may reasonably be considered a generation, despite some recent
scholarly objections to the term and despite the stunning originality
of each major figure. All responded to the poetic winds that blew
throughout the Western world in those times, decades of the many
isms of the vanguard of art: futurism, ultraism, creationism, cubism,
surrealism, and the others—all of which, of course, were proposing
a new realism, revelations of deeper realities, beyond the surface of
the bourgeois ones. The writers of this group, however, unlike those
of so many of these movements, were not propagandists and issued
no manifestos. The nearest thing to a statement outside their poetry
was the celebration and reevaluation they sponsored in 1927 (and
thus their name) on the occasion of the tercentenary of the great
baroque Spanish poet Luis de Góngora, with whose densely metaphorical poetry they obviously felt an affinity.

In 1925, José Ortega y Gasset published his *La deshumanización del
arte.* (Aleixandre had begun writing the poems of his first book the
previous year.) This term, "dehumanization," in many ways unfortunate and often misunderstood, nevertheless is a good springboard
for some generalizations about the poetry of the group to which
Aleixandre belongs. In consonance with Ortega's account of dehumanization, this poetry tends not to portray social or historical realities and rarely chronicles everyday social experience. It would not
be fruitful to look here for knowledge about Spain in the 1920s and
1930s. Except for the language in which they write, Jorge Guillén,

Pedro Salinas, the Aleixandre of those decades, would hardly be recognizable as Spaniards in their work. Although they often wrote poetry about common things, even about modern mechanical inventions, the reality that interests them is behind or beneath the surface. They see the world with the poet's eyes—those of the very special individual, not as you or I would see it—and they make us sense and appreciate the world in new ways. This other reality is the major theme of Salinas, as expressed in his "Mirar lo invisible" [To See the Invisible]: "Por un mundo sospechado / concreto y virgen detrás, / por lo que no puedo ver / llevo los ojos abiertos" [For what I cannot see, for a suspected concrete and virgin world on the other side, I keep my eyes always open]. (Translations are my own.) He therefore can see in a homely light bulb a crystal castle in which is imprisoned the poet's muse, a luminescent muse whose release is negotiated by flipping a switch. Daniel Murphy, in his second chapter, studies some poems of Salinas in great detail as a prelude to his application of similar approaches to the much more difficult poetry of Aleixandre. Both Salinas and Guillén are great vivifiers of reality, a lyric operation that these poets often carry out by concretizing the abstract: Salinas writes, "Me estoy labrando tu sombra / La tengo ya sin los labios" [I'm carving out your shadow, I've already removed your lips], while Guillén gives us lines like "El día plenario profundamente se agolpa / Sin resquicios" [The whole day rushes together in depth, leaving no cracks] or, speaking of an equestrian statue, "Permanece el trote aquí" [The trot stays here]. Federico García Lorca achieves this same life-giving effect with the animation not so much of abstractions as of the natural world: "Cuando las estrellas clavan / rejones al agua gris" [When the stars plunge spears into the gray water] or "una corta brisa ecuestre / salta los montes" [a light equestrian breeze leaps over the hills].

Two related matters, which will have been noted in the previous examples, are the importance of metaphor for all of these poets and the equal importance for the reader of visualizing those metaphors. Indeed, without accurate visualization, these poems, or parts of them, are often hermetic. In Lorca's famous elegy on the death of the bullfighter Sánchez Mejías we find a seemingly simple line, "El otoño vendrá con . . . / uva de niebla" [Autumn will come with grape of mist]. But what, fall weather aside, is a "grape of mist," or even a "misty grape"? Only our visual experience of seeing the waxy surface of a ripe grape will tell us. Thinking and interpreting will not help. Lorca's critics have often been deceived by those methods. In another poem of his we find "Por los ojos de la monja / galopan dos caballistas" [Two horsemen gallop across the nun's eyes]. Again, only correct visualization will tell us that only one horseman goes by, but is reflected in two eyes.

The visual nature of the metaphor is equally important for comprehending Aleixandre's poetry, as the following line from *La destrucción o el amor* suggests: "Soy el caballo que enciende su crin contra el pelado / viento" [I am the horse that sets fire to its mane against the bald wind]. The first thing we must do, of course, is visualize the horse's mane flying in the wind, taking on flame shapes, but many other things are happening simultaneously in this densely metaphorical poetic world. The invisible wind is made hard and smooth—something against which one might strike a match. That is, after all, the basic image. The choice of the word "pelado" [bald], which paradoxically suggests "pelo" [hair], is also intentional. Then behind this metaphorical complexity is the common expression "caballo fogoso" [fiery steed], an everyday-language metaphor. The line well illustrates the density of metaphor, the importance of visualization, and the ways of looking at the world that Aleixandre and other members of the Generation of '27 share. Lorca, for example, uses very similar images: "La higuera frota su viento / con la lija de sus ramas" [The fig tree rubs the wind with the sandpaper of its branches]. In this case one is not to visualize but to hear, with the mind's ear, the sound of the wind in the tree, made vivid by the comparison with sandpaper. Of course, Lorca has also turned things around a bit, since he makes the tree the active agent, while in fact it is the wind that moves, causing the rasping sound of branches rubbing together. This auditory image gives the reader a new esthetic experience which is very different from hearing a real wind in the trees, but which nevertheless lets us sense that reality with new ears. The term "defamiliarization" fits these metaphors admirably. That is, the poet is heightening our sense of the world, as we have it from personal experience, by making the ordinary strange and therefore available to us once again with the freshness of the unknown. The above-described characteristics, which apply to Lorca, Aleixandre, and others of the group, come close to constituting that much repeated New Critical definition of a good poem as one that is a well-made verbal object that says something significant about a reality we all know but which the poem perceives uniquely.

An important aspect of much of the poetry of Aleixandre's generation, one also subject to the phenomenon of dehumanization as Ortega y Gasset understood it, is its emphasis on love, the major subject of Guillén, Salinas, and Aleixandre. While all three are great love poets, they treat this age-old theme of the lyric in a decidedly avant-garde manner. They often do so by expanding it or making it abstract, frequently expressing it as the poet's relationship to the world or even the universe. In Salinas, the beloved is reduced to essence; that is what Salinas was doing in the previously cited sculptor's image of "carving out his love's shadow." The focus of Salinas's poetic vision of his lover is her "dulce cuerpo pensado"—the "sweet idea of her body"—rather than the body itself, which had kept love carnal and superficial. Guillén, in contemplating the nude body of his beloved—a very real woman—sees that body as a sculptor might and glories in its "masa" or bulk, denying all other feminine attributes of beauty or promise. He sings instead "¡Oh absoluto presente!" Love in Guillén is primarily directed, indeed, to the world around him, and in his major work, *Cántico* [Hymn of Praise], the world-as-creation takes God's place. While the title of "Más allá," the first poem of this book, may seem to mean "The Beyond" or "Afterlife," it refers instead to the immediate world that not only surrounds the poet but, in doing so, makes him its center. In another poem, Guillén says of the immediate paradise that he loves so well, "¡con cuerpo la gloria!" [glory, but with the body!]. This tendency to see the natural world as God and to find eternity and love as related concepts in it naturally presupposes that the Christian God of tradition is not a concern of these poets. Nonetheless, Guillén and Salinas glowingly express their wonder at the glory of the world, of a reality imbued with spiritual values. Only Lorca, in his Elegy, overtly denies the Christian afterlife and claims that art is its only substitute.

In his poetry of the 1930s, Aleixandre, like Guillén or Salinas, dehumanizes the beloved by way of a remarkably intense metaphorical process. Aleixandre typically metamorphoses his lover by converting her into a landscape, an erotically charged landscape, often of cosmic proportions. In one poem the lover is transformed into a burning star and in another into a volcano of searing lava into which the poetic narrator wishes to throw himself in order to become one with her. As these examples may suggest, Aleixandre conceives of love as a fusing force whereby lover and beloved become one and the same. This subject of the fusing power of love was to be the defining theme of Aleixandre's poetry, not only in these early decades, but also throughout his work. Carlos Bousoño, to date Aleixandre's major critic, classifies his work as erotic pantheism, and calls him a totalizing poet. By the time Aleixandre wrote *La destrucción o el amor* [Destruction or Love], published in 1935 and the subject of Daniel Murphy's book, the theme of amorous fusion had become dominant and inseparable from his technique and his metaphoric system. The title of this collection, Aleixandre's greatest pre-Civil War volume, is

itself an arresting emblem of that theme. The positive sense of
Aleixandre's death-through-love is frequently expressed as the ecstatic melding of the universe, whose elements—be they animal,
vegetable, or mineral—are metaphorical vehicles for the essential,
amorous human being. That is, the stone, the cobra, the beetle, the
tiger that through predation fuses with the gazelle, all these inhabitants of Aleixandre's lyric universe are expressive of amorous communion, of the human being's innate drive to fuse in love with another person. On the other hand, the barrier to love lies in the
overly rational or civilized side of human make-up. This, a sort of
artificially instilled conscience, impells the human being to reject
love, thus causing a vital segregation in which the individual unhappily remains divorced from instinctual essence, that is, the amorous
cosmos. These few examples may have served to intimate that the
thematic thrust of La destrucción o el amor is highly positive. Indeed,
Aleixandre not only sees love here as a happy annihilation of the self
and as a recuperation of one's cosmic essence, but he also views love
as an eminently achievable, rather than elusive, human goal. The loss
of love—and thus the human being's separation from his or her originary cosmic essence—is the subject of Sombra del paraíso [Shadow of
Paradise]. Here, in a poem entitled "El fuego" [Fire], Aleixandre rue-
fully exclaims, "¡Humano: nunca nazcas!" [Mankind, be not born!].

   In La destrucción o el amor, Aleixandre's particular conception of
love as cosmic fusion results in some very difficult poetry, a poetry
whose dehumanized nature stems from the fact that metaphor tends
to overgrow and thus obfuscate the human being, the primary referent and main concern of this poetry. Following the lead of the
semantically complex title—where the ambiguous "or" is simultaneously conjunctive and disjunctive—the poems are filled with fused
opposites wherein apparently disparate anthropomorphic images are
juxtaposed and metaphorically combined. The sea is amalgamated
with the earth and the jungle, the air with the water, up becomes
down, fish are hybridized with birds, stars with eyes, beasts of prey
with their victims, and of course, love is synonymous with death and
death with birth. We recognize that the lyric fusion of love/death is
not exclusive to Aleixandre. Saint John of the Cross, John Donne,
Richard Wagner, Walt Whitman, and many other creative artists pre-
ceded Aleixandre in this conception of love. What is quite new—and
a further impediment to the accessibility of the poems contained in
La destrucción o el amor—is Aleixandre's particular treatment of the
amorous death conceit. His elaboration of the theme is decisively
surrealistic and imbues the poems with an irrational and random-
appearing character that produces extraordinarily strong feelings in

us. One example, from "A la muerta" [To the Dead Girl] will suffice: "Vienes y vas ligero como el mar, / cuerpo nunca dichoso, / sombra feliz que escapas como el aire / que sostiene a los pájaros casi entero de pluma" [You come and go swift like the sea, never blessed body, happy shadow who escapes like the air that holding birds aloft is almost entirely of feathers]. Daniel Murphy's study of the surrealist dimension of Aleixandre's verse goes far toward the clarification of the processes by which theme and technique become one in these poems.

Literary generations (the very term has recently become suspect), like human generations, run their course and come to an end. The Generation of 1927 in Spain was abruptly interrupted by the Civil War, and when poetry again found its voice, the needs of art were perceived as different ones. As always, there was a rejection of what came before and a setting out in new directions with new intentions and different views about the nature of poetry. Gabriel Celaya claimed that poetry was not an end in itself, but an instrument for transforming the world. José Hierro believed that if by chance any poem of his should be read in a hundred years, it would not be for its poetic worth but for its documentary value. Victoriano Crémer said that there was no point in deceiving ourselves, that poetry was a strange cult supported by people who are of very little use in life. Blas de Otero dedicated a book "To the great majority," as a putdown, at least in part, of Juan Ramón Jiménez, who had earlier in the century dedicated a collection "To the minority, always." The seventeenth-century Góngora, idol of Aleixandre's generation, had similarly said that it was an honor to be unintelligible to the ignorant. Generation of '27 poetry does have a smaller potential audience, but only because it tends to be difficult, not because the poets themselves ever claimed to address only a minority.

In an era when a major poet, Blas de Otero, tries to write verse that can walk the streets, shake hands, and spit, the poetic values of an Aleixandre will have to bear adjustment; social values change. Poetry now becomes all the things it was not in the 1920s and 1930s: engagée, historical, social, circumstantial, actively anti-esthetic, unpolished, casual, easy, addressed to the common man in everyday language in an expression of solidarity with him, and intended to lead to social action. The major theme is injustice, and although the God of Christian theology returns, he is roundly denounced for his complicity in this injustice. Confronting these two generations in this way is not to praise one and condemn the other, but to recognize that different circumstances and the different winds that blow produce different art. Readers and critics of poetry are at this very moment of writing confronting one of those swerves, one that is diminishing the perceived value of poetry as a genre, presumably because it lends itself less well (or is thought to do so) to the currently favored socially instrumental role of criticism and literary texts.

Aleixandre alone among the major poets of his group remained in Spain after the Civil War, where he became the preeminent mentor of younger poets of note, much loved by them as a man and honored as a poet. The many volumes of poetry he published after *Sombra del paraíso* in 1944, the last being in 1974, make a fascinating comparative study with his earlier work. All of the remaining figures of his group continued, outside Spain, to produce fine work, only failing when they were tempted to write political poetry for which their talents or vision were not well suited. I think, however, that of those who lived on for many years, none was able to reconcile change with constancy quite so well as Aleixandre. He knew how to evolve while remaining true to his poetic vision.

Three things never disappear from Aleixandre's work: love, solidarity, and quality, but love and solidarity evolve to include man and everyday circumstantial life in ways not too different from those of other early postwar poets, despite his lack of overt gestures toward social action. This great and convincing change in his work is most often commented on in relation to the 1954 book, *Historia del corazón,* in which time and man become the central concerns, just as the cosmic force of love had been dominant before. *Story of the Heart* is a kind of poetic spiritual biography in terms of the ages of man. It uses everyday language with a realistic technique and projects both utter simplicity and deepest emotion. The poet has now become a man, not a unique visionary—"a poet of the inner eye," as J. M. Cohen called him (5)—set apart from others. Whether Aleixandre's earlier or later poetry (and he certainly continued to evolve beyond the postwar titles already mentioned) is at any given time more highly valued will, of course, depend not on him or on his art, but on the changes that the changing world imposes on his readers.

The bibliography on Vicente Aleixandre's works is by now immense, but most readers would probably name Carlos Bousoño's *La poesía de Vicente Aleixandre* (Madrid: Insula, 1950), as the most important global study of the poet. It continues, fifty years later, to be fundamental to anyone's first attempt at understanding this poet's very special world. The current book by Daniel Murphy might possibly be seen as the second great breakthrough into our understanding of this poetry. His analysis is the most extensive study to date of any single book by the poet. It studies the surrealist dimension of the poetry to a depth not previously attempted. Indeed, I suspect that Murphy opens up the whole subject of surrealism in Spanish poetry in ways that will illuminate that aspect of the work of a number of other poets. The subject has always been contested in Spain both by poets—including Aleixandre—and by critics. Along with surrealism, Murphy's work also characterizes in some detail the role of Freud, the movement's progenitor, in this poetry. And finally, the book outlines the intertextual dimension of Aleixandre's poems—a dimension previously dealt with only glancingly—in as thorough and persuasive a manner as one could wish. The findings in this area are perhaps the most revelatory of all, providing us with new insights into the literary history of Spain. At last we have an in-depth study that documents the extraordinary role of Gustavo Adolfo Bécquer in twentieth-century Spanish poetry, a role often referred to but seldom looked at closely. Above and beyond all of those substantive virtues, Murphy's book uses and warmly personalizes a range of theoretical approaches that have not often been applied to these texts, and he has done this with originality and without obfuscation. The utility of his method will be apparent to any reader. And Murphy expresses all of this in that rarest of things in critical studies, a lively personal style that truly enhances the discussion. In short, I suspect that *La destrucción o el amor* and its author will be forever changed in readers' minds, just as Carlos Bousoño once caused us to read Aleixandre's poetry differently and with greater pleasure and comprehension.

H. L. Boudreau
University of Massachusetts—Amherst

Introduction

THE FOCAL BOOK OF THE PRESENT STUDY, VICENTE ALEIXANDRE'S *La destrucción o el amor* [Destruction or Love], was published in 1935, having already been awarded the prestigious Premio Nacional de Literatura in 1933. *La destrucción o el amor,* Aleixandre's finest surrealist book, is, with Federico García Lorca's *Poeta en Nueva York,* Luis Cernudas's *Un río, un amor,* and Rafael Alberti's *Sobre los ángeles,* one of the most admired examples of surrealist poetry produced by Spain's gifted Generation of 1927. There is one incontrovertible fact about *La destrucción o el amor:* like surrealist texts in general, it is incomprehensible in the light of quotidian logic, it is—in line with André Breton's goal of what the surrealist poem should be—a "débâcle de l'intellect."[1] Following are three reader reactions that deftly encapsulate the shocking effects created by Aleixandre's surrealist poetry. Dámaso Alonso, in reference to *Espadas como labios,* the Aleixandrean book immediately preceding *La destrucción o el amor,* succinctly states that "Esos poemas no tienen—literalmente—sentido común, porque tienen sólo sentido poético" [Those poems literally defy common sense because they only make poetic sense]. For his part, Luis Cernuda emphasizes that the shock of the new produced by Aleixandre's surrealism appears to make the poet the founder of a completely original form of poetry: "Tiene el lenguaje de Aleixandre, además de un vigor singular, una también espontaneidad, siendo difícil pensar al leerle que el lenguaje con que nos habla sea el mismo, filtrado por siglos, de tantos poetas anteriores. El arcaísmo preciosista de Lorca, consciente o inconsciente, no aparece aquí, ni las reminiscencias de nuestro verso clásico, nada raras en los poetas de esta generación. Su lenguaje parece brotar, instintivo y casi a tientas, creando una tradición más que continuándola" [Besides possessing a unique vigor, the language of Aleixandre also has an appreciable spontaneity, and it is difficult to believe that the language with which he speaks to us is the same language, filtered through the centuries, of so many earlier poets. The elaborately wrought archaism of Lorca, whether conscious or not, does not appear in Aleixandre, nor do we find echoes of our classic verse, which are so common among the poets of his generation. His language seems to issue forth instinctively and even in a random manner, thus creating rather than carrying on a tradition]. Finally, years later, the Spanish poet and critic Luis Antonio de Villena pointedly reiterates the baffling feeling common among readers of Aleixandre's surrealist works: "cuando el lector termina la lectura de uno de estos poemas (de raíz subconsciente)—aunque ha sido arrastrado por el fluir extraño de las imágenes a lo largo de todo el proceso—siente que no sabe qué es aquello"[2] [When the reader finishes reading one of those poems (of subconscious origin)—and although he has been swept along by the strange flow of those images throughout the entire process—he feels that he does not exactly know what it was that he experienced].

Critical approaches to Aleixandre's surrealism have tended to face the textual penumbra in one of two ways. The first, from a formalist point of view, an approach that emphasizes Aleixandre's work, including his more accessible postwar poetry, as a largely autonomous system. Exemplary of this trend is Carlos Bousoño, whose pioneering *La poesía de Vicente Aleixandre: Imagen, estilo y mundo poético* of 1950 is the first and still the most complete treatment of the poet's work. Indeed, Bousoño's seminal study becomes the model for almost all following aesthetic analyses. Among other things, the inclusive scope of Bousoño's analysis—it takes into account all Aleixandre books written to that date—is repeated throughout many subsequent studies, which in one way or another approach Aleixandre's extensive lyric output as a trajectory.[3] The second theoretical trend is the psychoanalytic approach, which is exemplified in Paul Ilie's *The Surrealist Mode in Spanish Literature* (1968), or Kessel Schwartz's *Vicente Aleixandre* (1970). This nonaesthetic tack seems a most logical response to Aleixandre's surrealism which, like that of the French school, has roots in Freudian theory and is decidedly automatic in style.[4] However, the results of the psychoanalytic approach, in contrast to those produced by aesthetic studies of Aleixandre, tend to be unilluminating with respect to the specifically poetic nature of Aleixandre's surrealist works. In general, more attention is given to illustrating Freudian theory than to the literary aspect of the poems per se, an emphasis that often leads to textually unfounded conclusions.[5]

Like Bousoño's study, the present analysis is chiefly concerned with the aesthetic aspects of Aleixandre's work. But the theoretical orientation of this analysis comes by way of intertextual approaches to poetry, such as those put forth by Alastair Fowler, Harold Bloom, and Michael Riffaterre. Theoretical debt is also owed to Gérard Genette for his account of narrative structure, and to the geneticist Richard Dawkins for his theory of "memes." The work of Dawkins as well as that of Bloom and Riffaterre has been most useful toward defining the character and scope of intertextuality and serves as the basis for the prolegomena to the present study, which will be laid out in the first two chapters. The specific mission of this analysis is to explore the poetic logic that informs Aleixandre's surrealism. The poetic logic behind the markedly irrational and passionate book of love poems that is *La destrucción o el amor* is a logic based on the poet's recreative and highly original recombination and interpretation of extant materials. The materials that go into Aleixandre's textual amalgam come from a wide variety of sources and are to be found both in general and literary culture. The task of identifying the intertextual materials germane to Aleixandre's poetry is organized on the basis of two theoretical clusters. The first cluster is formed by chapters 2–5, which take as their point of departure the discursive structure of poetry. The discursive structure is a communal intertext of conventional means of poetic presentation and includes the inscribed point of view from which a poem is delivered and the generic type on which it is modeled. Chapter 2 is specifically dedicated to laying out a working typology of discursive structure and serves as the basis for the analysis of *La destrucción o el amor* carried out in chapters 3, 4 and 5. Chapters 6 and 7 focus on Aleixandre's relation to model poets, most especially Fray Luis de León and Gustavo Adolfo Bécquer but also Rubén Darío. Chapter 1 reviews the most widely held perception of Aleixandre's surrealism and discusses intertextual theory, specifically how the insights of intertextual theoreticians can further broaden our understanding of the poet's surrealism.

Vicente Aleixandre's Stream of Lyric Consciousness

1
An Intertextual Tack

> Reading . . . depends upon fundamental
> previsions of what is being read, so
> that in order to read a poem you
> necessarily start with an idea of what a
> poem is, or can be.
> —Harold Bloom, *Agon*

THE POET AND CRITIC CARLOS BOUSOÑO HAS PLAYED THE PIVOTAL role in Aleixandre criticism for nearly fifty years, since the publication of *La poesía de Vicente Aleixandre: Imagen, estilo y mundo poético* (1950). In this ground-breaking study, the critic puts forth a theoretical framework for approaching poetry and discerns the salient features of Aleixandre's often daunting texts. Bousoño's theory, which he further elaborates in *Teoría de la expresión poética,* derives from two assumptions about modern poetry. For Bousoño, the modern lyric— and especially Aleixandre's—stands as the culmination of two inter-related phenomena: irrationalism and individualism.[1] The critic explains individualism, a trend that he observes has intensified since Romanticism, as resulting from the poet's desire, and aesthetic ne-cessity, to differentiate himself from others. This will to be distinct manifests itself in the uniqueness of a modern poet's world, a world which is born of the poet's particular synthesizing of reality via his own subjective point of view. Talent aside, it follows that the more origi-nal a poet's conception of reality, the more unique his lyrical universe will be. In this, irrationalism is especially efficient for producing in-dividual and unique poetry since this technique not only affords a private perception of the world synthesized in the poet's imagina-tion but renders an image of it filtered through his subconscious as well. Bousoño, however, is careful not to label Aleixandre's irrational-ist poetry "automatic writing" since for him, as indeed for the poet himself, this method, originally propagated by André Breton, is syn-onymous with an erasure of aesthetic control and is characterized by arbitrariness rather than by artistic intention.[2]

Although he gives significantly more attention to *Sombra del paraíso*

25

than to *La destrucción o el amor* in his 1950 study, Bousoño nonetheless manages to show system, coherence, and structure in *La destrucción o el amor*. For one, the critic identifies the thematic binaries essential to comprehending the unity of the book and describes the rhythmic and phonetic effects created by Aleixandre's "versículos." In addition, Bousoño elaborates a thorough account of the poet's syntactic peculiarities and alerts the reader to some linguistic and poetic sources.[3] The showpiece and most influential aspect of Bousoño's theory lies in his account of the irrational metaphor, which he dubs "visión." Such a metaphor is an analogy whose elements are either implausible or contradictory as a figurative description of reality—which is the feature that distinguishes this figure from the traditional metaphor. The vision's divorce from quotidian logic supplies the formal evidence that such a metaphor is derived privately, within the imagination or affect of the poet. The critic underlines, however, that although the visionary poem is private in origin, it is neither inaccessible nor arbitrary. This may be witnessed in the emotional response that the visionary text produces in the reader. In the latter, such a text recreates the "emoción poética," the poetic emotion that originally generated the poem, including, most notably, its incongruous visions or metaphors. In Bousoño's assertion that the vision—and thereby the poem—is an autonomous product of the poet's imagination lies the strength—and the limitations—of his theory. His insistence that the text and its meaning are independent of the poet produces a close text-based reading of Aleixandre, a reading which has made the single most significant contribution toward the critical understanding of Aleixandre's poetic world. The strength, indeed the great utility of Bousoño's study, is witnessed by the fact that for nearly five decades the vast majority of Aleixandre studies, including the present one, have cited the critic's many insights. Like Dámaso Alonso's study of Góngora, Carlos Bousoño's analysis of Aleixandre is an analytical ground-breaker, a seminal work of criticism that marks out the way for following scholars of a great though obscure poet.

The limitations of Bousoño's study—and the limitations of formalist approaches in general—lie behind the otherwise insightful and productive notion that the poet's work constitutes an autonomous system. The result, which we need not belabor, is that Aleixandre's poetic originality and indeed the significance of his work is understood but only in part. The theoretical lacuna, the part missing in a theory like Bousoño's, is the tradition or greater context in which poetry is written and to which it makes reference. Because the traditional aspect of Aleixandre's poetry—most notably that of his most hermetic works—has largely gone unexplored, the poet is understood to be a sort of "poeta magus," but a rather lonely one, as Cernuda's assessment of Aleixandre as a creator of a new tradition might suggest. For his part, Aleixandre insists that truly revolutionary poetry is at the same time profoundly traditional: "en poesía, en algún momento, la línea revolucionaria, si de veras genuina, acaba mostrando ser, haber sido, la única línea tradicional" (*OC* 2:524) [at some point, the revolutionary path of poetry, if it is truly genuine, shows itself to be and to have been the single path of tradition]. What tradition and originality can be and what value they have toward comprehending a revolutionary poet like Aleixandre are questions that intertextual theories are instrumental in addressing.

The basic assumption endemic to intertextual perspectives of poetry is that originality is relative, that in order to create, the poet, or anyone for that matter, must imitate, no matter how devious that imitation might be. Harold Bloom, in referring to tradition in its general sense, insists on the inevitability of imitation: "You cannot write or teach or think or even read without imitation, and what you imitate is what another person has done, that person's writing or teaching or thinking or reading."[4] It follows, then, that in order to discern more fully either the significance or the originality of the individual poet, the reader must first recognize that poet's other, be that other a precursor poet or a rather broad conglomerate of less well-defined nonoriginal sources including the writer's language and culture. What the parameters of the intertextual other are or can be is a highly complex question. However, the theoretical labor of writers such as Harold Bloom, Richard Dawkins, and Michael Riffaterre provides a framework for addressing this question and for defining the present approach to Aleixandre's surrealist poetry.

The theoretical energies of Harold Bloom are invested in the exploration of genealogical intertexts, that is, in the relationship between ancestor poets and younger poets.[5] For Bloom, in such lyric genealogy lies the crux of poetic creation. The rule of his system is that one poet's verse is generated first and foremost as a reaction to the poetry of a "strong" forebear whose influence effectively forms the new poet. Bloom elaborates his concept of poetic genesis psychodynamically, as a family story protagonized by the individual writer, who both inevitably imitates his lyrical forebears and simultaneously struggles to overcome the strength of their personalities. The younger poet does so in much the same way as a child, in the process of establishing his or her own identity, might fight to erase the inherited and internalized parental personality. Like the child, the poet has to face and overcome the anxiety of influence of a father—or composite father figure, as the case may be. This is carried out by "introjecting" or internalizing the father, a process Bloom calls "apophrades," a term borrowed by the critic from psychoanalysis. The poetic analogue of apophrades is dubbed "misreading" by Bloom, who also employs "misinterpretation," "misprision," and "revision" synonymously. In the realm of poetry, misreading means that poetic influence does not consist of a more or less faithful reduplication of a model poet's verses and imagery, though this does not rule out that some ancestral verses may appear conspicuously. Rather, misreading entails the younger poet's interpretive rewriting of the ancestor, an effort to efface the elder's voice in order to establish his or her own strong lyric personality. In the light of misprision, Bloom insists that poems, "are necessarily about 'other poems'; a poem is a response to a poem, as a poet is a response to a poet, or a person to his parent."[6] Similarly, poems are loosely paraphrastic of their model—but, "however wildly speculative, they interpret a central text and hold a stance toward the precursor text, which is what constitutes their 'misprision' of that text."[7]

Whether Bloom's psychological model of the poet accurately describes how all poetry is created or not, his theory of the individual poet's stance toward particular ancestor poets is compelling both for its general poetic relevance and for its particular applicability to Aleixandre. Bloom's insistence that "sources" are the norm of poetry, its semantic core material, is an insight that refocuses the question of verse loans. Thus seen, even the humblest citation might well signal a transcendent relationship between poets and thus provide a specific and invaluable context for understanding a work's significance. By making influence the aesthetic norm of creation, Bloom greatly enhances its status, since in previous criticism influence had been largely viewed with anxiety. Loans—and the connoted debt—had often seemed to compromise the poetic solvency of the creative writer. Bloom's idea of poetry as a nonliteral imitation of other poetry is an incisive description of how one poem may formally and thematically mute rather than echo another. In this, he alerts the analyst to poetry's indirectness: what a poem appears to be alluding to—an object or a landscape, for example—may well be another poem. In summary, whether we believe that all poetry is actually the misreading of other particular ancestral verse or not, Bloom's theory serves as a graphic lesson on this type of intertextuality. What the critic makes clear is that the relationship between poets is not operant as reduplication, as unqualified imitation or echoing. Rather, a new poem is most likely a rather devious response, a cover-up, and a distortion of its source. Similarly, it is quite likely that the new poem may well contradict or in some way distort the ideological assumptions of the ancestral piece. Briefly, the new poem assimilates other poems and, in so doing, transforms their form and meaning.

In *La destrucción o el amor,* Aleixandre's clearest and most sustained response to his lyric ancestry is made to Fray Luis de León and Gustavo Adolfo Bécquer, who act as the poet's Mystic and Romantic alter egos.[8] Aleixandre's internalization of these forebears is often signaled via visible citation. As preliminary evidence of this relationship, a few examples will suffice. Fray Luis's "El aire se serena / y viste de hermosura y luz no usada"[9] [The air becomes serene and dresses in beauty and light unused], the opening verses of his well-known ode, "A Francisco Salinas," return paraphrastically in the most visible verses of *La destrucción o el amor.* The Luisinian quote is placed in the first two lines of Aleixandre's liminal poem, "La selva y el mar" [The Jungle and the Sea]: "Allá por las remotas / luces o aceros aún no usados"[10] [Beyond, along the distant lights or steels yet unused]. A noteworthy feature of this particular lyrical iteration is that the audibility of the ancestral voice is metrically enhanced, Aleixandre's opening lines reduplicating the seven/eleven syllable scheme of the Augustine's first two verses. Here, in most visible display, Aleixandre's paraphrase and metrical reduplication of the ancestor poem heralds his close poetic kinship to the Mystic forebear. Aleixandre's Luisinian ancestry is in fact signaled rather openly on several occasions. One such example is "A ti, viva" (*La destrucción* 149) [To You, Living Woman], where the Novalis epigraph—"Es tocar el cielo, poner el dedo sobre un cuerpo humano" [To place a finger on a human body is to touch Heaven]—advertises the text's structural metaphor, body/sky. While Aleixandre's opening verse—"Cuando contemplo tu cuerpo extendido" [When I contemplate your reclining body]—metaphorically follows the epigraph's lead, it also clearly recalls "Noche serena" [Serene Night], the Luisinian ode which begins, "Cuando contemplo el cielo / de innumerables luces adornado"[11] [When I contemplate the heavens adorned with innumerable lights].

"A ti, viva" not only invokes the presence of Fray Luis in Aleixandre, it also serves as a concrete example of the principle ancestral confluence of this poet and Bécquer in *La destrucción o el amor.* Whereas the ancestral presence in the first verse is that of Fray Luis, the title of this poem quotes Bécquer's Rima 11, which is openly paraphrased in the titles of three other texts in *La destrucción o el amor* ("Ven, ven tú," "Ven siempre, ven," and "No busques, no"). The three stanzas of Rima 11, it may be recalled, are in dialogue form, each consisting of the speech of one of three beauties. In order, the three are the passionate "morena," the tender and pallid blonde and the intangible woman of dream. In the last verse of each stanza, the poet, in his quest for love and beauty, replies in turn to the brunette, the blonde, and the disembodied: "'¿A mí me buscas?' 'No es a ti, no.'" ['Is it me who you seek?' 'No, it is not you']; "'¿A mí me llamas?' 'No; no es a ti.'" ['Is it me who you beckon?' 'No, it is not you']; "'soy incorpórea, soy intangible; / no puedo amarte.' '¡Oh, ven; ven tú!'"[12] ['I am formless, I am intangible; / I cannot love you.' 'Oh, come, do come!']. The confluence of Fray Luis and Bécquer in "A ti, viva" is complex and is determined by a previously established relationship between Aleixandre's lyric progenitors. This relationship lies immanent in the first verse itself. A kind of pun or poetic homophone, Aleixandre's "Cuando contemplo tu cuerpo extendido" not only refers to the first verse of "Noche serena" but, in so doing, slyly reiterates the Bécquer genealogy announced in the title. Obliquely cited here is Rima 8, whose anaphoric structure and figural development also echo the ancestral voice of "Noche serena." Consider the first verses of Rima 8's two octets, which repeat Luisinian syntax and circumstantial motifs: "Cuando miro el azul horizonte / perderse a lo lejos" [When I watch the azure horizon fading into the distance] and "Cuando miro de noche, en el fondo / oscuro del cielo"[13] [When at night I watch the dark depths of the heavens].

The point of all this is more than to carry out a source-hunt based on tracking down quotes and quotes of quotes. That it is possible to perceive that Aleixandre's poetry takes up and demonstrates an affinity with lyrical forebears is clear preliminary evidence that he is far from being a poet without a specific lyric genealogy. What is more, the triadic ancestral relationship seen in "A ti, viva," suggests Aleixandre's place in and consciousness of the preestablished Fray Luis-Bécquer tradition. Harold Bloom explains the dynamics of such a tradition in this way: "Tradition is perpetuated when a fresh author is simultaneously cognizant not only of his own struggle against the forms and presence of a precursor but is compelled also to a sense of the precursor's place in regard to what came before."[14] Citation, whether conspicuous or covert, may possibly be but the tip of the intertextual iceberg, as happens to be the case in Aleixandre's relation to Fray Luis and Bécquer.

Suffice it to say for now that these samples of Fray Luis and Bécquer citations act as clearly audible signals of Aleixandre's systematic misreading of his Mystic and Romantic forebears. The examples specifically indicate that a good deal of the poetic sense of Aleixandre's surrealism is to be found in reference to these family poets, poets in whom *La destrucción o el amor* has a substantial investment.

What precise thematic and formal ends this misreading serves is a question considered at length in chapters 6 and 7.

In order to more graphically define how ancestral internalization works in Aleixandre, consider *Historia del corazón* [Story of the Heart] (1945–53), whose initial composition was begun over a decade after that of *La destrucción o el amor* (1932–33). In *Historia del corazón*, Aleixandre's ancestral misprision is typically layered or palimpsestic, an intertextual complexity owed to a double and simultaneous internalization of ancestors. First, Aleixandre responds to a particular ancestor who, as in *La destrucción o el amor*, is Bécquer. Second—and this is a possibility not taken up by Bloom—the poet becomes his own ancestor, a former poetic self whom he reinterprets in retrospect. Thus, if misreading—as Bloom asserts—is a family affair, it could well be said, repeating Wordsworth, that "The Child is father of the Man."[15] In "El niño y el hombre" [The Child and the Man] *(Historia del corazón)* Aleixandre expresses this very idea, "El niño comprende al hombre que va a ser" (*OC* 1:729) [The child contains the man that he is going to be]. This type of intertextual misprision—in which the poet makes direct response to his former lyric self—is carried out in the first section of *Historia del corazón*. This section, which is entitled "Como el vilano" [Like the Airborne Seed], acts as a poetic prelude to the entire book. Here, Aleixandre recalls and reevaluates *La destrucción o el amor* as a moment in his poetic history. More specifically, the liminal "Como el vilano" section constitutes a poetic examination of conscience wherein the poet darkly contemplates a personal sense of solitude and the irrecoverableness of the Edenic love sung in *La destrucción o el amor*. It is from this vantage that *Historia del corazón* departs, after closing with the brief transitional poem, "Sombra final" [Final Shadow]. At this juncture, Aleixandre thematically reorients his poetry via a series of "miradas," or gazes, whose lyric focus is now the present. It is within this chronological perspective that the poet finds consolation and hope, and a role for his poetry, which is now chiefly concerned with human solidarity rather than with love. Whereas in other books Aleixandre regarded art and his own poetry as but a remnant of life, as a "naturaleza muerta," or still life, inferior to living itself, poetry is now thematized as having a vital function. Indeed, Aleixandre's poetry becomes a sort of Unamunian "intrahistoria," a lyric story of timeless human aspirations. Thus, in "El poeta canta por todos" [The Poet Sings for Everyone]—a metapoem from "La mirada extendida" [The Extended Gaze], the second section of the book—Aleixandre portrays his poetry as a hymn through which the eternal human spirit sings itself:

Como una montaña sube. Es la senda de los que marchan.
Y asciende hasta el pico claro. Y el sol se abre sobre las frentes.
Y en la cumbre, con su grandeza, están todos ya cantando.
Y es tu voz la que les expresa. Tu voz colectiva y alzada.
Y un cielo de poderío, completamente existente,
hace ahora con majestad el eco entero del hombre.

(*OC* 1:718)

[It rises like a mountain. It is the path of those who march along.
And it ascends to the clear peak. And the sun shines upon their brows.
At the top, in their grandeur, all are now singing.
And it is your voice that expresses them. Your collective and elevated
    voice.
And a mighty heaven, completely existent,
Now majestically sounds the full echo of man.]

Consider, in greater detail, how the "Como el vilano" section sets the stage for *Historia del corazón*. Its seven poems—"Como el vilano" [Like the Airborne Seed], "Mano entregada" [Surrendered Hand], "La frontera" [The Border], "Otra no amo" [I Do Not Love Another], "Después del amor" [After Love], "Nombre" [Name], and "Coronación del amor" [Coronation of Love]—are derived as an interpretation of, and hold a stance toward, *La destrucción o el amor*. They also respond anew to Bécquer, who, also transumed therein, again plays an important role in the thematic and structural sense of these Aleixandrean poems. Following are stanzas 1–3 of "Como el vilano," the first and titular poem of the section:

Hermoso es el reino del amor,
pero triste es también.
Porque el corazón del amante
triste es en las horas de la soledad,
cuando a su lado mira los ojos queridos
que inaccesibles se posan en las nubes ligeras.

Nació el amante para la dicha,
para la eterna propagación del amor,
que de su corazón se expande
para verterse sin término
en el puro corazón de la amada entregada.

Pero la realidad de la vida,
la solicitación de las diarias horas,
la misma nube lejana, los sueños, el corto vuelo
del juvenil corazón que él ama,

todo conspira contra la perduración sin
descanso de la llama imposible.

(*OC* 1:683)

[Beautiful is the realm of love,
But it is also sad.
Because the lover's heart is sad
In the hours of solitude,
When at his side he sees the beloved eyes
That inaccessibly repose among swift clouds.

The lover was born for bliss,
For the eternal propagation of love
That, expanding from his breast,
Endlessly spills over
Into the pure heart of the surrendering beloved.

But the reality of life,
The demands of time from day to day,
The distant cloud itself, the dreams, the brief flight
Of the youthful heart he loves,
All of this conspires against the inexhaustible
Perpetuation of the impossible flame.]

In these lines, Aleixandre reinterprets the ecstatic passion of love portrayed in *La destrucción o el amor*, the "dicha" for which the archetypal lover was born and destined. The earlier book consciously sings of love as a very positive, tangible, and attainable goal, as is stated in a poem of the same name, "La dicha" [Bliss]:

Canto el cielo feliz, el azul que despunta,
canto la dicha de amar dulces criaturas,
de amar a lo que nace bajo las piedras limpias,
agua, flor, hoja, sed, lámina, río, viento,
amorosa presencia de un día que sé existe.

(*La destrucción* 180)

[I sing the happy sky, the dawning azure,
I sing the bliss of loving sweet creatures,
Of loving that which is born under pure stones,
Water, flower, leaf, thirst, lamina, river, or wind,
The amorous presence of a day that I know exists.]

"Como el vilano" misreads its predecessor book by placing the latter's thematization of ecstatic and timeless love in a different chronological frame, one that now recognizes love's limits, specifically that love is fleeting and that solitude is inevitable. The poems of this section of *Historia del corazón* sing not "el día que existe" but rather recall that day, its happiness or "dicha." The realm of love is beautiful but also "triste," a sentiment virtually absent in *La destrucción o el amor,* a book that rejects all forms of idealized love, including love as a poetic "naturaleza muerta," converted into an artifact by the very poem that celebrates it.

The poems of "Como el vilano" chronicle the history of the "amante"—the archetypal lover and poetic protagonist of Aleixandre's works. The eternal lover is celebrated in the closing poem, "Coronación del amor," wherein Aleixandre qualifies amatory destruction, one of the nuclear conceits informing *La destrucción o el amor.* We read in "Después del amor" that, "Momentánea destrucción es el amor" [Love is but momentary destruction]. The misreading of the precursor text in *Historia del corazón* constitutes an understated interpretation, an effect coherent with the now much more muted and somber vision of love that the newer book portrays. The same change may be witnessed in the situational configuration of "Después del amor," whose base poetic scene is identical to that of many poems in *La destrucción o el amor.* The setting derives from a minimal anecdote, from the poet's contemplation of his lover after love-making:

Tendida tú aquí, en la penumbra del cuarto,
como el silencio que queda después del amor,
yo asciendo levemente desde el fondo de mi reposo
hasta tus bordes, tenues, apagados, que dulces existen.
Y con mi mano repaso las lindes delicadas de tu vivir retraído
y siento la musical, callada verdad de tu cuerpo,
que hace un instante, en desorden, como lumbre cantaba.
El reposo consiente a la masa que perdió por el amor su forma continua,
para despegar hacia arriba con la voraz irregularidad de la llama,
convertirse otra vez en el cuerpo veraz que en sus límites se rehace.

(*OC* 1:693)

[You lie here, in the darkness of the room,
Like the silence that remains after love.
I weightlessly ascend from the depths of my repose
To your dim and extinguished edge, which sweetly exists.
And with my hand I touch the delicate margin of your retracted life
And I sense the musical, but now faint, truth of your body that
But a moment ago chaotically sang like a flame.
Repose allows your form, which through love lost its usual mass,
Shooting upward in the voracious irregularity of fire,
To assume its true body, now reshaped within its borders.]

Love's destruction of limits, and the concurrent unity in love celebrated in the earlier work, is now represented as a fluttering moment which passes like a "vilano" in the air. The imminent loneliness
hovering about the poem is reflected in its setting, which is the
"penumbra del cuarto," a dark and limited space wherein the poet
construes his contemplation of the lover. This melancholy point of
departure stands in stark contrast to that of the poems of *La destrucción o el amor*, where solitude can be vanquished. This difference
is patent in "Ven siempre, ven" (*La destrucción* 134) [Come always,
come], a poem whose point of departure is also based on the poet's
contemplation of the lover. Here, "soledad" sylleptically generates
two antithetical series of images based on the structural metaphor
lovers/celestial orbs. In the first five strophes, which are introduced
by the anaphora, "No te acerques" [Do not come near], the poet rejects the light of loneliness, "La soledad que destella en el mundo
sin amor" [The solitude that shines in the loveless world]. In the remaining three, which are headed by the titular phrase, "Ven, ven . . ."
[Come, come . . .], the poet opts for the blazing "soledades" of
love. These "soledades"—the Petrarchan eyes-like-suns of the lovers—
collide and produce "imperiosas llamadas" [imperious flames], an
eternal amorous destruction uniting poet and beloved.[16]

Structurally and thematically, Aleixandre's interpretation or misprision of *La destrucción o el amor* in "Como el vilano" responds anew
to the Bécquerian model poem, Rima 11. This piece, as mentioned,
is arranged on an optative format in which the poet rejects ostensibly concrete lovers in favor of a disembodied "fantasma de niebla y
luz" [specter of mist and light] whom he summons with the words,
"¡Oh, ven; ven tú!" *La destrucción o el amor* rejects Bécquer's amorous
choice, electing instead the non-ideal, earth-bound "viva" as lover.
Aleixandre summons this carnal being with Bécquer's own words,
"Ven, ven tú," an apostrophe suggestive of one of the essential speech
acts of this book, the exhortation to take this same amorous, and
vital, option. The five opening poems of *Historia del corazón* all develop on the Bécquerian dichotomy of tangible versus intangible love,
and vacillate, like a "vilano," between the two poles of the opposition. However, in the context of Aleixandre's history of misreading
Bécquer, these pieces represent an ironic twist of theme, itself
brought about by the passage of time, by "la realidad de la vida"
mentioned in the first, and titular poem, "Como el vilano."

The amorous choice is still the "viva" sung in the earlier book.
However—and as the fourth poem, "Otra no amo," intimates—the
carnal "viva" has herself become, in the time elapsed between *La destrucción o el amor* and *Historia del corazón*, an ideal and thus intangible

"otra" similar in this to Bécquer's choice in Rima 11. The once carnal "ella" is now shadow, memory, or a mere echo, a "nombre" as the poem of the same name indicates. Her counterpart, the new "viva," who is portrayed in "Otra no amo," is eclipsed by the memory of her predecessor, the now disembodied but once tangible "otra." The poetic voice says of the present lover, "Desde mi cansancio de otro amor padecido / te miro, oh pura muchacha pálida que yo podría amar y no amo" (*OC* 1:690) [From the weariness of other amorous suffering I see you, oh pure, pale girl whom I could love but do not]. Aleixandre's dismissal of this pallid lover brings his interpretation of Bécquer full circle. In an ironic twist, he rejects the tangible presence that, in direct opposition to the forebear, he had so enthusiastically embraced in *La destrucción o el amor.* In this way, Aleixandre's thematics of love would seem to have become aligned with that of Bécquer, to whom he had responded so differently in his poetic youth. In the light of Bloom's theory of misprision, "Como el vilano" constitutes a poetic identity crisis brought about by discovering an unwanted identity with the father. Whether this is the actual psychological dynamic behind the poems or not, the new consolation for life and poetry subsequently expressed in *Historia del corazón* certainly suggests a necessity on the poet's part to free himself of his ancestral past and instead to set for himself a new goal and vision. Aleixandre undertakes this directional change in the remainder of this book by responsively misreading Antonio Machado. Aleixandre's "caminante," or wanderer, is assured that there is a "camino," a path whose outline is quite discernible. The perpetuation of humanity and the individual's eternal unity within its bosom is itself the path whose beginning and end are both well defined. A most powerful example of Aleixandre's communal vision may be seen in "En la plaza" [In the Square], an ode in which the poet exhorts his anonymous addressee to bathe in the swirling sea of humanity:

> no te busques en el espejo,
> en un extinto diálogo en que no te oyes.
> Baja, baja despacio y búscate entre los otros.
> Allí están todos, y tú entre ellos.
> Oh, desnúdate y fúndete, y reconócete.
>
> (*OC* 1:712)

> [Do not look for yourself in the mirror,
> In an extinct dialogue in which you do not hear yourself.
> Descend, descend slowly and look for yourself among the others.
> There they all are, and you are among them.
> Oh, cast off your clothes, dissolve, see yourself.]

We have considered the theory of Harold Bloom, whose concept of misprision casts intertextuality as relation among poets. Bloom's theory is especially suggestive of what a poem can be: it can be a response to its ancestors, a nonliteral interpretation in which the new poem is generated in relation to other poetry. This, too, is one way a particularly hermetic book like *La destrucción o el amor* can become coherent for the reader. But *La destrucción o el amor* is more than a transumption or misreading of Fray Luis and Bécquer or even of a composite precursor who, among others, would include San Juan de la Cruz, Góngora, Espronceda, and Darío. *La destrucción o el amor* is also inextricably bound to a broader and less well-defined culture. This culture consists of a kind of murky intertextual gene pool and is a source of a great deal of the book's formal and semantic intelligibility. Mixed in that pool are the intertextualities of language, art, science, philosophy, religion, folklore, literature, and particularly poetry itself. It is reasonable to assume that Aleixandre's work contains and reflects his culture, given that the poet, not unlike other humans, is intellectually nourished and formed by culture's influence. To approach Aleixandre's work from this broad intertextual perspective might seem impossible, considering the daunting magnitude of cultural materials which could potentially be inscribed in the work. But from experience we know that no novel, no invention, and no poem exists as a compendium of civilization. Rather, such artifacts are manufactured from a finite store of materials, beliefs, or ideas reflective of the particular concerns of their artificer and connected to his or her historical, aesthetic, and cultural circumstances. We now turn to intertextual theories that treat the collective and often anonymous components that can go into the text.

Richard Dawkins, who by profession is a geneticist rather than a literary critic, discusses the transmission and evolution of the type of collective materials that are the central concern of many intertextual theories of poetry. In "Memes: The New Replicators," Dawkins identifies culture and its rapid transmission as unique to the human being among all other earthly species. He underlines that whereas innate human characteristics are received via gene transmission, culture is propagated intellectually, by means of the "meme," which Dawkins defines as a "unit of cultural transmission," or a "unit of imitation." Memes may be tunes, ideas, cliches, architectural designs, and so on, whose manner of replication is to "leap from mind to mind in a broad process of imitation." Dawkins goes on to note that "memes as replicators are—unlike genes—subject often to mutation and are often passed on in altered form" though he adds that certain complexes of memes—similar to genes—have high survival values.[17] One such example of a hardy survivor in the cultural meme pool is the idea of God. According to Dawkins, the God meme owes its longevity to two factors. The first is the "fecundity" of this meme— that is, the concept of God has been widely acceptable and therefore broadly distributed. The second is a complex of "coadapted memes," which are fostered, in turn, by the Church, through its rituals and doctrine, sacred art and architecture, and literature, for example. Toward fathoming the irrationality of *La destrucción o el amor,* recognizing the traces of such cultural intertexts is fundamental.

In order to suggest how Dawkins's theory of memes can illustrate the scope of intertextuality and be of utility in approaching Aleixandre's poetry, let us cite but one example of a meme, a very productive one in Aleixandre, which might be called the "mortality meme." This meme is definable as the specific, and ancient, Western concept of human mortality, as predetermined by man's essential substance, that of earth or clay. Reducible to the formula man = dust, this equation has countless variants and is no doubt internalized in the Western psyche via one or more memetic variants. Before specifying exactly what role the mortality meme plays in Aleixandre, let us examine how this particular meme is predisposed to poetic elaboration even before it is received by him.

The mortality meme's suitability for poetry can be explained in the light of the qualities that Dawkins ascribes to the high survival values of memes in general. These qualities, drawn up by Dawkins as part of the gene/meme analogy, are "fecundity," "longevity," and "copying-fidelity." The fecundity of the mortality meme is directly proportional to the profound emotional impact that it creates and to its acceptability as a formula by which we conceptualize our existence.[18] The man=earth equation is supercharged with import. It darkly resonates mortality, earth, ashes, dust; it echoes Alpha and Omega, cradle and grave, and is the plot summary of human existence, the circle of mortal destiny. We need not search very far for examples of how this meme came to be imprinted on our collective psyche. Most Catholics recall those childhood Ash Wednesdays on which the priest, as he applied the dark ash to our still unfurrowed brows, solemnly admonished, "Memento, homo, quia pulvis es, et in pulverem reverteris." The office of the Ash Wednesday mass was not the only way the concept of mortal ontology was assisted on that first day of Lent. Seemingly, it was reduplicated ad infinitum: on the street, in class and on the playground, nuns, parishioners and playmates wore that ashen sign of humanity's collective doom, a graphic repetition of "Remember, oh man, that dust thou art, and into dust thou shalt return."[19] Ash Wednesday was also an early lesson in juxtaposition, the cruciform application of the ash being at once the sign of doom and the emblem of promised immortality, the ultimate triumph of life over death. Both body and spirit, that mixture of dust and divine breath, as Genesis portrays our being, are members of a greater cluster of memes that might be called the "human ontology complex." This complex is itself subject to shifts, according to how our idea of what we are alters through time. A concrete example of a widely accepted and quite recent addition to the human ontology complex is the "Freudian psyche meme." In the light of this scientific model, the subconscious has come to replace the divine mystery of God and is conceptualized as an enigma within that powerfully motivates human behavior. It bears mention that the Freudian permutation of the human ontology complex is central to surrealism, which as an aesthetic and ideological movement misreads the theories of Freud.

The second and no less remarkable quality of the mortality meme is its longevity, no doubt aided by its sheer importance. The man/earth formula is ancient, having served as a conventional formula of mortality in Western culture for at least as long as the Bible has been disseminated. Indeed, the meme's most illustrious variant is to be found in Genesis, the opening book of the Old Testament wherein the Judeo-Christian creation myth is contained. Here we are told, "the Lord God formed man of the dust of the ground, and breathed into his nostrils the breath of life; and man became a living soul" (Gen. 2:7). Later, when the proscribed fruit from the tree of knowledge of good and evil had been consumed by Adam and Eve, they were not merely expelled from Eden but were also reminded of the humble origins to which they were now condemned to return: "In the sweat of thy face shalt thou eat bread, till thou return unto the ground; for out of it wast thou taken: for dust thou art, and unto dust shalt thou return" (Gen. 3:19). The last phrase of Jehovah's speech takes us from Paradise to Ash Wednesday Mass where, millennia later, we still shudder before this simply phrased formula of our fate.

In addition to the fecundity and longevity of the mortality meme, the factor that also makes it successful in the great cultural meme pool is its copying fidelity. This virtue of the man=earth equation is owed to its simple, almost motto-like formula, which, akin to a catchy tune, is most memorable, a quality perfect for dissemination. And also like a good tune, the mortality meme lends itself to variations such as the biblical and liturgical ones cited above or to other countless reduplications and distortions. A popular variant of the mortality meme exists in the phrase, "estoy hecho polvo" [I am pulverized], a hyperbolic expression of fatigue synonymous with "estoy muerto" [I am dead]. Examples of this meme's use by poets are common and serve to witness both the mortality meme's powerful thematic charge as well as its linguistic pliability. As a few examples will confirm, this meme, by the time it reaches Aleixandre, is a poetic "déjà lu" of considerable emotional impact. One has only to call to mind the memorable closure of the Góngora sonnet, "Mientras por competir con tu cabello." Here, the mortality meme is repeated in two variants, "tierra" [earth] and "polvo" [dust] and is expanded to "nada" [nothingness], the very last word of the poem. The chilling effect and memorableness of this line are owed to two factors. The first is the initial and central position of the mortality meme paraphrases. The second is the stark contrast of this basic human minerality—the double finality of the poem—with the much brighter, but no less conventional, metallurgic, floral and aquatic metaphors preceding it:

> Mientras por competir con tu cabello
> oro bruñido al sol relumbra en vano,
> mientras con menosprecio en medio el llano
> mira tu blanca frente el lilio bello;
>   mientras a cada labio, por cogello,
> siguen más ojos que al clavel temprano,
> y mientras triunfa con desdén lozano,
> del luciente cristal tu gentil cuello;
>   goza cuello, cabello, labio y frente,
> antes que lo que fue en tu edad dorada
> oro, lilio, clavel, cristal luciente,
>   no sólo en plata o vïola troncada
> se vuelva, mas tú y ello juntamente
> en tierra, en humo, en polvo, en sombra, en nada.[20]

> [While in order to compete with your tresses
> Polished gold shines vainly in the sun,
> While with disdain your fair brow
> Gazes on the beautiful lily of the plain;
>   While more eyes pursue the harvest of your lips
> Than seek to pluck the spring carnation,
> And while with haughty disdain your gentle neck
> Triumphs over the shimmering fountain;
>   Take joy from neck, tresses, lip and brow
> Before what was in your gilded youth
> Gold, lily, carnation, and shimmering font
>   Not only into silver or harvested violet
> Be changed, but you and all of that together
> Into earth, into smoke, into dust, into shadow, into nothing.]

Quevedo also employed the hombre/polvo meme in some of his most exquisite "conceptista" [conceit-based] sonnets, in the development of both religious and amorous themes. In one psalm, a eucharistic prayer, the poet, as he addresses Christ, describes himself as an ever humbler vessel for the Savior. First, he is a "monumento" [tomb], then a "pesebre" [manger] and, finally, in the tercets, is the essential man/dust variant whose body, being earth, is both its own grave and, paradoxically, the earthly and mortal "monumento" that is to contain and inter Christ's immortality.

> Hoy te entierras en mí, siervo villano,
> sepulcro a tanto huésped vil y estrecho,
> indigno de tu Cuerpo soberano.

> Tierra te cubre en mí, de tierra hecho;
> la conciencia me sirve de gusano;
> mármol para cubrirte da mi pecho.[21]

> [Today You inter Yourself in me, an unworthy servant,
> To such a guest as You I am a vile and narrow sepulcher,
> Unworthy of Your sovereign Body.

> Earth covers You in me of earth made;
> Conscience is my worm;
> My breast is the marble that covers You.]

In Quevedo, this meme continually resurfaces, though perhaps its most well-known mutation is to be found in the love sonnet entitled "Amor constante más allá de la muerte" [Love Constant Beyond Death]. In this poem, Quevedo employs the man/dust meme along with allusions to the classical Underworld. Here, as in the preceding sonnet, the human body/dust finality dramatically concludes the work in a play of sharp paradox:

> Alma, a quien todo un Dios prisión ha sido,
> Venas, que humor a tanto fuego han dado,
> Medulas, que han gloriosamente ardido,

> Su cuerpo dejará, no su cuidado;
> Serán ceniza, mas tendrá sentido;
> Polvo serán, mas polvo enamorado.[22]

> [Soul, who has been imprisoned by a sovereign god,
> Veins, which have fed so great a fire,
> Marrow, which has gloriously blazed,

My soul will abandon this body but not its cares;
Veins and marrow will be ash, but passionate ash;
Dust will they be, but loving dust.]

In Aleixandre's poetry, the hombre/tierra meme carries out a fundamental thematic and formal mission. The significance of the mission is due, to a large extent, to the cultural history of the meme which the above examples suggest. The mortality meme serves two purposes in Aleixandre's poetry. First, having arrived from tradition as a shorthand for human destiny—the matrix idea of Aleixandre's poetry—the meme may be found spliced onto a cluster of other thematically similar motifs such as love, death, paradise, unity, and solitude. Second, this meme and others act to signal the thematic tradition to which Aleixandre's poetry belongs. Namely, the poet's work is concerned with the transcendent questions of existence, a thematic feature coherent with both Aleixandre's choice of specific ancestry and the rhetoric and length characteristic of his verse. The poet's work is engaged in singing the plight of one main character, who, as Aleixandre has remarked "es siempre el mismo, porque la poesía, sin que le sea dable escoger otros términos, empieza en el hombre y concluye en el hombre" (*OC* 2:538) [is always the same, since poetry, having no other option, begins and ends in man]. For the poet—and this is but a prose paraphrase of the mortality meme so often rendered in Aleixandre's poetry—man is an "elemento de ese cosmos del que sustancialmente no se diferenciaba" (*OC* 2:538) [element of that cosmos from which he is substantially indistinct]. Formally, the mortality meme plays an incisive role as a primary trope and lies directly behind the generation and development of a significant quantity of images and metaphors.

Following are a few examples of how this conventional meme is manifest and how perceiving it assists our reading of Aleixandre's poetry. Like the presence of specific ancestors, that of the mortality meme is signaled quite openly at times as, for example, in *Hombre de tierra* [Man of Earth], the original title of *Pasión de la tierra* [Passion of Earth], or in "Al hombre" [To Man] (*Sombra del paraíso* [Shadow of Paradise]). In the ode, "Al hombre," humankind—variously addressed as "barro" and "arcilla"—is admonished in the closure: "mira tu cuerpo extinto cómo acaba en la noche. / Regresa tú, mortal, humilde, pura arcilla apagada, / a tu certera patria que tu pie sometía. / He aquí la inmensa madre que de ti no es distinta. / Y, barro tú en el barro, totalmente perdura" (*OC* 1:576) [See how your extinct body goes out in the night. Return, humble mortal, oh pure extinguished clay, to your true native land that your foot lately trod.

Behold the immense mother who from you is indistinct. And you, clay in that clay, totally endure]. Such overt and prominent paraphrases of the human/earth meme alert us to more covert elaborations of the same. In more obscure instances, the formula is poetically misread or subverted in much the same way as happens with ancestral texts. Consider the change of title previously cited, *Hombre de tierra* → *Pasión de la tierra*. While the original titular phrase, "hombre de tierra," is an open paraphrase of its intertextual relatives—the biblical citations and both the Góngora and Quevedo poems—"pasión de la tierra," the Aleixandrean variant, is both a defamiliarization of the meme and a concrete example of its poetic pliability. In this example, the mortality meme undergoes a type of mutation, common in Aleixandre's poetry, that exploits the congenital troping potential of man/earth. Namely, this equation is a metonym, a formula that defines the whole (man) by its part (earth). The Aleixandrean metamorphosis is realized by retroping both of the constituents of the traditional equation. Man, the first element and metonymic tenor of the formula, is replaced by his chief spiritual feature, "pasión" or eros. Passion is the human element that Aleixandre sees as the driving force behind the human, as the human being's "fuerza del sino," or force of destiny. The conventional metonymic vehicle—"tierra"—is likewise refigured, a poetic operation carried out with the addition of the determiner "la" before "tierra." This conversion allows for an ambivalent reading of man—"la tierra"—who is both a categorical substance (earth, dust, etc.) and the planet Earth, which the determiner "la" commonly designates.

In the context of this memetic ambiguity, we can find many paradigmatic variants of the base hombre/tierra meme. Typically, the human is refigured, having been replaced with an aspect of his own affect or with an emblem thereof. This process may be seen in several Aleixandrean titles—*Espadas como labios, La destrucción o el amor, Mundo a solas, Sombra del paraíso* and *Historia del corazón*—wherein "pasión" or "humano" appears in the guise of affective emblems, as "labios" [lips], "amor" [love], "a solas" [alone], "sombra" [shadow], and "corazón" [heart]. For its part, the mineral vehicle—the definitive element of human mortality—is retroped via abstraction, reduction, or expansion. In this way, "la tierra" becomes "destrucción" [destruction], "mundo" [world], "paraíso" [paradise]. The "historia" of *Historia del corazón,* is a noticeable departure from the paradigm, a change which is coherent with Aleixandre's new thematic focus. In this book—the last of the five alluded to—the poet's "mirada," or gaze, is extended to include humankind's social, rather than passionately tellurian, destiny.

The titular eminence of the mortality meme now brings us to the much commented Aleixandrean landscape, to whose development this meme is crucial. But before considering the important role that this metonym plays in the construction of the poet's world, let us pause in order to cite a final example of intertextual theory, that of Michael Riffaterre. In two books—*Semiotics of Poetry* and *Text Production*—and in numerous articles, Riffaterre has intrepidly set out, literary magnifying glass in hand, in search of poetry's significance. Although he does not use the word, "meme," Riffaterre convincingly argues that a poetic text is both produced from, and so becomes significant in relation to, other extant, meme-like materials, its intertexts. In order to perceive the coherence of a poem, its sense or logic, the reader must undertake to identify those intertexts, the basic memetic material that the poem refers to, typically in an oblique or transumptive manner. Riffaterre emphasizes that the primary composition of such material is linguistic, language itself making up the poem's intertextual meme pool.

If and when Riffaterre is knighted for his scientific endeavor, his heraldic motto might well read: "Poetry says one thing but means another," for it is on the assumption of poetry's indirectness that his theory of meaning is based. According to Riffaterre, poems do not make sense as unmediated representations of reality. On the contrary: when taken as such they produce "ungrammaticalities," semantically incompatible, inaccurate, or strange results. The unity of the poem—a characteristic the critic underlines as one of its primary features—must therefore not be sought at the level of mimesis but rather at the higher level of significance. It is this move, from what the poem seems to say to what it means, which is at the heart of semiosis.

For Riffaterre, the primary generative source of a poetic text is its "matrix," a kind of deep structure or hypothetical kernel. The matrix is actualized through processes of expansion or conversion, which produce poetic rather than mimetic signs. These signs, labeled "hypograms," are preexistent word groups such as cliches, quotations, or descriptive systems—complexes of conventionally associated elements. The hypogram is then a type of meme, or a cluster of memes present in language. Riffaterre insists—and this is the test of intertextuality—that an intertextual relationship exists between text and intertext when a poetic sign in the focal poem not only refers to a hypogram but has in common with it the same matrix. Thus, in order for the reader to grasp the significance of a poem, a bit of sleuthing is necessary, for not only must he or she search for an often occult hypogram but must also locate the common matrix central to intelligibility. Riffaterre's theory might seem more like a puzzle solver's guide than a description of reading poetry. But his interpretations, guided by this enigma model of poetry, are compelling and persuasive. What is more, Riffaterre's model of poetry is especially well-suited to the obscurity of Aleixandre's surrealism, as the critic's readings of Breton and Eluard illustrate.[23] While maintaining the man/earth metonym as an example, consider how Riffaterre's perception of poetry can aid our reading of Aleixandre.

Riffaterre points out that ungrammaticalities in a poem serve to signal that its coherence is not to be found by reading it as a reference to real life. Instead, such semantic dissonances are a sign of an enigma, of a mystery that the reader might pose in this way: How can this poem make sense? We can begin unraveling that mystery by searching through language itself for those preexistent word groups that Riffaterre labels "hypograms." The hombre/tierra meme, a highly productive formula in Aleixandre, is such a hypogram. Its common variant—the biblical "Man is dust and to dust he shall return"—neatly exemplifies Riffaterre's hypogram requirements. It is an extant formula, one which exists in language and literature beyond Aleixandre's work. Its matrix—mortality or human destiny—is a semantic constant detectable both in the variants of the equation and in Aleixandre's poetry.

The human/earth hypogram is a highly productive means through which the human destiny matrix is translated in Aleixandre, especially from *Pasión de la tierra* to *Sombra del paraíso*. With respect to form, this equation serves to produce two complementary types of figurative structures common to the poet's early period. The first kind is produced by expanding the metonymical potential of the human/earth equation, a process like that which generates the titular mutation of *Hombre de tierra* into *Pasión de la tierra*. By such expansion, the tenor of the man/earth metonym becomes figuratively overgrown, and is "enterrado," or interred, in his own essence—the vehicular "polvo" or "tierra." This common type of figuration may be seen in "En el fondo del pozo" [At the bottom of the Pit] (*Espadas como labios),* where the human referent effectively acts as his own "pozo" or grave. The human may also be figured as a mine, as in "Mina," or as a volcano, in "Unidad en ella" [Unity in Her] (both from *La destrucción o el amor*). Equally common in this play on the hypogram's metonymical potential is the hyperbolic expansion of the human into a terraqueous paradigm of vast proportions. Since the human "tierra" can also be taken as the planet Earth, so the tenor can be expanded, as in *La destrucción o el amor,* into an astral system complete with shooting stars ("Ven siempre, ven") or a vast "locus

amoenus" populated with a descriptive system of jungle flora and
fauna ("La selva y el mar"). In these cases and in many more, the world
described by Aleixandre is derived from and becomes grammatical
only in view of this underlying hypogram. That is, Aleixandre's
world is not the universe of our daily experience but an artificial system strikingly similar to the surrealist "l'une dans l'autre" [the one
in the other] wherein an object—the human—is described in terms
of what it may potentially be—planet, paradise, or tomb. The resulting obfuscation of the human referent is owed to this figurative
overgrowth, which is based on exploiting the metonymic potential
of the human/earth hypogram.

The second type of figurative structure directly relatable to the
human/earth hypogram is complementary to the Aleixandrean
"l'une dans l'autre" described above. Its effect is closely akin to "pa-
thetic fallacy," the projection of human sentiment onto nature that
is associated with Romanticism. In this case, the figurative expansion
of the hypogram could be described as an anthropomorphization
of the natural world, again the outcome of exploiting the structural
potential of the hypogram. By this means, Aleixandre creates a
highly sentient poetical universe whose components—firmament,
sea, land, fauna and flora—are strangely impossible as descriptions
of nature. Rather, they serve as emblems of the human, of that
"tierra," "mundo," or "paraíso" who is imbued with basic instincts,
the chief of which is desire or love. This poetic tack may be seen in
Aleixandre's early poetry, for example in "Mar y noche" [Sea and
Night] (*Ambito* [Ambit]). A markedly Gongorine poem, "Mar y
noche" exemplifies Aleixandre's extreme anthropomorphization of
natural imagery on the basis of the man/earth hypogram. Here, as
recounted in the closure, the heaving sea erotically strains toward
the coquettish, beautiful, but indifferent night sky:

> Parece atado al hondo
> abismo el mar, en cruz, mirando
> al alto cielo, por desasirse,
> violento, rugiente, clavado al lecho negro.
>
> Mientras la noche rueda
> en paz, graciosa, bella,
> en ligado desliz, sin rayar nada
> el espacio, capaz de órbita y comba
> firmes, hasta hundirse en la dulce
> claridad ya lechosa,
> mullida grama donde
> cesar, reluciente de roces secretos,

pulida, brilladora,
maestra en superficie.

$$(OC\ 1{:}132)$$

[The sea seems to be lashed to the deep
Abyss and, spread out, is gazing into
The heavens above as, violently groaning,
He struggles to free himself from the dark bed.

Meanwhile, the night turns about
In peace, graceful and lovely,
Stealing away, leaving no trace
In the firmament, free to orbit and curve
Until she sinks into the sweet
Milky-white clarity,
The soft grasses where
She will halt, shimmering in secret caresses,
Immaculate, radiant,
Mistress of surfaces.]

As these examples may have served to suggest, Aleixandre's poetry is in a close communicative relationship with both specific ancestors and with a larger cultural and poetic tradition. The examples may also have served to illustrate the utility of intertextual theory in approaching the poet's work and to define the theoretical orientation of this study. The focus of the following four chapters is poetry's discursive structure, a communal intertext related to the ways in which a poem may be presented.

2
Poetry's Discursive Logic

. . . difficulties return us to fundamentals.
—Alastair Fowler

As SUGGESTED IN CHAPTER 1, VICENTE ALEIXANDRE'S PRE–CIVIL
War poetry creates the impression that it is unique and nearly unfathomable. From an intertextual point of view, however, the
uniqueness consequent with Aleixandre's surrealist aesthetic is not
unqualified uniqueness at all; nor is the obscurity of his surrealist
poetry unfathomable. Rather, such impressions result from the poet's
highly creative reworking of extant poetic materials—like the previously cited man/earth meme—which are defamiliarized by the
"automatism effect," deemed by Riffaterre to be the earmark of the
surrealist text.[1] It is in the context of Aleixandre's creative combination of the old and the new that the logic, and the significance,
of his work can be discerned. An appreciable portion of the difficulty, and of the rationale, informing *La destrucción o el amor* lies in
Aleixandre's revolutionary reelaboration of "discursive structure,"
a term I have coined to designate some of poetry's primordial materials. Briefly defined, discursive structure is a complex of lyric elements which, related to "point of view" and genre, constitutes an
intertextual repertoire of how poems can be discursively presented.

The present chapter, which develops a working typology of discursive structure, serves as a theoretical preface to the following three,
wherein Aleixandre's surrealist treatment of that structure is analyzed in detail. This theoretical exposition, illustrated with poems of
Antonio Machado and Pedro Salinas, is necessitated by several factors. As previously indicated, the first is Aleixandre's surrealism, a
poetry whose substantial difficulty is due, to a large degree, to the
poet's subversion of many of poetry's basic and time-honored elements, including, in particular, elements associated with what I label
discursive structure. Indeed, the "qué es aquello" query posed by Villena can easily be expanded to include a cluster of questions directly
related to that structure. Among such questions are those concerning

48

the identity of both the persona and the primary referent of Aleixandre's poems, the perspective informing those texts, their generic makeup, and even what happens in them. The latter, a query that might seem more germane to prose fiction or narrative poetry, is, like other discursive ingredients, of key import to the poetic sense of the lyric in general and to Aleixandre's surrealism in particular.

The second factor compelling me to put forth this typology is the need to address systematically—that is, by means of a formal model—questions like those cited above. Specifically, the discursive model provides a concrete point of departure that takes into account the internal relationship among the constituents of individual pieces and the communal relationship of those elements to the greater ambit of poetry and culture. This sort of ecological tack, which reflects the intertextual orientation of the present study, differs from the tendency among theoretically diverse critics to approach Aleixandre's poetry by focusing on specific poetic elements, which are often gathered from different poems and studied in isolation from their original lyric context. Of such elements, the image—doubtless the most arresting figure in Aleixandre's surrealist poetry—is the feature most frequently studied in this manner. Notwithstanding the insights that image-based analysis can afford, by considering this lyric ingredient apart from its original poem—and from the attendant discursive context—one runs the risk of understanding only partially the function and sense of that ingredient and of the poem in which it appears.[2] To illustrate briefly this assertion, I cite "Mina" [Mine] (*La destrucción* 132), one of whose outstanding features is its metallurgical imagery. A partial list of the same includes "hierro" [iron], "alzar un pico" [to raise a pick], "hendir a la roca" [to cleave the rock], or "acero" [steel].

In tandem, these images serve to provide concrete evidence of the tellurian nature of the poem and, indeed, of the earthy character of *La destrucción o el amor* in general. However, the verses in which this imagery appears—"Dejadme entonces, comprendiendo que el hierro es la salud de vivir" [Let me, then, because you understand that iron is the health of life], "Dejadme que alce un pico y que hienda a la roca" [Let me raise a pick and cleave the rock], "dejadme que se quiebre la luz sobre el acero" [let me make light break on the steel]—surround the metallurgical figures in a rich and decidedly mysterious discursive atmosphere. Indeed, these three verses indicate that the imagery is part of a rather specific locutionary circumstance: there is a narrator who, cast in the role of miner, asserts that the plural addressee understands the vital worth of "hierro" and therefore petitions that addressee to allow him to cleave the rock.

Leaving aside for now the poetic significance of the mining story—
and of "Mina"—this cursory example may have suggested that poetic figures—be they metaphorical or discursive in nature—function
in a symbiotic relationship, a relationship essential to the lyric sense
of a poem. "Mina" itself is analyzed in detail in chapter 4. The final
consideration for sketching the discursive model—and specifically
for citing non-Aleixandrean texts for that purpose—is to illustrate,
via practical example, the communal functioning of that model,
which is re-elaborated from generation to generation and modified
according to different poetic personalities. The particular choice of
Machado and Salinas—the elder and the contemporary; the member of the Generation of '98 and Aleixandre's fellow "vanguardista"—
not only provides samples of discursive structure under the pen of
two appreciably different poets but, of equal importance, furnishes
a most useful point of reference and comparison toward discerning
with precision the discursive features characteristic of Aleixandre's
surrealist art, the task of chapters 3, 4, and 5.

From a bird's-eye view, poetry's discursive structure comprehends
two interrelated types of conventional models. The first is a work's
narrative model, which orients a poem as a "point of view." By this
means, a poem develops as a close association between persona
and poetic world in which the perspective of the persona or poetic
voice typically overshadows its chosen subject. Normally inscribed in
a poem as a rather brief situational fiction—the poet, alone in old
age, rues the absence of past love, for example—the narrative model
provides a poem with a self-contained story of its own genesis.
Thanks to this sort of fiction a poem not only assumes an aesthetic
autonomy from its actual creator but also supplies the reader with
a most important context for naturalizing a text that, when taken
as an unmediated rather than as a mediated representation, might
seem impersonal if not strange or even incomprehensible. The
second component of the lyric's discursive framework is its generic
model, which places the individual piece in the context of traditional poetic prototypes. Genre functions as poetry's genetic code
of discursive acts which are accompanied by other conventions associated with the generic type at hand.[3] For example, the elegy begins as an act of eulogizing, and it is from this discursive nucleus
that it typically develops as a philosophical consolation for the living based on the exemplariness of its dead subject. Reflecting the
nature of its poetic mission, the elegy is a poetic type characterized
by serious tone and high poetic diction. Similarly, the extension of
the elegy tends to be relatively lengthy, as befits the grand theme that
this generic sort sets out to address. A work's generic affiliation is

valuable as a kind of guiding light—or "horizon" as Alastair Fowler terms it[4]—by which something of an older, more familiar world is still available and against which the reader can see how a new work conforms to or deviates from generic conventions. In tandem, the generic and narrative models—joined here as the components of the lyric's discursive framework—encode a poem with a contextual logic that serves the reader as an invaluable key toward comprehending a poem, especially if that poem is in some way obscure or unfamiliar. While attention to the discursive structure is not the complete answer to understanding poetry, it is an essential first step toward discerning a poem's design, including its troping and thematics.[5]

Turning now to a more detailed description of the form and function of poetry's discursive structure, we begin with the subject of a work's genre, an aspect of poetry that, in comparison to the lyric's narrative dimension, has been given thorough and systematic consideration by theorists. In high school or early college literature courses we may have been left with the impression that genre is either an academic construct of neatly ordered pigeonholes in which professors place works of literature or else pertains to the rules of rhetoric adhered to by neoclassical writers of the Enlightenment. We might also be under the impression that, in the age of Romanticism, genre, given the logic of form and order it implies, was abandoned by poets in favor of imagination and formlessness. But genre's usefulness and longevity have been vindicated, to say the least. Genre has been shown to be an extremely important and useful concept not only for poets of all periods but also for readers. Rather than existing as either a prescriptive set of rules or as an abstract category, genre, as Alastair Fowler emphasizes, "enables a poet to orient his composition to previous work. And, more creatively, it extends a positive challenge or 'invitation to form'."[6] That is, genre serves as an important context in which a poem's individuality can be measured against the conventions of type that the work conforms to, rejects, or in some way transforms. Fowler explains that a work's degree of difficulty, or of intelligibility, is tied to its generic affiliation. Indeed, he observes that, "Innovative works tend to be obscure precisely because their generic context is not yet obvious," and, in the same vein, "No work, no matter how avant-garde, is intelligible without some context of familiar types."[7] Once a poem's type—or its "generic horizon"— becomes visible, one can see in what ways that poem conforms to or deviates from the conventions of genre. Not only can the piece's general formal sense become clearer, but locating a particular work's genre is also an essential step toward perceiving other configurations, including basic figurative and thematic structure.

Chosen to illustrate the functioning of genre is Pedro Salinas's "Fe mía" [My Faith], whose final verse encases the title of the book in which it appears, *Seguro azar* [Sure Chance] (1924–28):

> No me fío de la rosa
> de papel,
> tantas veces que la hice
> yo con mis manos.
> Ni me fío de la otra   5
> rosa verdadera,
> hija del sol y sazón,
> la prometida del viento.
> De ti que nunca te hice,
> de ti que nunca te hicieron,   10
> de ti me fío, redondo
> seguro azar.[8]

> [I do not put my faith in the rose
> Of paper,
> No matter how many times I made
> It with my own two hands.
> Nor do I put my faith in the other one,   5
> The true rose, daughter of sun and season,
> The betrothed of the wind.
> In you, whom I never made,
> In you who was never created,   10
> In you I put my faith, round
> Sure chance.]

This poem, when compared to the irrationality and extension that typify Aleixandre's surrealist poetry, appears to be rather straightforward. Nonetheless, a close examination of its generic horizon serves to reveal the formal and semantic complexity of this svelte piece. "Fe mía" develops as a meditation on the rose, a time-honored poetic act. This act, which serves as a generic signal, would lead one to contextualize "Fe mía" as a metapoem, a poetic sort with which the rose—the central image—is perfectly coherent, this flower being a traditional emblem of poetry, and of poetic concern with form and creation. As its paradoxical closure demonstrates, "Fe mía" treats this convention in an unconventional manner. It does so by poeticizing, and thus giving form to "el azar," or chance, the ultimate and essential rose whose superior order determines the uncertain existence of both natural and artificial roses. In view of the poetic type of "Fe mía," we would begin to frame the poem and its elements as intelligible as a self-conscious statement on poetry itself. Nevertheless,

2: POETRY'S DISCURSIVE LOGIC

the work's generic horizon is more complex. As well as being a metapoem, "Fe mía" pertains to a specific liturgical genre, that of the devotional "Credo," of which there are several variants or "Acts of Faith." The generic signals that connect the Salinas poem to the liturgical genre are two: the titular "Fe mía," itself a personalized paraphrase of the "Credo"; the repeated "(no) me fío," which echoes the "yo creo" [I believe] formula framing the entire contents of a prayer like the Nicene Creed, the best known credo, memorized by Catholics worldwide. On one hand, recognizing this additional generic information explains Salinas's formal articulation of his poetics as an act of faith, which is the essential speech act of the model genre and of the modern copy; on the other, the credo connection heightens the already paradoxical relation between poetry and universal order. The former, the "rosa de papel," is an existential ordering of "azar," the essential disorder. The poetics-credo hybrid casts "Fe mía" as a prayer, a sharply ironic one that misreads a liturgical genre whose purpose is to express unlimited faith in a divinely created order. The generic duplicity of "Fe mía" as metapoetry and credo is reflected, too, in the poem's central image. Roundness, which binds paper rose and garden rose and is here imposed on chance, is introduced in one swift poetical stroke, by the adjective "redondo" hanging off the end of the penultimate verse. It would seem to derive exclusively from the stereotyped shape of the rose but is also coherent with the central idea of ordered creation and perfection behind Salinas's ecclesiastical intertext. The divinely ordered cosmos that the "Credo" espouses has for centuries been pictorially represented in Church art as a circle, a symbol of the perfection of God's creation. Now lyrically reinterpreted by Salinas, the circle serves to express the poet's faith in the principle of chance.[9] As this example may have served to illustrate, taking genre into account is a most useful means of perceiving the sense and the form of a poem. "Fe mía" also supplies graphic evidence that poems, regardless of their extension, may well be generically complex. Indeed, the generic information to which "Fe mía" alerts us is essential to comprehending *La destrucción o el amor,* a significant portion of whose surrealist penumbra can be fathomed in light of genre and generic hybridization.

Giving an account of poetry's narrative model is a bit more problematic than considering the question of genre. This is because, in marked contrast to the novel, whose narrative structure is subject to a great deal of theoretical scrutiny, the narrative aspect of the lyric has been given little thorough attention.[10] The reasons for this theoretical lacuna go beyond the scope of this study, though I suspect that the conventional categorization of poetry into "narrative"—the ballad and epic poetry—and "non-narrative"—the lyric, or basically all other poetry—predisposes students of literature generally to overlook or take for granted the relation between the contents of a poem and its discursive presentation. The fact that we label the poem's narrator "persona" and not "narrator"—this despite the fact that both carry out the task of mediating their respective fictions—may well reflect the same type of conventionally drawn division that conditions us to ignore fundamental similarities between types of literature. Nevertheless, lyric poetry, like a novel or short story, develops as a narrative form whose discursive framework, though less extensive than that of a novel, serves to contextualize poems as autonomous discursive presentations.

Most useful to the present endeavor to describe the form and effects of narrative structure in poetry is Gérard Genette's narratological study of the novel, *Narrative Discourse: An Essay in Method.* In this book, Genette reconsiders "point of view," one of the most frequent points of departure for discussing narrative mediation. Objecting to the theoretical imprecision of this notion, Genette splits point of view in half, dividing it conceptually into "voice" and "mood," each of which, the theoretician points out, have variously been used to describe point of view.[11] Roughly speaking, voice addresses the question of "Who speaks?," that is, the vocal source of narration. Mood addresses the question of "Who sees?," or whose is the perspective or sensibility through which the narration is focalized. The utility of Genette's scheme, amply illustrated in *Narrative Discourse,* lies in its efficacy for describing different effects within narrative fiction, which the theorist convincingly accounts for as modulations in voice and mood.

That voice and mood are basic aspects of poetry's discursive format can be seen in the following narrative prototype, perhaps the narrative structure most frequently employed by poets since Romanticism. Here, the poem represents itself as the delivery of a persona who, first, in speaking or singing, both gives voice to the poem and conjures up the work's subject. Secondly, this narrator, rather than translating a somewhat accurate description of the invoked subject, transmits mood by projecting his or her own psychic or poetic concerns on that subject. Thus, what the lyric persona sees is effectively transformed into his or her own vision. In this way, the text assumes a mimetic appearance chiefly as an act of discourse or poetic mediation, which frames the poem and sets its contents beyond mere description. A poem's narrative scheme therefore offers the reader a built-in context or circumstantial fiction for naturalizing a text whose contents, as mimesis, might seem inaccurate or odd. In this way, any textual inconsistencies or breaches in mimesis can be rationalized as the outcome of an act of vocalizing and perception that determines and explains the subjective character of the text. Obviously, this rather abstract example hardly gives a very concrete idea of how individual poems, in the light of voice and mood, vary in form and effect, even when they are informed by this same narrative prototype.[12] For the purpose of concretizing what has so far been said about poetry's narrative structure, let us consider rather closely two examples—one from Pedro Salinas, another from Antonio Machado—that make vividly clear how mood and voice can function in the lyric. These two particular examples prove to be most useful toward discerning with precision Aleixandre's particular manipulation of narrative structure in *La destrucción o el amor.*

First a consideration of mood, as it is elaborated in "Don de la materia" [The Gift of Matter], a Pedro Salinas poem which, like "Fe mía," is from *Seguro azar.*

> Entre la tiniebla densa
> el mundo era negro: nada.
> Cuando de un brusco tirón
> —forma recta, curva forma—
> le saca a vivir la llama.   5
> Cristal, roble, iluminados
> ¡qué alegría de ser tienen,
> en luz, en líneas, ser
> en brillo y veta vivientes!
> Cuando la llama se apaga   10
> fugitivas realidades,
> esa forma, aquel color,
> se escapan.
> ¿Viven aquí o en la duda?
> Sube lenta una nostalgia   15
> no de luna, no de amor,
> no de infinito. Nostalgia
> de un jarrón sobre una mesa.
> ¿Están?
> Yo busco por donde estaban.   20
> Desbrozadora de sombras
> tantea la mano. A oscuras
> vagas huellas sigue el ansia.
> De pronto, como una llama
> sube una alegría altísima   25
> de lo negro: luz del tacto.
> Llegó al mundo de lo cierto.

Toca el cristal, frío, duro,
toca la madera, áspera.
¡Están!   30
La sorda vida perfecta
sin color, se me confirma,
segura, sin luz, la siento:
realidad profunda, masa.[13]

[Midst the dense shadows
The world was dark: nothing.
When with a sudden stroke
—straight form, curved form—
The flame brings it forth to life.   5
Glass, oak, illuminated.
What joy of being they possess
In light, in lines, existing
In living luster and grain!
When the flame goes out   10
Fugitive realities,
That form and that color,
Escape.
Do they live here or in doubtfulness?
What slowly ascends is a nostalgia,   15
Not for moon, nor love,
Nor for the infinite. A nostalgia
For a pitcher on a table.
Are they here?
I search for where they were.   20
The hand, that dispeller of shadows,
Gropes. In the dark,
Longing follows a vague trail.
Suddenly, like a flame,
Rises up the highest joy   25
Of obscurity: The light of touch.
It reached the world of the certain,
It touches the hard and cold glass,
Touches the rough wood.
They are here!   30
The silent perfect life
Without color makes itself known to me,
Sure, without light, I feel it:
Profound reality, mass.]

   This Salinas piece is a graphic example of what mood is and of
how its manipulation can affect poetic intelligibility. Structurally,
"Don de la materia" is a variant of the previously mentioned narrative

prototype, being framed as the voicing and perspective of a persona who mediates the poetic world of the poem. Furthermore, this text is a type of metapoem that, by transposing some object of art—here, the "naturaleza muerta," the still life of a table and water jug—thematizes its own poetic concerns. But neither the generic model, nor the attendant fictive scene of the poem, are apparent at first glance. Indeed, one might well feel left in the dark as to what "Don de la materia" says, let alone as to what it means, to paraphrase Riffaterre. This is because the work alters the prototype by emphasizing mood, which is done by fixing the focal perspective of the text as an interior "vision avec" (Genette's phrase) through the consciousness of the narrator. More particularly, the entire text is limited to the field of vision and sensibility of the narrator, who recounts in the course of his elliptical narration his step-by-step adventure in the penumbra of a dark room. The perspective through which the text is focalized is further complicated by the narrator's peculiar character. Unlike the more sentimentally round personality expected of traditional personae, Salinas's lyric protagonist, judging from the visual quality of the poem, seems lens-like or even mechanical. In tandem with the restricted focalization, this trait defamiliarizes the contents of the poem and effectively imbues it with a noticeably rebus-like flavor. The textual riddle—and Salinas's lyric rendering of mood—is developed through techniques of indirection. One of the most noteworthy of those techniques is circumlocution by which the narrator, rather than directly naming the objects which he perceives, instead depicts them fragmentarily, as clusters of minimal features. This quick and incomplete manner of describing the objects serves to simulate mood by suggesting rapid visual perception, that is, the narrator's quick glance in the dark environs in which he finds himself. It bears emphasizing that the circumstantial fiction from which the poem generates—the narrator's striking of the match in verses 3–5—and the subsequent illumination of the poem's primary referent—the table and jug referred to in verses 6–9—is obfuscated by this mode of presentation. Owing to such descriptive ellipsis, the reader is forced to search out clues elsewhere in the text which might help to fill in the onomastic blanks that are crucial to the coherence of the poem.

But even these structural clues, namely the nuclear poet-subject relationship, are presented indirectly. First, even though the water jug and table, unlike the match striking, are indeed explicitly named, this contextual information is hardly crystal clear, being given, as if in passing, at the end of the anaphoric "nostalgia" series of verses 15–18. Here, the homey still life is collocated in the curious paradoxical phrase, "Nostalgia / de un jarrón sobre una mesa." Second, the persona, whose presence is not made explicit until more than half way through the poem by the sudden introjection of a first person form—"Yo busco"—remains, even at that, depersonalized and abstract rather than well-rounded and human. Salinas deftly dehumanizes the lyric narrator by detaching or isolating from him both sense and sentiment. For example, "nostalgia," "alegría," "duda" are presented via impersonal formulas that, in contrast to more personal syntagms—"me entra una nostalgia, una alegría," "dudo," and so on—defamiliarize the conventional narrative model in which the persona is clearly the affective source of the poem. Striking in this is the detachment, and subsequent abstraction, of the narrative hand, which serves both as a synecdoche for the full-blown narrator and as the sentient, and finally victorious, protagonist of the poem. Reminiscent of the cinematographic artifice whereby the cameraman's hand appears momentarily on the screen, the hand of the narrator suddenly comes into view, via hyperbaton, in verse 22, after breaking off from the personal, "Yo busco" form immediately preceding it. The textual appearance of the hand at this juncture is a graphic reminder of the effect worked on the text by mood. In particular, the poem simulates—and playfully so—the restricted perspective of a narrator who, groping about in the dark, is necessarily reduced to tact, that is, to a hand. From here, the appendage, driven by "el ansia," tracks down the ephemeral vision of water jug and table. The existence of these objects is sensorially confirmed, as suggested by the unusual synesthesia, "luz del tacto." In the following three verses (27–29), the hand, or rather its abstracted tactile form, is made to disappear altogether, being formally elided as the subject of all three. This pattern of progressively dissolving the narrative persona is slightly reversed as "Don de la materia" closes. In the final four verses, the passive dative construction, "se me confirma," gives way to the personal "siento" which, with its colon, heralds the poem's conclusion.

Together with the "Yo busco" of verse 20, the explicit first person form of "siento" is the clearest clue to this poem's underlying narrative structure and to the circumstantial anecdote that rounds it out. In marked contrast to the strange and fragmented vision worked on the surrounding text by restricting mood to the interior and nonverbal perspective of the groping narrator, these brief and relatively explicit incursions of voice—dubbed "alterations" by Genette—signal that this poem, like so many other narrative family members, is a first person form to be taken as the speech and perspective of its poetic I. This sort of vocal clue, which acts to shed light on the textual obscurity wrought by emphasizing mood, also proves to be of great utility toward discerning the basic discursive structure underlying some of Aleixandre's most challenging poems, including "La selva y el mar" and "Sin luz." Returning to the matter at hand, the concluding "la siento" both stipulates perspective—through "siento," a verb of perception—and emphasizes mediation, which is done by joining this active first person form to "la," or "realidad," the grammatical and poetic object ultimately transformed through the particular vision of Salinas's narrator in "Don de la materia." The "yo busco" and the "la siento," again together, also mark the pivotal moments in the poem's plot, a discursive plot played out as a drama of perception wherein the poem assumes coherence and is naturalizable. Briefly put, this plot consists of two events of perception. The first is the fleeting vision of jug and table afforded momentarily, and as if by chance, by the short-lived illumination of the match. In doubt as to the reality of the objects, the protagonist sets off on a "búsqueda," a quest that occupies two thirds of the text.

The second event is that of tactile illumination ("luz del tacto"), which resolves the narrator's search by confirming the existence of the jug and table. This encounter, the poem's denouement, is portrayed in the final third of the poem and is summarized in two words, "la siento." In this highly sentient and interior context, the oral character of the interrogative and exclamatory sentences act to alter mood and can feasibly be taken as bits of interior monologue. As the above may have served to illustrate, the key, and the first step, toward the intelligibility of "Don de la materia," lies in recuperating the discursive act which simultaneously structures the work and defamiliarizes it. The effectiveness of Salinas's use of mood in "Don de la materia" is reflected in the reading activity that it triggers, a reading activity mirroring the action of the poem itself. The reader, initially disoriented by the textual shadows that are created by restricting the text to the perspective and sensibility of Salinas's narrator, must search for the narrative logic informing the poem. Once encountered, the narrative system opens the text up to the reader's perception, and is now available to his or her imaginative and interpretive re-creation. The search that is launched in the wake of Salinas's manipulation of perspective is likewise an integral part of the reading experience in Aleixandre, whose surrealist manipulation of mood tends to create even greater semantic barriers.

As well as illustrating the impact that narrative technique can have on the sense of a poem, "Don de la materia" also sharply exemplifies the pivotal role that discursive structure can play in a text's thematic development. In this particular case, the poem comes to define itself to an appreciable degree as a response, a la Bloom, to Romantic variants of the aforementioned narrative prototype. The poem's Romantic ancestry is evoked in verses 15–17, where the intertextual fragments "nostalgia," "luna," "amor," and "infinito" specifically recall Romantic poems whose scene is built around such topoi.[14] The setting suggested by the modern poem might be summarized like this: the poet, alone midst the darkness of night, rues the loss and impossibility of love; the poet's only companion is the moon—itself an emblem of absence—the light of which dimly illuminates the scene. Though focalized through the lyric narrator and naturalizable as projections of his or her emotional and philosophical concerns, the nocturnal backdrop of such a scene is represented, nonetheless, as exterior to or even beyond the reach of that narrator. Toward defining its own significance, "Don de la materia" contorts this ancestral model, an operation which is carried out by simultaneously inverting, reducing and generically recontextualizing that model, a transumptive pattern also noticeable in Salinas's internalization of the "Credo" in "Fe mía." The Romantic ancestor is inverted first, and foremost, by Salinas's particular exploitation of mood which, in foregrounding the perspective of the persona, narratologically turns the discursive structure of the intertextual model outside in. Owing to this, as has been seen, the new poem blurs the distinction between the narrator and the contents of the poem, thus troubling the identification of both. This focal difference between the Salinas poem and its Romantic intertext serves to define the difference between modern and Romantic notions of subjectivity, the anti-empirical premise from which both depart. "Don de la materia" also inverts the prototype by moving the scene of its discourse from the open and natural immensity of the cosmos, where the Romantic poet ponders the infinite, to an interior, man-made space in which the poet now searches for the finite and tangible. The latter brings us to the reductive pattern of the Salinas poem, a pattern whereby the formal and thematic grandness of Romanticism is replaced by the much humbler scope of the new poem. This lyric opposition is most openly expressed in Salinas's triple negation of the Romantic in verses 15–18, where lunar, amorous, and infinite nostalgia is rejected in favor of a nostalgia for the tangible and homey vision of jug and table, a subject hardly suitable to the much loftier Neoplatonic aspirations of the Romantics who sought an absolute reality hidden from the senses and open—even when only partially so—to orphic insight. In marked contrast to such goals, the objects sought in Salinas are eminently attainable, not solely because of their ostensible concreteness but even more so because their reality is contingent upon the poet's perception of them. The relatively brief extension of the poem and even its meter—here predominantly ballad meter—is a most tangible sign of this "sotto voce" response to the typically more extensive forms of Romanticism. Salinas's reaction to Romanticism, including his narrative recasting of the prototype, is a feature shared by Aleixandre who, in *La destrucción o el amor*, also interprets the cosmic mystery of Romanticism but relocates it in the penumbral region of the subconscious.

In addition to inverting and reducing the discursive scheme of the Romantic prototype, Salinas reinterprets that model—and thereby defines the lyric sense of his own poem—by way of generic recontextualization. This process is realized by casting "Don de la materia" as a mock epic, a generic type whose parodic ambience is the characteristic most obviously at odds with the melancholy atmosphere of the Romantic model. The parody is signaled by invoking the biblical epic of creation in the introit and by diminishing, in subsequent verses, the heroic dimensions of that story.[15] In particular, there is a dramatic stylistic contrast between the dark and heavy tone of the first verses, which befits Jehovah's "fiat lux," and the light and agile style of Salinas's domestic "fiat lux" portrayed in the remainder of the work. As an epic of creation, the Salinas poem plays out its adventure as a search and encounter plot, as already noted. Thanks to the heroic efforts of individual perception, the poem victoriously, if only artificially, imposes its own creative light on the otherwise dark formlessness of chaos, the "seguro azar" which both spurs artistic activity and makes its false order possible. The epic context serves to underscore the differences between "Don de la materia" and the Romantic stereotype alluded to in the text. The latter, unlike the Salinas poem, develops as the passive reception and internalization of an outer illumination, not as the willful projection of an inner creative light, Salinas's "luz del tacto." As for the lunar light of the Romantic stereotype, it shines from another descriptive system, that of the nocturnal firmament, wherein stars, moon, and darkness symbolize fate, a higher fixed order that, lying beyond the poet, can only be partially fathomed. The tasks of Romantic and modern poets reflect their notions of universal order and how that order is perceptible. One of the common roles of the Romantic poet is that of gifted receptor or seer who communicates his or her glimpses of that higher and mysterious order. Such may be seen in Bécquer who, as in Rima 1, casts the poet as receptacle of "un himno gigante y extraño" [a strange and immense hymn], the poem being, "cadencias que el aire dilata en las sombras" [cadences that the air disperses among the shadows], but which, nonetheless, are impossible for poetry to translate perfectly.[16] This Romantic role is taken up and playfully inverted in "Don de la materia," where the poetic visionary is now a "non-seer" who explores a darkness rich in poetic possibilities. This anti-Romantic stance is also an outstanding feature of "Vocación" [Vocation] *(Seguro azar)*. The following stanza records the denouement, an epiphany of obscure enlightenment:

> Cerrar los ojos. Y ver
> incompleto, tembloroso,
> de será o de no será,
> —masas torpes, planos sordos—
> sin luz, sin gracia, sin orden
> un mundo sin acabar,
> necesitado, llamándome
> a mí, o a ti, o a cualquiera
> que ponga lo que le falta,
> que le dé la perfección.[17]

> [Close the eyes. And see
> Incomplete, tremulous,
> What may or may not be,
> —graceless forms, voiceless planes—
> Without light, without grace, without order,
> An unfinished world,
> Needy, calling me,
> Or you, or anybody
> To supply what is lacking,
> To give it perfection.]

As the discussion of "Don de la materia" may have served to illustrate, narrative structure and mood in particular can play a decisive formal and thematic role in poetry. In this piece, there is a direct correlation between the manipulation of mood—the technique of perspective as Genette defines it—and Salinas's elaboration of perspectivism, an ideological constant of his work. Moreover, the particular intertextuality of Romantic and modern narrative types suggests that the morphology of modal point of view is diachronically subject to change, a change reflecting aesthetic and ideological shifts in how reality is perceived and with regard to the mission of poetry itself. The perspectivism that Salinas translates via mood indicates an increasingly skeptical secular culture in which the idea of an absolute order—whether divine or not—is no longer tenable. Artistically, the poet shows a strong affinity both with "arte puro," the aesthetic ideal which values the aesthetic over the representational, and with the European avant-garde whose "deshumanización del arte" is achieved, according to Ortega y Gasset, by focusing the work of art through unaccustomed perspectives.[18] From what has been said, it would seem that the major technical and thematic function of mood is to translate consciousness, be it orphic or existential. While mood does fulfill this mission, it is also through this technique of rendering perspective that the dynamics of the subconscious mind can be simulated. This specific application of mood, which makes a poem especially resistant to intelligibility, is one of Aleixandre's outstanding lyric innovations.

Voice, as previously indicated, is the aspect of narrative structure that responds, roughly, to the question of who speaks. Whereas mood frames a poem as an act of perception, voice contextualizes the lyric as a vocal happening or event of discursive delivery. It is worth noting that voice, rather than mood, is the aspect of narrative structure to which we most often appeal in naturalizing poetry. There are several reasons for this. For one thing, it is through voice that both a poem's speaker-subject relation and its attendant spatiotemporal frame are figured, the latter functioning as a circumstantial fiction in which to place a text that might otherwise seem strange or impersonal. For its part, the persona, who is most overtly translated via voice, serves as an especially powerful device for explaining the genesis of a poem. Voice also plays a crucial role in creating a poem's autonomy. In its sounding, voice constitutes a feat of ventriloquy through which verse speaks for its creator, whose own voice may well be silent. This function of voice is made explicit in much poetry, including Garcilaso's "Egloga tercera" [Third Eclogue]. By means of "la voz a ti debida," the voice owed to his lady, the poet promises to celebrate her virtues in death as well as life. Garcilaso claims that his singing soul, as it is ferried across the Stygian lake, "celebrándote irá, y aquel sonido / hará parar las aguas del olvido[19] [will go about celebrating you, and that sound will halt the waters of forgetfulness].

To illustrate the role that voice can play in poetry, I have chosen Antonio Machado's "Las moscas" [Flies] (*Soledades* [Solitudes]).

> Vosotras, las familiares,
> inevitables golosas,
> vosotras, moscas vulgares,
> me evocáis todas las cosas.
> ¡Oh, viejas moscas voraces   5
> como abejas en abril,
> viejas moscas pertinaces
> sobre mi calva infantil!
> ¡Moscas del primer hastío

en el salón familiar,   10
las claras tardes de estío
en que yo empecé a soñar!
  Y en la aborrecida escuela,
raudas moscas divertidas,
perseguidas   15
por amor de lo que vuela
   —que todo es volar—, sonoras
rebotando en los cristales
en los días otoñales . . .
Moscas de todas las horas,   20
  de infancia y adolescencia,
de mi juventud dorada;
de esta segunda inocencia,
que da en no creer en nada,
  de siempre . . . Moscas vulgares,   25
que de puro familiares
no tendréis digno cantor:
yo sé que os habéis posado
  sobre el juguete encantado,
sobre el librote cerrado,   30
sobre la carta de amor,
sobre los párpados yertos
de los muertos.
  Inevitables golosas,
que ni labráis como abejas,   35
ni brilláis cual mariposas;
pequeñitas, revoltosas,
vosotras, amigas viejas,
me evocáis todas las cosas.[20]

  [You, the familiar ones,
Inevitable sweet tooths,
You, common flies,
In me you evoke all things.
  Oh, voracious old flies   5
Like bees in April,
Old obstinate flies
Upon my bald baby head!
  Flies of that very first tedium
In the family parlor,   10
On those bright summer afternoons
When I began to dream!
  And in the detested school house,
Swift amusing flies,
Pursued   15

By the love of flying things
    —everything is flight—, with sweet sound
Bouncing against the windows
On autumn days . . .
Flies of every hour,   20
    Of infancy and adolescence,
Of my golden youth;
Of this second innocence
That leads one to believe in nothing,
    Of always . . . Common flies   25
Who, because you are so familiar,
Likely haven't a worthy singer:
I know you have lighted
    On the enchanted toy,
On the closed school book,   30
On the love letter,
On the lifeless eyes
Of the dead.
    Inevitable sweet tooths,
You who neither labor like the bee,   35
Nor shine like the butterfly;
Tiny, mischievous,
You, old friends,
Evoke in me all things.]

"Las moscas" is a seemingly straightforward poem which, not unlike the Romantic narrative prototype mentioned earlier, takes shape
as a discursive act in which the narrator both delivers the poem and
mediates its contents from his particular point of view or perspective. The outstanding vocal feature of this Machado piece is apostrophe, an aspect of voice that permeates the text and contributes
to its overall clarity. Apostrophe is itself of special interest to this
discussion of poetry's narrative structure since it not only graphically
illustrates the function of voice in poetic discourse but is also the
tonic note of voicing in *La destrucción o el amor*. Briefly, apostrophe
is a rhetorical device whereby a speaker directs him- or herself to
another, whether the intention of the address be vocative, imperative,
or interrogative. One of the most often cited effects of apostrophe is
the sense of life and immediacy that it lends a poem. As indicated,
"Las moscas" is a highly apostrophic poem. Apostrophe occupies the
entirety of both the opening and closing strophes and is reiterated
on five other occasions in the central sections. The overarching
rhetorical mission of apostrophe in this Machado work is lexically
stipulated in the phrase "me evocáis," which defines evocation as

the text's nuclear speech act or its "happening," as Jonathan Culler, in "Apostrophe," describes the enlivening effect of this device. "Las moscas" not only exemplifies how apostrophe enlivens a poem but also serves to illustrate that there is much to be said regarding its role, particularly in regard to poetry's temporal and thematic structure.

To be examined first is the part played by apostrophe in a poem's temporal scheme. The outstanding feature of apostrophe's verbal mood, whether it be couched as interrogative, imperative, or optative, lies in its atemporality, apostrophe working as the poem's "eternal here and now" in the context of which all other deictics are to be taken into account. In "Las moscas" the almost obsessive repetition of the eternal by way of apostrophe stands in marked contrast to the equal degree with which temporal deictics saturate the poem. The "me evocáis," the poem's atemporal introit, leads the way to an anaphoric progression of time, which is encapsulated in the subsequent adverbials, "en abril," "tardes de estío," and "los días otoñales." The adverbials themselves are summarized and expanded upon in the sixth stanza, where the temporal-seasonal circle is filled out and the demonstrative "esta" allows us to construe an image of the poet looking back on life from old age. In the penultimate stanza, again constructed anaphorically, the temporal deictics undergo a last imagistic transformation culminating in the final "de los muertos." Both "de los muertos" and the preceding "de siempre" refer us to the flies conjured up in the poet's memory, the seminal anecdote inscribed in Machado's poem. The "forever" suggested by these phrases also points back to the atemporal frame of the poem established by apostrophe, the figure to which the insects, and the entire poem including all temporal markers, are ultimately bound. These deictics remind us that the "present" and actual ontology of the evoked insects is artificial, a lyric eternity implicitly promised by the poet—"no tendréis digno cantor"—and made good by "Las moscas" itself. The poem's technical play on time and eternity is squarely in line with Machado's "arte poética," which, attributed to the poet's fictional alter ego, Juan de Mairena, is condensed in "Cancionero apócrifo" [Apocryphal Songbook]:

> Juan de Mairena se llama a sí mismo "el poeta del tiempo." Sostenía Mairena que la poesía era un arte temporal—lo que ya habían dicho muchos antes que él—y que la temporalidad propia de la lírica sólo podía encontrarse en sus versos, plenamente expresada. . . . El poeta pretende, en efecto, que su obra trascienda de los momentos psíquicos en que es producida. Pero no olvidemos que, precisamente, es el tiempo (el tiempo vital del poeta con su propia vibración) lo que el poeta pretende intemporalizar, digámoslo con toda pompa: eternizar[21]

[Juan de Mairena calls himself "the poet of time." Mairena maintained that poetry was a temporal art—which many before him had already said—and that the temporality particular to the lyric could only be found fully expressed in his verse. . . . In effect, the poet's goal is that his poetry transcend the psychic moment in which it is produced. But, to be precise, let us not forget that time (the poet's lifetime with its particular reverberation) is what the poet sets out to detemporalize or, as we might say with great pomp: to eternalize].

It bears mention that Aleixandre, whose surrealist poems are highly apostrophic, is also, and not coincidently, keenly aware of the eternalizing power of poetic discourse. However, as there will be occasion to appreciate, his personal reaction to this lyric topic is quite different from that of Machado.

In addition to acting as the nuclear element of the deictic system, apostrophe plays a central role in the poem's figurative development wherein it functions as a prosopopeia or enmasking.[22] What apostrophe figuratively enmasks is a presence, the apparently dichotomous presence of the poetic I and the addressee, which in the Machado example is naturalizable as "poeta" and "moscas." The separateness of narrator-subject is one of the illusions created by such poetic voicing. As Culler puts it, "the vocative of apostrophe is a device which the poetic voice uses to establish with an object a relation which helps constitute him."[23] Machado expressed the same notion in aphorism: "Con el tú de mi canción / no te aludo, compañero; / ese tú soy yo"[24] [With the you of my song, I am not alluding to you, my friend. That you is me]. The ontological ambivalence that apostrophe entails is of major thematic importance in Aleixandre whose invocation of his ancestry—especially Bécquer and Darío—involves a complex psychological dynamic related to the younger poet's identification with his elders. In any case, what both parts of the figurative mask do in "Las moscas," besides aiding the reader to naturalize the work, is to masquerade for the poetic tenor that they represent. The tenor that the poet-flies vehicle enmasks is time itself, the matrix idea prompting the entire poem. In this, the particular raison d'être of the insects lies in their appropriateness for representing specific temporal aspects: for one thing, these winged creatures perfectly incarnate the hypogram, "el tiempo vuela" [time flies], an aphorism spelled out almost verbatim within the poem ("—que todo es volar—"); furthermore, by directing itself to "las moscas" rather than to "unas moscas," the poem categorizes its ostensible subject, thus marking its flies as an abstract and atemporal class coherent with its own vocal modality. The poetic persona, who throughout life is variously amused, entertained, and bothered by these alar spots of time, figures apostrophe or poetic voice and, in relation to the omnipresent and fugitive insects, incarnates the poetically eternal pitted against an awareness of temporality. In the light of the poem as a whole, the thematic concern raised by voice, and by the subject it pretends to invoke, is that of the "temporality of writing,"[25] namely the inextricable relationship between poem and time, a traditional concern of poetry and a specific preoccupation of Machado, who describes poetry as "la palabra en el tiempo" [the word within time].

As the presence of apostrophe in "Las moscas" illustrates, voice can play a central narratological role in poetry. Not only does the device work in tandem with other deictics toward establishing the chronological orientation of the poem; apostrophe also contributes to the construction of poetic persona and the attendant point of view informing a poem. In addition, apostrophe can act as a generic signal, a point which brings us full circle to the first topic of the present exposition on discursive logic and poetic orientation. In the particular case of "Las moscas," apostrophe signals the tradition of the ode, one of whose outstanding and definitive features is evocation.[26] Indeed, one way the Machado piece makes sense is in the light of this particular tradition. Like its many family members, it starts as a meditation on an addressee whose value lies not so much in its own particular status but rather in its idealness as a vehicle for translating the poet's philosophical concerns. This movement toward transcendence is an odic feature that may even be made explicit, as in the opening verses of Shelley's "To a Sky-Lark," an ode which dispels any illusion of referentiality that its title might suggest: "Hail to thee, blithe Spirit! / Bird thou never wert—."[27] Machado's apology for the selection of the "moscas" as poetic subject ("Moscas vulgares / que de puro familiares / no tendréis digno cantor:") is more than a ploy, since flies and other unpoetic insects, including the flea, have been sung by poets; it is as well a response to the ode motivated by the apparent inappropriateness of its subject in a genre standing as the paragon of high poetic diction and elevated tone. Nevertheless, "Las moscas," like most of its family members, addresses through poetic enmaskment the grand themes of human import including death, life, destiny, and the role of poetry itself in voicing such concerns. It comes as no surprise that Aleixandre, who also addresses via apostrophe questions concerning the nature and destiny of humankind, should be, like Machado, a poet who employs the ode as one of his favored lyric vehicles.

3

Narrating the Subconscious

Las hojas no dejan ver el bosque.
[You can't see the forest for the trees]
—Popular adage

THIS AND THE FOLLOWING TWO CHAPTERS EXAMINE *LA DESTRUCCIÓN*
o el amor in light of discursive structure. Mood, voice, and genre are
to be treated, in that order. The selection of particular poems is
based on the representative value of those pieces for the discussion
of Aleixandre's surrealism and because each piece in one way or
another illustrates that the often baffling obscurity that invites the
question, "¿Qué es aquello?" is to an appreciable extent the result
of the poet's innovative treatment of poetry's primordial discursive
stuff. To put the matter in another way, the shock produced by
Aleixandre's poetry is the shock elicited by much avant-garde art of
the period. Robert Hughes, in speaking of Picasso's "Les Demoi-
selles d'Avignon," observes that "No painting ever looked more
convulsive. None signaled a faster change in the history of art. Yet
it was anchored in tradition, and its attack on the eye would never
have been so startling if its format had not been that of the classical
nude."[1]

"Don de la materia" served to illustrate that there is a direct correlation between a poem's narrative presentation, its intelligibility,
and thematics. With respect to narrative structure in particular, the
Salinas piece acts as an example of how emphasizing mood defamiliarizes an otherwise familiar poetic type by restricting the narrative
perspective to that of an individual focal mind, whose point of view
and sensibility subjectively skew the poem's contents. Obversely, as
also seen, this same narrative technique holds the key to the work's
basic poetic structure in the light of which the contents of the piece
become intelligible as mediated lyric representation. The shadows,
and a good deal of the logic, of many Aleixandre poems are also
directly related to mood, which is technically elaborated by the poet
in order to simulate and poetically reify the subconscious and its

69

functioning. Such is the case of some of the poet's most anthologized
poems, including "Sin luz" and "Las águilas," pieces in which mood
plays a key formal and thematic role. First, "Sin luz" [Without Light]:

El pez espada, cuyo cansancio se atribuye ante todo
  a la imposibilidad de horadar a la sombra,
de sentir en su carne la frialdad del fondo de los
  mares donde el negror no ama,
donde faltan aquellas frescas algas amarillas
que el sol dora en las primeras aguas.

La tristeza gemebunda de ese inmóvil pez espada cuyo   5
  ojo no gira,
cuya fijeza quieta lastima su pupila,
cuya lágrima resbala entre las aguas mismas
sin que en ellas se note su amarillo tristísimo.

El fondo de ese mar donde el inmóvil pez respira con sus branquias un
  barro,
ese agua como un aire,   10
ese polvillo fino
que se alborota mintiendo la fantasía de un sueño,
que se aplaca monótono cubriendo el lecho quieto
donde gravita el monte altísimo, cuyas crestas se agitan
como penacho—sí—de un sueño oscuro.   15

Arriba las espumas, cabelleras difusas,
ignoran los profundos pies de fango,
esa imposibilidad de desarraigarse del abismo,
de alzarse con unas alas verdes sobre lo seco abisal
y escaparse ligero sin miedo al sol ardiente.   20

Las blancas cabelleras, las juveniles dichas,
pugnan hirvientes, pobladas por los peces
—por la creciente vida que ahora empieza—,
por elevar su voz al aire joven,
donde un sol fulgurante   25
hace plata el amor y oro los abrazos,
las pieles conjugadas,
ese unirse los pechos como las fortalezas que se aplacan fundiéndose.

Pero el fondo palpita como un solo pez abandonado.

De nada sirve que una frente gozosa   30
se incruste en el azul como un sol que se da,
como amor que visita a humanas criaturas.

De nada sirve que un mar inmenso entero
sienta sus peces entre espumas como si fueran pájaros.

El calor que le roba el quieto fondo opaco,   35
la base inconmovible de la milenaria columna
que aplasta un ala de ruiseñor ahogado,
un pico que cantaba la evasión del amor,
gozoso entre unas plumas templadas a un sol nuevo.

Ese profundo obscuro donde no existe el llanto,   40
donde un ojo no gira en su cuévano seco,
pez espada que no puede horadar a la sombra,
donde aplacado el limo no imita un sueño agotado.

(La destrucción 30–31)

[The swordfish, whose fatigue is above all attributable to a failure to bore
    the gloom,
To feel in its flesh the chill of the ocean bottom where the darkness does
    not love,
Where there is none of the fresh yellow seaweed
That is gilded on the surface by the sun.

The plaintive melancholy of that immobile swordfish whose eye   5
    does not turn,
Whose blank stare harms its pupil,
Whose tear slips away through the water itself
With no trace of its sad yellow having been noticed.

The floor of that sea where the immobile fish breathes a mud with its gills,
That water like an air,   10
That fine dust
That only grows excited in feigning the fantasy of a dream,
That is monotonously placated when its still bed is covered in silt
Where the highest mountain bears down its weight and whose crests shake
Like the plumage—yes—of a dark dream.   15

Above, the tresses of foam, dispersed,
Take no heed of the deep feet of silt,
Of that impossibility to break free from the depths,
To rise up with verdant wings above the dry abyss
And elope fearlessly with the ardent sun.   20

The white tresses, the youthful bliss
Populated with fish, hotly roil
—with the expanding life that now begins—,
Struggling to raise a cry to the youthful air,
Where an effulgent sun   25

Makes love silver and embraces, gold,
Two skins as one,
That union of breasts like forces that through fusion find repose.

But the depths beat like a solitary and abandoned fish.

It is vain for a desirous brow   30
To encrust itself in the azure like a surrendering sun,
Like a love that visits human creatures.

It is vain for the immensity of an entire sea
To feel its fish among the foam as if they were birds.

The heat stolen from the sea by the still, dark depths,   35
The immovable base of the millenary column
That crushes the wing of a drowned nightingale,
A beak that once sang of love's elusiveness,
Content in its plumage warmed under a new sun.

Those obscure depths where weeping does not exist,   40
Where an eye does not turn in its dry pouch,
A swordfish that cannot penetrate the shadow,
Where, placated, silt does not imitate a spent dream.]

"Sin luz," like other pieces in which Aleixandre emphasizes mood, stands among the most baroquely conceived poems in the entirety of the poet's work. Simply put, the seascape of "Sin luz"—like the paradisal wilderness of "La selva y el mar"—is not, as it seems, the work's primary referent or subject. Rather, this maritime panorama is an elaborate figurative overlay beneath which lies submerged the poem's subject: a human whose preverbal psychic life serves as the text's referential core and as the focus of its lyric narration. As a result, this manner of narrative presentation—a highly innovative one in the lyric—creates considerable textual difficulties, which will be discussed before proceeding. From the standpoint of reading, the text of "Sin luz" effectively constitutes a sort of rebus in which, like the surrealist game of "l'une dans l'autre," an unnamed object is described in terms of another descriptive system. The objective of the puzzle is to guess the identity of the circumlocuted referent.[2]

The general clues indicating that "Sin luz" is not a description of the natural world and that its coherence is therefore to be found elsewhere lie in the systematic anthropomorphization of its natural imagery, from the "tristeza gemebunda" of the swordfish to the hairlike waves of the ocean surface beneath which this creature is submerged.[3] More specifically, these anthropomorphic signs indicate that the primary referent and poetic tenor of the poem is a human, a human lyrically garbed in elaborate maritime raiment. The most overt signals of the structural human/sea analogue are sounded, though not until more than half-way through the poem, in verses 29–31: "Pero el fondo palpita como un solo pez abandonado" and "De nada sirve que una frente gozosa / se incruste en el azul. . . ." The first line straightens out the work's otherwise inverted metaphorical structure—sea as human, rather than human as sea—which is realized by way of placing the poetic vehicle, the swordfish, after "como." Now couched in a more conventional figurative syntax, the metaphor indicates that the swordfish serves to figure cardiac depths, that is, human affect. Such figurative inversion, which may be seen in the titles of *Espadas como labios* and *La destrucción o el amor,* is an important Aleixandrean device and is symptomatic of the poet's penchant for creatively reworking basic poetic materials. As if in passing, this verse and the following two also reveal—both via "palpitar," connoting heart and love, and through "frente" to which the maritime "cabelleras" of the preceding strophes are attached—that the sea and its depths—the "fondo"—figure an interior reality, a subliminal reality existing beneath the surface of the wavelike tresses of the poem's subject. While establishing this human nether world as the ambit to which "Sin luz" refers, the same verses contain essential structural information regarding the poem's circumstantial and narrative point of departure. Most revealing of that starting point are "frente" and "cabelleras," words whose lexical specificity signals traditional love poems wherein such words are frequently employed to describe the beauty of the beloved. In "Sin luz" these lexical vestiges of the past, which stand as the sole physical descriptions of the human subject, intimate that the text's point of departure, like that of innumerable amatory ancestors, is a sort of poet-before-the-beloved scene. In Aleixandre, this kind of situational nucleus is quite frequent.[4] What is highly innovative in Aleixandre's contemplation of the amorous subject in "Sin luz" is the discursive and thematic approach that the poet takes toward this traditional model, an approach that radically affects the configuration of this type of poem.

The factor that plays the central role in reconfiguring this time-honored sort of love poem is Aleixandre's manipulation of mood. Indeed, mood is of key formal importance in creating the baroque double vision of beloved/seascape and in translating the poet's surrealist conception of love. With respect to narratological structure, "Sin luz" is generally akin to "Don de la materia" in that it is framed as an interior focalization or "vision avec," a perspective which, as noted, carries with it certain restrictions of field (i.e., what we read is largely limited to what the focal character sees, feels, thinks, and so on). Notwithstanding this overall narrative similarity, "Sin luz" diverges from Salinas's poem in its particular narrative configuration of mood. Borrowing Dorit Cohn's expressive coinage, "Sin luz" is a "psycho-narration," a narrative form of mood in which an omniscient narrator mediates, via his or her discourse, the inner preverbal life of a focal character.[5] In contrast, "Don de la materia" is construed as a sort of first-person type of narrative wherein the lens-like persona focuses the text through his own perspective which, as there has been occasion to see, is an eminently conscious one. Generally speaking, the application of psycho-narration to poetry is highly innovative. Many traditional love poems, such as the type on which "Sin luz" is based, are delivered by a persona who limits the description of the beloved to potentially observable moral or physical traits. The latter can include, for example, "cabelleras" [tresses], "frente" [brow], "labios" [lips], or "ojos" [eyes]. Additionally, this lyric exteriority, which tends to sketch a clear line between poet and subject via pronouns and verbs, is presented as focalized through the sensibility of the bard, not through the inner workings of the beloved's preverbal mind. By employing psycho-narrative technique Aleixandre radically recasts such traditional narrative structure by making the psychic recesses of the human subject the focus of the text and the materia prima of its lyric plot. Thus, while there are scant physical references to the subject, allusions to that subject's psychic world are relatively abundant. In "Sin luz" such references include "cansancio," "sentir," "fondo," "tristeza," "fantasía," "sueño oscuro," and "palpita." Before a closer examination of "Sin luz," it bears noting that the employ of psycho-narration complicates the Aleixandrean text in two general ways. First, as suggested above, psycho-narrative technique effectively blurs the formal distinction between persona and subject, a fictional division important for naturalizing a poem, and for discerning its figurative development. Consequently, we are faced with the questions To what extent "Sin luz" can be taken as the mediational activity of the narrator, and, To what extent it can be understood as the account of the working of the poetic subject's mind?[6] One of the chief means by which the poem blocks access to this structural information is by totally eliding any overt pronominal or verbal clues. There is no lexicalized "yo-tú" delineation nor does the narrator explicitly make his presence felt through voicing, a stylistic exception in La destrucción o el amor where voice, in particular apostrophe, is a central feature in the vast majority of the poems, in roughly 80 percent by my own calculations.

The second way in which psycho-narration complicates the text of "Sin luz" has to do with the very nature of the representational task associated with this particular narrative mood. Specifically, it is through this technique that Aleixandre sets out to translate the subconscious, an otherwise unverbalized and hidden inner human reality. Perhaps the most immediately appreciable way in which the subconscious is simulated is through the fluid character of the text, which seems to develop associatively. Added to this complication is the medium of poetry itself, in whose already indirect language of metaphor and image Aleixandre conceptualizes the psychic arcanum of the subconscious. At any rate, Aleixandre's recasting of poetic form in the contours of the subconscious obscures both the primary referent and the situational nucleus of the poem and thereby poses a considerable barrier to comprehension.

Now to a more detailed look at Aleixandre's narrative recasting in "Sin luz," a poem in which a familiar situational kernel—the poet before the lover—is transformed into a highly elaborate maritime "engaño," or double vision. "Sin luz" begins quite abruptly, as do many Aleixandrean poems in *La destrucción o el amor*. The "pez espada," described in two of the book's longest verses, introduces, in medias res, the work's psychic mediation. The "cansancio," or malaise, of this mental denizen of the deep is reflected in the stasis of the first three strophes, a lifelessness reinforced by the lack of main verbs and repeated throughout the poem by images of dust, darkness, and stagnation. The first two strophes, in which the affectively mired fish is most directly described, have an especially peculiar air about them, owing to the stylistic disparity between bookishness and irrationality. While the anaphoric pronoun, "cuyo," and the impersonal construction, "se atribuye," couch the ostensible piscatorial subject in a rather encyclopedia-style language, the grammatical incompleteness of the following description, its lengthy, associative meanders and odd contents imbue the text with a markedly automatic flavor. This syntactic antithesis acts to enunciate the core anecdote of the poem, an instinct vs. intellect conflict within the focal human subject. The appreciable irrationality itself is a stylistic sign that the poem is to be naturalized as deriving from the subconscious, an impression reconfirmed by the seemingly unprepared for and strange disappearance of the fish who, after verse 9, is named only twice: first, in the vehicle slot of "Pero el fondo palpita como un solo pez abandonado" and then in the last strophe. Actually, Aleixandre's "poisson soluble" dissolves gradually, in a syntactical series that, in the first verse of each of the work's first three stanzas, place him in positions of decreasing importance: the swordfish goes from highly visible subject ("El pez espada, . . ."), to prepositional object ("La tristeza gemebunda de ese inmóvil pez espada . . .");

thirdly, he is relegated to a subordinate clause, itself imbedded in a prepositional phrase ("El fondo de ese mar donde el inmóvil pez respira . . ."). The three metaphorically key words—"pez espada," "tristeza," and "fondo"—are variants of human affect, which is repeated and made patent in the cardiological "palpita" of verse 29. The stagnant and penumbral submarine world depicted in the first three stanzas stands as a poetic x-ray of the focal beloved's instinctual depths; it also establishes the particular conflict played out therein. In essence, this plot consists of the ancient story of unrequited love which Aleixandre re-thematizes a la Freud as the repression of erotic instincts. Generally, the psychosexual turmoil within the focal human is conceptualized as "la fantasía de un sueño"—as an impinging erotic fantasy—and later as a millenarian column crushing the wing of a drowned nightingale—civilization in emblematic form as it antagonistically represses surfacing sexual instinct. In this, it is worth recalling that Aleixandre spoke of his surrealist work as a "ruptura" from previous poetry, a breaking-off which he explained as the consequence of writing poetry from a psychic point of view. The poet summarizes this poetics in a way that nearly encapsulates the anecdote underlying "Sin luz." His poetic world—he says—is, "Un mundo de movimientos casi subterráneos, donde los elementos subconscientes servían a la visión del caos original allí contemplado, y a la voz telúrica del hombre elemental que, inmerso, se debatía" (*OC* 2:541) [A world of almost subterranean movements, where subconscious elements went into the original chaos therein contemplated and into the telluric voice of man who, submerged, was struggling with himself].

The fourth and fifth stanzas logically complement the first three by providing, in a reversed order of cause and effect, an explanation for the initial melancholy atmosphere of the poem—"la tristeza gemebunda." This is done by way of filling out the poem's psychological plot, which is prepared for by means of descriptive change. This change is initiated in the third strophe where the poem leads us up the submarine mountains of the subconscious to the peak of a dark dream. For their part, stanzas four and five narrate not the penumbral and stagnant affective depths of Aleixandre's human subject but rather cognition, which is figured as a dynamic ocean surface—"arriba"—bathed in amorous light. These stanzas develop as a miniature, a brief anecdote in the style of the Golden Age that casts sea and sky as lovers. The pair, in amorous idyll, would potentially unite in fiery mystical love-death, expressed here in a mixed metallurgical and military conceit, "ese unirse de pechos como las fortalezas que se aplacan fundiéndose." However, the main verbs of both stanzas—the cognitive "ignoran" and the sentient "pugnan"—negatively frame the miniature as an impossible daydream, as a mental exercise in futility on the part of the focal character who wistfully imagines this sort of amorous fable. Here lies the explanation for the depressive ennui portrayed in the greater part of the first three stanzas: the romantic "cabelleras"—a synecdoche for the fantasizing focal character—imagine love as an idealized and therefore impossible form while ignoring and thereby suppressing the deeper reality of erotic instinct. The struggle for love—ethereal, idealized love—is a vain one, a thematic motif iterated throughout the work of Aleixandre. To this point, the figurative development of "Sin luz" systematically mirrors the unconscious-conscious binary at the heart of the narrated psychic conflict. The entirety of the first three stanzas poetically conceptualizes human instinct as a "fondo," as depths, an oceanic heart of darkness in which the repressed sexuality of its main occupant is effectively equivalent to a nonlife. The following pair of stanzas figure consciousness in a way diametrically opposed to the subconscious. Here, albeit in the context of futile mental activity, all is light, sky, and air.

The narrative task of the first five stanzas, then, is to portray the basic heart-mind conflict of the poem, which is figuratively foregrounded at the beginning of each strophe: "El pez espada . . . ," "La tristeza gemebunda de ese pez . . . ," "El fondo de ese mar . . . ," "Arriba las espumas . . . ," "Las blancas cabelleras. . . ." In the context of psycho-narration, in which the omniscient persona is primarily engaged in chronicling the psychic activity of the unhappy focalizer, the insertion of the following triple series of verses—"Pero el fondo . . . ," "De nada sirve que . . . ," "De nada sirve que . . ."—stylistically halts the poem. What is most arresting about the series is not so much the separate typographical space given each. What disturbs the poem is the style of their introits, which foregrounds rhetoric rather than image. This bit of stylistic invasiveness effects a brief but significant alteration or breach in the up-to-now unbroken focal pattern of "Sin luz." It does so—though not in a manner as direct as apostrophe—by bringing to our attention voice and the mediational activity of the omniscient and otherwise formally invisible narrator. On one hand, this wispy voicing suggests the narrator-subject relation at the structural bottom of "Sin luz" and encases the clearest clue to the poem's base metaphor, the human/sea indicated in the synechdochic palpitating heart/swordfish analogy. On the other hand, this verse heralds the discursive task of the remainder of the poem. Aleixandre's omniscient narrator is henceforth charged with evaluating and concluding the psychic plot recounted in the preceding

text. In this, "pero" is the key transitional word. It rejoins the immediately preceding daydream with the "fondo" narrated in the first
three strophes of the text, thus bringing the poem full circle. By this
means, too, the psychic cause and effect narrated to this point is reiterated and the poem is now ready to start off on the analytical leg
of its rhetorical mission. As indicated, this is launched via "pero" and
the aphoristic sounding "De nada sirve que." Together, these phrases
negatively frame the head vs. heart story, thus qualifying the stance
taken by the omniscient narrator toward the focal "tú." For this purpose, each of the two "De nada sirve que" verses thematizes that story
as a lesson in "vanitas" by reintroducing each of the psychic plot
components, which return as periphrastic miniatures. The ethereal
imagining of the focal character is subordinated to the first "De
nada sirve que." Here, the narrator stresses the artificiality and futility of the maiden-in-distress-waiting-for-her-lover topos suggested in
the "cabelleras" section, stanzas 4 and 5. The precious and jewel-like
brow connoted by "se incruste," the pleasurable but necessarily unreal and fleeting daydream set in "el azul," and the passivity that en-
compasses these motifs recall a specific intertext, Rubén Darío's
"Sonatina," his well-known Modernista work whose sad, bejeweled
princess stares into the azure ether waiting for her prince.

In citing this particular poem, "Sin luz" responds to and qualifies
the amorous theme of the Nicaraguan ancestor. In fact, it is by virtue
of the Darío connection that "azul," one of the very few chromatic
motifs in Aleixandre, is most often negativized, standing for futile
illusion. The second "De nada sirve que" subordinates the now abstracted "fondo" section of the poem, continuing the elaborate
maritime figuration of the first three stanzas: "De nada sirve que
un mar inmenso entero / sienta sus peces entre espumas como si
fueran pájaros." The two verses, given their brevity as well as their
formulaic beginning, have an especially aphoristic air about them.
The word "pájaros" brings to mind the popular adage, "Más vale pájaro en mano que cien volando" [literally, A bird in hand is worth
more than a hundred on the wing]. The thematics of the concrete
vs. the ethereal that is translated by the saying's airborne and un-
reachable birds may indeed play a part in the intertextuality of Aleixandre's verses. When translated from the poetic language of "Sin luz,"
these verses render a tautological lesson: It is vain to feel/live one's
desire in the imagination as if desire were—like the imagination—
ethereal. The textual proximity of these verses to Rubén Darío—particularly the "azul" fragment of the preceding three verses—offers
additional intertextual territory for deciphering the message of "Sin
luz." Pasted together, "azul" and "pájaros" approximate the title of

another Darío work, "El pájaro azul" [The Blue Bird], a prose poem narrating the death of a romantic poet whose imagination—the pájaro azul—effectively causes his unhappy demise.[7] This same bird also flies through the narratological and thematic ether of "La selva y el mar" where, in the closing stanzas, this emblem of futile psychic activity—"azul pájaro o pluma" [azure bird or plume]—is described as inventing the highest branches ("inventa los ramajes más altos"), where he remains above the erotic wilderness below. Like the distant azure ether, birds, especially diminished, aloof birds that do not alight, are messengers of Aleixandre's negative stance toward idealized love, itself one of the equivalents of death or "destrucción" in *La destrucción o el amor.* Shortly we will turn our attention to other psychic birds—"Las águilas"—birds of a complementary thematic and narratological feather.

The rhetorical mission of the penultimate stanza of "Sin luz" is to offer a final commentary on the psychic drama played out within the focal subject. This closing observation is initiated in verses 33–34, where the omniscient narrator refers to the focal subject in its most expansive metonymic form, the human as "un mar inmenso entero," to which the "le" of verse 35 subsequently refers. The penultimate stanza proceeds to reexamine the depths of the human sea by insetting one more miniature into the poem, an exemplum iterating the theme of repressed love, though this time putting it in a cultural perspective. The antagonist, the "milenaria columna"—an emblem of the artificial or civilized—is itself firmly ensconced in the oceanic depths of the focal beloved. Crushed beneath this symbol of the "cooked" lies the now flightless and silent nightingale, the literary bird of love and antithesis of the "pájaros" of the preceding text. The anecdote implicit in this section is suggested by three fragments: the nightingale, a traditional motif in amorous literature such as the pastoral; the only past tense in the poem, "cantaba," which, by contrast with other temporal deictics, emphatically casts the song of the nightingale in a world that used to be, an erotic Arcadia with its "sol nuevo"; and the "evasión del amor," a plot fragment common in classical mythology and repeated throughout Western literature. The amorous evasion conjured up in this context, like the relation "pájaros"-"ruiseñor," is antithetical both to the main plot of "Sin luz"—the psycho-narration of the focal subject's inner sexual repression—and to the ancillary miniatures with which that plot is qualified—the Daríoesque fragments. The difference lies in the mental versus physical quality of their respective story lines. Whereas the latter are emphatically psychological quests for an idealized, and thus impossible, amorous goal, the target of the "evasión del amor" suggested in the final inset is overtly carnal and, therefore, attainable, at least in theory. In mythology, for example, there are many variants of the amorous pursuit, all charged with erotic content: Zeus and Europa, Apollo and Daphne, Polyphemus and Galatea, and so on. The column of civilization—of science, of art, of the rationalized and sublimated—thus stands as the ultimate cause of the story of sexual repression narrated in "Sin luz" and of erotic repression in general. The locus of the column, its entrenchment precisely in the very depths of the maritime human, is the perfect image of the superego, the internalized mores of civilization which crush the id, the psychic node of inborn and therefore natural erotic impulses. The final strophe of the poem emphasizes the triumph of the superego over the id by repeating the stagnant atmosphere of the first section (strophes 1–3). This closure not only brings the poem full circle to the dark "fondo" and to its denizen, the "pez espada"; it also adds one final and ironic note to the psycho-narrative denouement. The repression of desire—and the sublimation of its libidinous force in futile Romantic-style daydream—results in complete affective and sensual numbness. The terraqueous substance—"limo," desire or carnal longing—is, in a pejorative sense, "aplacado," a necessarily false placation of the physical and instinctual quite unlike the realized erotic quest or nondream to which "un sueño agotado" of the last verse refers.

Aleixandre's particular choice of the structural human/sea metonym for the figural translation of the psyche in "Sin luz" is directly related to the poet's idea of the id. As suggested in the poem, the inborn and ineluctable erotic impulses contained therein are tantamount to destiny. The poet's election of the sea as vehicle could not be more traditional, given that the sea is a time-honored symbolic shorthand for destiny. Intertextual traces of the destiny/sea pairing are scattered throughout Western culture and are quite visible in poetry, including Aleixandre's own. One of the most memorable examples of this symbolic function can be seen in "Soy el destino" where destiny—the very protagonist of the piece—voices itself, and the lovers which it contains, as a simultaneously circular, floral and sonorous sea:

> Soy el destino que convoca a todos los que aman,
> mar único al que vendrán todos los radios amantes
> que buscan a su centro, rizados por el círculo
> que gira como la rosa rumorosa y total.
> (*La destrucción* 192)

[I am the destiny that summons all who love,
The unitary sea to which will come all radiant lovers
That, as they seek their center, are rippled by the circle
that in gyres turns like the sonorous and absolute rose.]

The structural rationale behind the maritime expansion in "Sin luz" is based on an expansion of the vehicular component of the hombre/tierra meme. That the human tenor is primarily mapped via a maritime descriptive system in "Sin luz" concords with the particular thematic concern of this piece, which, again, is to emphasize that humanity's instinctual essence—the id—is also its destiny, its sea, or font of both life and death.

Before proceeding to "Las águilas," the second example of how mood functions in *La destrucción o el amor,* there remain a couple of general points to be made about what has been said regarding psycho-narration, the narrative technique whereby an omniscient narrator mediates the preverbal psychic life of a focal character. Partly due to its sheer novelty in the lyric, and partly because of its potential for skewing narrative structure in general, psycho-narration effectively defamiliarizes conventional poetic form including the situational nucleus or scene—the poet-lover relation—and the primary tenor/vehicle structure, hombre/mar. Left unmentioned in the preceding discussion of "Sin luz" is the considerable role that this narrative mode plays in obfuscating the piece's generic horizon. Like many other of Aleixandre's poems, "Sin luz" shows a very strong affinity with the ode. Its triadic structure—akin to "strophe," "antistrophe," and "epode" of many traditional odes—its didactic tone and grand formal and thematic conformation all point toward the ode. However, apostrophe, one of this genre's most important generic signals, is elided, the result of the strong narrative emphasis on mood over voice. As we shall see at every turn, such recasting of the traditionally poetic is at the heart of Aleixandre's poetics. What Aleixandre's use of psycho-narration also reflects, and quite graphically, is the considerable formal and ideological investment that the poet had made in the concept of the subconscious by the time he wrote *La destrucción o el amor* in 1932–33. In his endeavor to portray this subterranean (i.e., intra-human) world, Aleixandre falls plainly in line with surrealism, the avant-garde dedicated to the meliorative interpretation of Freud, whose scientific theory of the subconscious acts as a seminal concept from which surrealism launches its vindication of the irrational.[8] What also becomes clear in the light of the narrative structure of "Sin luz" is that Aleixandre's surrealist method can justifiably be described as "automatismo controlado" [controlled automatism], though not as "psychic automatism in its pure state," the famous Breton formula often taken as synonymous with all surrealist poetry.[9] The strongest justification for adding control to automatism lies in the evident combination of traditional lyric materials and narrative technique, which suggests not a free-associative method but one based on artistic and cultural association designed to create the poem's noticeably irrational and automatic ambience.

Now to "Las águilas" [The Eagles], a second example in which Aleixandre employs psycho-narration to render the preverbal world of his poetic subject.

El mundo encierra la verdad de la vida
aunque la sangre mienta melancólicamente
cuando como mar sereno en la tarde
siente arriba el batir de las águilas libres.

Las plumas de metal,   5
las garras poderosas,
ese afán del amor o la muerte,
ese deseo de beber en los ojos con un pico de hierro,
de poder al fin besar lo exterior de la tierra,
vuela como el deseo,   10
como las nubes que a nada se oponen,
como el azul radiante, corazón ya de afuera
en que la libertad se ha abierto para el mundo.

Las águilas serenas
no serán nunca esquifes,   15
no serán sueño o pájaro,
no serán caja donde olvidar lo triste,
donde tener guardado esmeraldas u ópalos.

El sol que cuaja en las pupilas,
que a las pupilas mira libremente,   20
es ave inmarcesible, vencedor de los pechos
donde hundir su furor contra un cuerpo amarrado.

Las violentas alas
que azotan rostros como eclipses,
que parten venas de zafiro muerto,   25
que seccionan la sangre coagulada,
rompen el viento en mil pedazos,
mármol o espacio impenetrable
donde una mano muerta detenida
es el claror que en la noche fulgura.   30

Aguilas como abismos,
como montes altísimos,
derriban majestades, troncos polvorientos,
esa verde hiedra que en los muslos
finge la lengua vegetal casi viva.   35

Se aproxima el momento en que la dicha consista
en desvestir de piel a los cuerpos humanos,
en que el celeste ojo victorioso
vea sólo a la tierra como sangre que gira.

Aguilas de metal sonorísimo,   40
arpas furiosas con su voz casi humana,
cantan la ira de amar los corazones,
amarlos con las garras estrujando su muerte.
                                  (*La destrucción* 216–17)

[Earth holds life's truth,
Even though blood may sadly feign
When, like a calm afternoon sea,
It senses the narrowing swoop of free eagles.

The metal feathers,   5
The powerful talons,
That thirst for love or death,
That urge to drink from eyes with iron beaks,
To be able to kiss at last the surface of the earth,
Flies like desire,   10
Like penetrable clouds,
Like the radiant azure, the heart exposed,
Opening its freedom to the world.

The serene eagles
Will never be skiffs,   15
Nor dream, nor bird,
Nor a box for forgetting sadness,
A place to keep emeralds or opals.

The sun that coagulates in the eyes,
That freely gazes into the eyes,   20
Is an everlasting bird, a victor of breasts
That sinks its rage into a bound body.

The violent wings
That flog eclipsing countenances,
That open veins of defunct sapphire,   25

That split coagulated blood,
Shatter the wind into a thousand pieces,
Marble, or an impenetrable space
Where, in restraints, a dead hand
Is the clarity that flashes in the night.   30

Eagles like abysses,
Like the highest mountains,
Overthrow majesties, trunks veiled in dust,
The green ivy that, clinging to the thighs,
Imitates the almost living vegetable tongue.   35

The day is at hand when bliss will consist
Of divesting human bodies of skin,
When, victorious, the celestial eye
Will only see the earth as a gyre of blood.

Eagles of most resonant metal,   40
Furious harps with their almost human voice,
Sing the ire of loving hearts,
Of taloned love squeezing out death.]

"Las águilas" affords fertile territory for the further exploration of the poetic logic behind Aleixandre's surrealism. It not only serves as a second example of psycho-narrative mood and of the disruptive effect that this novel perspective works on an otherwise conventional, and thus intelligible, sort of poem. This particular piece also offers a graphic illustration of the poet's penchant for defamiliarizing the human subject, a marked textual characteristic throughout Aleixandre's surrealistic period.[10]

At first sight, "Las águilas" may well seem rather unproblematic when compared to "Sin luz." While "Sin luz" seems to overpower and disorient with its copious imagery, "Las águilas" may quite well give the impression that it is rather clear-cut. Judging from outward appearances, this piece, which is figuratively structured on the analogy desire/eagles, seems to be a sort of animal poem to be read symbolically, the eagles standing for desire in much the same way that Machado's flies incarnate time in "Las moscas." The impression of clarity comes by way of the second stanza, where the raptors' symbolic function is indicated quite explicitly, and is maintained throughout, the aquiline figuration being developed with relatively few digressions. While the symbolic mission of the eagles is certainly not insignificant, the poem's seemingly streamlined metaphorical conformation as an "imagen continuada" [extended image]—Bousoño's term—is as deceptive as the baroque outline of "Sin luz." In brief, the poem's primary referent is not an outer aquiline landscape but rather the interior and preverbal psychoscape of the work's human subject. As in "Sin luz," it is this occult instinctual ambit—the inner world of the focal "tú"—that the omniscient narrator mediates in the course of the poem. That the setting is not geographic per se is belied by the anthropomorphic signs that permeate the poem, including "sangre," "siente," "sueño," "la ira de amar," and so on. To these affective allusions we need to add two structurally revealing physical references, both ocular: "ese deseo de beber en los ojos" of verse 8 and "El sol que cuaja en las pupilas, / que a las pupilas mira libremente," of verses 19–20. Constituting but a swift break or alteration in narrative modality (from the tonic inner focus to an exterior one), these bits of outer description, like the "cabelleras" and "frente" of "Sin luz," elliptically afford a brief overview of the human referent and intimate the attendant situational kernel from which the piece arises. Gathered together, the fragments suggest an embryonic eyes-meet-eyes love story, in particular the ensuing erotic surge thereby produced in the focal beloved. That libidinous surge, or "deseo," is figuratively incarnate in the eagles. The eye reference and the accompanying situational fiction that these fragments hint at exist both as traditional motifs in amorous poetry, and as commonplaces in our collective lore of love. Consider, for instance, the following Santa Teresa "villancico." As in "Las águilas," the amorous denouement of eyes-meet-eyes is meliorative destruction:

> Véante mis ojos,
> dulce Jesús bueno;
> véante mis ojos,
> muérame yo luego.[11]

> [May my eyes see You,
> Sweet, good Jesus;
> May my eyes see You,
> So that I may die at once.]

The Petrarchan conceit, "eyes like suns," is also manifest here—as in other Aleixandrean poems such as "Unidad en ella"—in the pairing of eyes and sun, condensed in verses 19 and 20, "El sol que cuaja en las pupilas, / que a las pupilas mira libremente." Also at play in the plot of desire are commonplaces like "El amor entra por los ojos" [love enters through the eyes], "amor a primera vista" [love at first sight], and "beber en los ojos del amado" [to drink from the eyes of the beloved], the latter being actualized in verse 8, "ese deseo de beber en los ojos con un pico de hierro."[12] Finally, it should be noted that the eye is in itself a perfect device for launching psycho-narration: the eye is the "espejo del alma," a mirror-like point of access to the human inner world, wherein the spirit—or its modern counterpart, the psychic complex of id, ego, and superego—abides. In surrealist art, the most memorable example of the eye as the focal point for narrating the psychosexual world of the subconscious is to be found in the opening scene of the Luis Buñuel-Salvador Dalí film, "Un Chien Andalou" [An Andalusian Dog]. Here, thanks to the neat razor-made incision of the focal character's eye, we become privy to an incongruous inner world, replete with bizarre dreamlike images set in a plot similar to that of "Sin luz" or "Las águilas," in which erotic instinct is pitted against the internalized repressive forces of the superego.

Both from the previous discussion of "Sin luz" and the present one of "Las águilas," it is certainly not unfair to claim that mood, psycho-narration in particular, is the primary factor in disrupting our comprehension of these poems. We have seen quite clearly that this narrative manner of x-raying the subconscious inner world of a poem's human subject defamiliarizes some of the basic structures on which we rely for orienting poetry. To wit, by recasting the poem as a largely interior rather than exterior representation, Aleixandre all but erases the primary referent and surrounding circumstantial fiction that are so important to the initial naturalization of the text. Nonetheless, a traditional poetic scene is still inscribed, though obliquely so, in both pieces. It functions, when recuperated, as an important point of departure toward perceiving the poem's target mimesis, the psychosexual drama played out within the recesses of the focal subject. The strongest evidence for psycho-narration's effectiveness in poetic rearrangement is the careful sleuthing that this technique requires on the part of the reader: both in "Sin luz" and in "Las águilas" we have literally had to piece together the situational nucleus. In "Las águilas," reconstruction of the familiar has been greatly aided by retrieving the aforementioned eye references, which not only suggest that the poem is born of a familiar sort of poetic anecdote—the eyes-meet-eyes story—but also serve as a referential clue signaling the poem's interior rather than outer focus. More generally, the obscurity of these Aleixandrean pieces dramatizes the functional importance of basics—whether we are fully aware of them or not—to the reading of poetry.

Let us now take a more detailed look at how Aleixandre defamiliarizes his human subject in "Las águilas." This analytical task must endeavor to answer one central question: How, or by what logic, does the conventional and potentially full-blown human subject become metamorphosed into air-borne raptors? This tour de force of Ortegian "deshumanización" begins with the basic composition or ontology of Aleixandre's human, who not only acts as the primary referent and focalizer, but also as the poem's semantic and figural nucleus around which all other constituents are organized. In "Las águilas"—and this is applicable to all of *La destrucción o el amor*—the human subject is quite "flat" and reducible to a small cluster of traits.[13] In effect, the human might well be defined as the Freudian era version of the biblical human ontology complex discussed earlier. Human essence, though still hinging on the flesh-spirit binary, has been altered, the age-old spiritual component—the Judeo-Christian soul or divine breath of life—having been replaced with the id, the psychosexual instinct and innate life force impelling human behavior. The only further human ingredient to be added is the superego, which is an acquired and thus a nonessential set of internalized social mores roughly equivalent to civilization, as seen in "Sin luz." At odds with humankind's primitive psychosomatic character, the superego acts as the most imposing barrier to the fulfillment of human destiny, the carnal-spiritual union of human with human which Aleixandre, echoing his cultural and linguistic patrimony, still calls "el amor," as advertised titularly in *La destrucción o el amor.*

In "Las águilas," the trinal scheme of flesh, spirit and superego is condensed in the first strophe where the two congenital components of the human ontology complex are translated metonymically. "El mundo," an expanded variant of the biblical source metonym of "arcilla" or "barro," stands for flesh; spirit or id is figured as "sangre" and "mar," both metaphoric shorthand for innate instinct and destiny. In Aleixandre, amorous instinct and destiny are inextricably bound together and are inseparable from the terraqueous vessel of the human in which they are enclosed. The superego, and the potential conflict that this nonessential element may cause, are summed up in "mienta," whose meaning of dissimulation or repression is modally cast here, via the subjunctive, as a potentiality. The closing strophes, which lexically announce the imminence of desire's fulfillment ("Se aproxima el momento . . ."), answer to and resolve the "maybe" implicit in the "mienta" of the introit. In this way, and in marked contrast to "Sin luz," "Las águilas" narrates an inner story chronicling the victory of the id—the "pasión de la tierra" [earth's passion]—over the superego. The happy erotic outcome of the psycho-narration is directly reflected in the lively rhythm of the poem and in its epic-flavored imagery. Consequent with the abstraction of the human to a cluster of essential traits is the omission of any concrete identity, including gender. Not only in this poem but throughout *La destrucción o el amor* and its predecessor, *Espadas como labios,* there are only exceptional pieces in which clear reference is made to male or female identity. Such a stylistic elision is very unusual and even a bit unnerving in love poetry, a fact echoed among readers who have naturalized such poems by supplying gender. Seen another way, Aleixandre's use of a collective and generic human model bereft of particulars falls squarely in line with the project of surrealism as a whole, one of whose central goals is to vindicate the universally human, namely our collective irrational patrimony. In this, Aleixandre belongs to the tradition of "poetas radicales" [radical poets], as he himself calls those poets who address, "no a lo que refinadamente diferencia, sino a lo que esencialmente une" (*OC* 2:525) [not what finely differentiates, but that which essentially unifies].

As indicated, the defamiliarization of the human subject in "Las águilas" involves several steps. The first is narratological and involves the omniscient persona's focalizing the text through the preverbal world of the human subject, a maneuver that restricts the text to the sentient perspective of the latter. The second step consists of the reduction of the human to a cluster of essential traits, in effect, to a modern version of an ancient ontology complex. The third step toward the "deshumanización" of the human referent consists of an expansion of the aforementioned traits, which serve as the poem's formal and semantic *materia prima.* It is finally, through this expansive process of figurative "arborización" [arboreous expansion]—Bousoño's coinage—that the primary referent and attendant scene nearly disappear from sight. In "Las águilas," the figurative interment of the focal subject begins, as in many other Aleixandrean pieces, with the expansion of the underlying human=earth formula, which here produces an expanse of sea, land, and sky. However, "Las águilas," as opposed to other psycho-narrations such as "La selva y el mar" or "Sin luz," visibly emphasizes one trait, the erotic force of the id. Here, the id in aquiline guise functions as a synecdoche for the human focalizer and protagonizes the text. The figural contract for the desire/eagles analogy is drawn up by the "como" simile of verse three and is overtly detailed in the second stanza where eros/ eagles is paraphrased in each of the first four verses. The analogy comes full circle in the aeronautical main clause, "vuela como el deseo," which repeats "ese deseo de beber en los ojos." Although the psychic anecdote narrated in the poem is a simple one—paraphrase-able as "desire impinges on flesh"—the metamorphosis of that desire into eagles is complicated and might even seem far-fetched or randomly produced. Nonetheless, these Aleixandrean birds are not without a greater cultural and poetic genealogy, and come to the poem as structural vehicle by way of a rather complicated conflu-ence of associated intertextualities. One source—a time-honored source for conceiving love or its variants as winged—is the demigod Amor, who is portrayed plastically and in literature as a winged boy armed with bow and darts, ready to send mortals into the dizzying and irrational throes of desire. The arrows of the hovering rascal could easily be hyperbolized as beaks and talons borne aloft on the wings of eagles which, as the verb "batir" suggests, are narrowing in on their prey. This intertext may well be at play both here and in the "caza de amor" [hunt of love], a figurative model more specifically akin to that of "Las águilas." The "caza de amor" is a traditional con-ceit in which love, though still winged, is mapped as falconry, em-phasizing the violent and destructive character of this emotion. The "caza de amor" has been employed in both secular and "a lo divino" Spanish poetry. In the former, the "caza de amor" portrays love as elusive and dangerous. The poet, casting himself as falcon, gives aerial chase to the beloved, a beautiful but ferocious prey, often a heron. The inevitable result of this amorous falconry is destruction, a destruction caused by the lady's disdain and aloofness, which is figured as a fruitless ethereal pursuit. Aleixandre, in direct line with the Mystics, responds to the use of the "caza de amor" in courtly love poetry by rearranging its traditional plot and sense. While main-taining the basic ornithological hunt motif and the attached pairing of love-death, he, like the Mystics, both places the amorous quarry within reach of his destructive raptors and meliorates the sense of the imminent love-death promised in the poem.[14]

While the "caza de amor" conceit does take us a way toward per-ceiving how the focal human—now reduced to the psychosexual eros—becomes enmasked as birds of prey, it does not satisfactorily account for the specific choice of eagles—vs. hawks, owls, vultures, or other raptors—as the metaphorical vehicle for the id. The ra-tionale for electing this species as a psychic incarnation is to be found in the light of two associated textual features: the first is narrato-logical and involves the nature of the speech act framing the poem; the second feature is lexical and has to do with the verb "mienta," which has already been cited in reference to the superego. What "Las águilas" does, as well as mediating the brief though intense psychic happening within its human subject, is to predict the fulfillment of eros, the happy denouement of the psychic plot. The speech act of prophesy, in which the psycho-narration is ensconced, is most clearly uttered in the opening and closing strophes. As mentioned, the penultimate answers the opening strophe, assuring that "Se aproxima el momento en que la dicha consista / en desvestir de piel a los cuerpos humanos." Notice, too, that the third strophe explicitly iterates the poem's visionary mission, the anaphoric series, "no serán," foretelling what love will not be, which is carried out via a brief paradigm of artificial or ethereal counter examples, including the bird of daydream—"pájaro o sueño"—a relative of the "pájaro azul" of "Sin luz" and "La selva y el mar." The lexically disembodied persona of "Las águilas," who we may deduce is a kind of seer, bases these divinizations on a universal truth, expressed in the aphoristic and high sounding opening verse, "El mundo encierra la verdad de la vida." When decoded from Aleixandre's poetic language, this verse roughly renders: the human contains his or her own destiny, an erotic destiny inextricably bound to the human's terraqueous, rather than ethereal, condition. In the context of the poem as prophetic speech act, the choice of eagles as metaphorical vehicle for a bellicose and victorious id is determined by association with Jupiter, the lusty god whose sacred bird is the eagle, considered an omen of his favor, especially as a sign of impending martial victory. The verb "mienta" of verse two sounds an additional—and quite revealing—intertextual signal reinforcing the id-eagles-Jupiter connection. Besides occupying a highly visible position in the poem—the central element of the second verse—"mienta" is quite arresting because of the restricted and quite rare poetic sense it has here, meaning to feign or to belie true form. Poetically charged in this way, "mentir" in Aleixandre recalls a specific ancestor text, Góngora's celebrated "Soledad Primera" [First Solitude], where the variant "mentido," again found in the central position of the second verse, is used, as are other elements, to give a mythical cast to the poem's scene and plot:

> Era del año la estación florida
> en que el mentido robador de Europa
> —media luna las armas de su frente,
> y el Sol todos los rayos de su pelo—,
>   luciente honor del cielo,
> en campos de zafiro pace estrellas;
> cuando el que ministrar podía la copa
> a Júpiter mejor que el garzón de Ida,
> —náufrago y desdeñado, sobre ausente—
> lagrimosas de amor dulces querellas
>   da al mar; que condolido,
>   fue a las ondas, fue al viento
>   el mísero gemido,
> segundo de Arión dulce instrumento.[15]

[It was the flowery time of year
When the feigned robber of Europa
—the crescent moon, the weapons of his brow,
And the Sun, the resplendent beams of his coat—,
    The shining pride of heaven,
Grazes on stars in fields of sapphire;
When he who was more worthy to bear the cup
Of Jupiter than even Ida's attendant,
—shipwrecked and unhappy in love—
Tearful and sweet plaints of love
    Makes to the sea; moved to compassion,
    The waves and the wind are stirred by
    His unhappy sighs,
Arion's second sweet instrument.]

The Gongorine scene is given as the dawning spring sky which, in Taurus, is described through allusion to Jupiter's rape of Europa in the guise of a bull, "el mentido robador"; the taurine horns are the crescent moon while the lustrous coat is the rays of the rising sun. The protagonist—a lovesick and shipwrecked victim of fate—emerges from the sea and is compared to Ganymede, the beautiful youth sequestered by the libidinous Jupiter in aquiline form. Aleixandre, in enmasking the id, has absorbed and rearranged several Gongorine motifs: the id is effectively apotheosized, having been cloaked in the aquiline form of the erotic divinity alluded to in Góngora; in Aleixandre, the human referent is a Ganymede-like victim of winged desire, and is subject to its "rapto," an abduction which is both fated, by virtue of the human's own carnal condition from whence eros springs, and which is to deliver the mortal out of "soledad," to amorous union.

The Gongorine intertext also plays an important generative role in Aleixandre's figurative dramatization of the id's augured victory over the superego. Toward this end, Aleixandre assimilates two fragments from the "Soledad": the first is the word "zafiro" for sky, which appears in the fifth strophe; the second is the Gongorine ambient motif of sunrise which, in Aleixandre's penultimate stanza—"celeste ojo victorioso"—triumphantly heralds the new day of amorous freedom.[16] "Zafiro," because of its additional gemological association, acts as point of departure for Aleixandre's pejorative description of the superego. The internalized antagonist or superego—another minimal trait comprising the human referent of "Las águilas"—is first figured as a faux sky, an internalized and artificial barrier to the focalizer's erotic instinct. The libidinous eagles' destruction of the superego is narrated as a systematic rampage beginning with the sky-smashing of verse 27 ("rompen el viento en mil pedazos") and continues through strophes 5 and 6, in a string of associated variants that further chronicle the imminent annihilation of the superego. Exemplifying the imagistic fluidity of Aleixandre's surrealist art, the sapphire firmament grows into the mixed funerary sculpture-moon metaphor of verses 28–30, and into the statuary of verses 34–36. Taken together, the fragments form a collage of literary and artistic motifs reminiscent of the stereotypical forlorn-love-in-the-garden-under-the-moon scene. These images both flesh out the superego in Aleixandre's poem and serve as dramatic backdrop to the id's ultimate and ecstatic victory, a light over darkness story in which the happy dawn of Góngora's "Soledad" is metamorphosed into the id-eagles-Jupiter-sun's light and song filled destruction of darkness.

Is Aleixandre an obscure poet? I think that the discussion of mood in *La destrucción o el amor* exacts an affirmative reply to this question. Both "Sin luz" and "Las águilas" provide the occasion to see that one of the key ingredients of Aleixandre's surrealism is a narrative technique employed in order to reify in lyric form the strange inner arcanum of the subconscious. Realized by way of psycho-narration, the inner perspective to which such poems are restricted radically mutates traditional poetic structure and creates the impression that Aleixandre's poetry is unique if not unfathomable. Conversely, the poetic logic and sense of such poems are to be found in the light of innovation and tradition which, as further consideration of *La destrucción o el amor* reveals, lie at the heart of Aleixandre's surrealism.

4

The Voice of Desire

Dime, dime quién es, quién me
llama, quién me dice, quién clama . . .
[Tell me who it is, who is calling me,
who is speaking to me, who clamors . . .]
—Aleixandre

As "Sin luz" and "Las águilas" may have served to illustrate, Aleixandre's use of mood, in particular of psycho-narration, casts such poems as psychic anecdotes wherein the texts, mediated by an omniscient and apparently unobtrusive narrator, portray the pre-verbal inner life of a focal human. From the reader's perspective, these poems suggest that taking narrative technique into account can prove to be invaluable toward discerning the structure and sense of otherwise hermetic and daunting pieces. But whereas mood responds to the "¿qué es aquello?" quandary by answering Genette's question of who sees, voice sheds light on yet another portion of Aleixandre's surrealist penumbra by replying to the no less important question of who speaks. Indeed, and as Machado's ode, "Las moscas," made patent, voice can play a pivotal lyric role. In particular, voice contextualizes a poem as a discursive happening or event whose interrelated elements lie at the core of lyric intelligibility. In order to illustrate the utility of voice for comprehending Aleixandre's surrealism, I have chosen "Mina," a most intriguing poem and a graphic example of the form and function that this discursive category assumes in *La destrucción o el amor*. In "Mina," voice not only carries out an essential orientational mission common among the many other voiced pieces of the book; this particular instance of voice also encapsulates the primary rhetorical and ideological task undertaken by *La destrucción o el amor* on the whole, including that of apparently nonvoiced poems such as those discussed in relation to mood in the last chapter. Below, the text of "Mina" [Mine]:

Calla, calla. No soy el mar, no soy el cielo,
ni tampoco soy el mundo en que tú vives.

93

Soy el calor que sin nombre avanza sobre las piedras frías,
sobre las arenas donde quedó la huella de un pesar,
sobre el rostro que duerme como duermen las flores   5
cuando comprenden, soñando, que nunca fueron hierro.

Soy el sol que bajo la tierra pugna por quebrantarla
como un brazo solísimo que al fin entreabre su cárcel
y se eleva clamando mientras las aves huyen.
Soy esa amenaza a los cielos con el puño cerrado,   10
sueño de un monte o mar que nadie ha transportado
y que una noche escapa como un mar tan ligero.

Soy el brillo de los peces que sobre el agua finge una red de deseos,
un espejo donde la luna se contempla temblando,
el brillo de unos ojos que pueden deshacerse   15
cuando la noche o nube se cierran como mano.

Dejadme entonces, comprendiendo que el hierro es la salud de vivir,
que el hierro es el resplandor que de sí mismo nace
y que no espera sino la única tierra blanda a que herir como muerte,
dejadme que alce un pico y que hienda a la roca,   20
a la inmutable faz que las aguas no tocan.

Aquí a la orilla, mientras el azul profundo casi es negro,
mientras pasan relámpagos o luto funeral, o ya espejos,
dejadme que se quiebre la luz sobre el acero,
ira que, amor o muerte, se hincará en esta piedra,   25
en esta boca o dientes que saltarán sin luna.

Dejadme, sí, dejadme cavar, cavar sin tregua,
cavar hasta ese nido caliente o plumón tibio,
hasta esa carne dulce donde duermen los pájaros,
los amores de un día cuando el sol luce fuera.   30
                              (*La destrucción* 132–33)

[Quiet. I said be quiet. I am not the sea, I am not the heavens,
Nor am I the world in which you live.
I am the warmth that without name moves along cold stones,
Over the sands where a trace of sorrow was left,
Over the face that sleeps like flowers sleep   5
When, in dreams, they understand that they were never iron.

I am the sun that beneath the earth struggles to break the surface
Like a most solitary arm that at last breaches its prison
And rises, clamoring, while birds take flight.

I am that clench-fisted threat to the heavens,   10
The dream of a mountain or sea that no one has transported
And that one night escapes like a swift-footed sea.

I am the shimmering of fish that on the water a net of desires feigns,
A mirror where the trembling moon looks at herself,
The glimmering of eyes that can dissolve   15
When the night or cloud closes like a hand.

Let me, then, because you understand that iron is the health of life,
That iron is the splendor that of itself is born
And does not wait but for the single piece of soft earth to wound like
    death,
Let me raise a pick and cleave the rock,   20
The immutable face that the waters do not touch.

Here on the shore, while the deep blue is almost black,
While there is lightning or funereal darkness or even mirrors,
Let me make light break on the steel,
An ire which, love or death, will sink into this stone,   25
Into this mouth or teeth that will come flying out without a moon.

Let me, yes, let me dig, dig ceaselessly,
Dig down to that hot nest or warm plumage,
Down to that sweet flesh where birds slumber,
The loves of a day when the sun shines forth.]   30

In overview, "Mina" poses some of the same textual difficulties encountered in the poems discussed in relation to mood. That is, this
piece is mapped out as a strange anthropomorphic landscape whose
contours, rather than well-defined and stable, are untidy and seem
to shift from verse to verse. Such fluidity, a marked feature throughout Aleixandre's surrealism, may be appreciated in the narrator's
initial appellation, "calor," which metamorphoses, in the following
three strophes, into "sol," "amenaza," and "brillo de los peces." In
turn, each of those four pseudonyms gives way to an embedded and
figuratively complex inset, a brief fable spawned by process of association. Again, what the poem refers to is problematic. "Mina" explicitly poses additional questions, questions directly related to the
markedly vocal nature of this text: Who is the "yo" self-defined as
"calor," "sol," "amenaza," and "brillo de los peces"?; who is the addressee, or addressees, to whom the narrating voice directs itself both
in the opening verse and, again, repeatedly in the last three stanzas?;
finally, where does this vocalization take place and what figurative

and thematic purpose might this strange locution serve? Toward answering such fundamental questions, a scrutiny of this poem's introit proves to be most useful.

Like many other poems in *La destrucción o el amor,* "Mina" abruptly commences with an "in medias res" vocalization, the "Calla. Calla. No soy el mar, no soy el cielo, / ni tampoco soy el mundo en que tú vives."[1] This vocal onset is richly charged with narrative information. Its curt phrasing intrusively intimates the rhetorical kernel spawning the entirety of "Mina," which consists of an initial question followed by a rather elaborate and elusive answer. The question, which precedes the text proper, may be deduced from the narrator's first words, the "Calla, calla. No soy el mar." The off-stage query is either the yes/no, "¿Eres el mar? [Are you the sea?], ¿el cielo? [the sky?], ¿el mundo?" [the world?], or a simple "¿Quién eres?" [Who are you?]. The response of the narrating persona suggests several other pieces of narrative information: the addressee is an inquisitive "tú," a seeker of knowledge who is bid to be silent; the information sought is not to be found in the expansive scape of sea, heavens or earth, before the immensity of which, we may surmise, the interrogative "tú" stands; the narrating persona is an apparently unseen or unobservable source, a speaking enigma "sin nombre" who eludes the seeker's quest for knowledge; the enigmatic speaker appears to hail from a cosmos other than the one observed by the addressee. Appropriately, then, the response of the arcane speaker (i.e., the entire poem) does not provide a clear notion of vocal identity but poses a riddle whose contents are restricted to what that mysterious entity says. Also noteworthy is the tone of the homey "Calla, calla" imperative, which suggests, ironically enough, a familiar relationship between the enigma and its inquisitor. Indeed, the curt phrasing of this particular imperative might well lead one to suspect that the enigma is a bit fed up with the sort of question posed by the "tú." Lastly, the first two verses encapsulate the poem's subsequent rhetorical structure which, in reverse order of initial imperative followed by "no soy," consists, first, of self-definition (strophes 1–4) and, secondly, of exhortation (strophes 5–7).

One of the principle clues toward fleshing out the identity and origin of the poem's elusive persona comes by way of the narrative outline of the poem itself. The self-defining arcanum design of the first four strophes orients "Mina" in the direction of Bécquer, whose Rima 5 is built on this exact scheme. The intertextual kinship is confirmed in "Mina" by iterating the model's imagistic titanism, its insistent "yo soy" anaphora, and via other citational fragments, such as the phrase, "sin nombre," which is prominently displayed in both

poems.[2] Following are the first and final two pairs of the twenty quat-
rains that make up Rima 5:

> Espíritu sin nombre,
> indefinible esencia,
> yo vivo con la vida
> sin forma de la idea.
>
> Yo nado en el vacío,
> del sol tiemblo en la hoguera,
> palpito entre las sombras
> y floto con las nieblas.
>
> . . . .
>
> Yo soy el invisible
> anillo que sujeta
> el mundo de la forma
> al mundo de la idea.
>
> Yo, en fin, soy ese espíritu,
> desconocida esencia,
> perfume misterioso
> de que es vaso el poeta.[3]
>
> [Spirit without name,
> Indefinable essence,
> I live in life
> Without the form of thought.
>
> I swim in the void,
> In the blaze of the sun I tremble,
> I quiver among the shadows
> And I float on the mists.
>
> . . . .
>
> I am the invisible
> Ring that binds
> The world of form
> To the world of thought.
>
> I, in sum, am that spirit,
> An unknown essence,
> A mysterious fragrance
> Of which the poet is the vessel.]

Rima 5 contains the features basic to the "yo" of "Mina": this latter "yo," like its Romantic counterpart, is roughly "espíritu" or "esencia," an absolute which, while beyond the intellect and language— "sin nombre"—is an omnipresent entity vital to life and available to the senses. In both pieces, the perceptible though intellectually impalpable nature of the arcane persona is translated through sense-based imagery, including the very sonority inherent in the "yo" itself, who in each case speaks. But even a summary comparison of the imagery shows that Aleixandre's mysterious speaker is anything but a carbon copy of Bécquer's. On the contrary, the "yo" of "Mina" is born as a Bloomian misprision of its forebear and effectively inverts Bécquer's Neoplatonism. While the speaker of Rima 5, an ineffable spirit present in the immensity of the universe, is lyrically conceptualized via ephemeral sense imagery such as "el fleco de oro / de la lejana estrella" [the wispy golden strand of the distant star] or "la ignota escala / que el cielo une a la tierra" [the unknown scale joining heaven to earth], Aleixandre's persona, who negates cosmic origin, is self-defined by a string of concrete and sensuous images. Variously, this being is a subterranean sun violently struggling for release, a clench-fisted threat to the heavens, a miner hacking away toward "esa carne dulce donde duermen los pájaros, / los amores de un día cuando el sol luce fuera." The key word that both explains the difference between narrators and establishes the identity of Aleixandre's is "calor" of verse 3, a time-honored analogue for passion. Far from being a disembodied and impalpable spirit, the narrator of "Mina" is desire itself, the id poetically incarnate as voice and as forceful protagonist, to which the previously cited images attest. Thus, the id-narrator, since it is beyond intellectual comprehension and observation, resists the impertinent query of the inquisitive "tú." From our reading of "Sin luz" and "Las águilas," we are already familiar with this erotic personage and may therefore suspect that "Mina," though in different narratological guise, again recounts the fortunes of the id as it is engaged in struggle with the superego within the psychosomatic world of the human. Such is indeed the case, as will be seen upon lending attention to poetic scene and to the identity of addressee.

First, the poetic scene of "Mina." The most visible reference to locus is to be found in the opening verse of the second strophe, "Soy el sol que bajo la tierra pugna por quebrantarla." Containing Aleixandre's seminal hombre/tierra hypogram, this verse at once explains the referential problem of verses 1 and 2, identifies the site from which the poem's voice issues, and illuminates the meaning of the title: the world referred to and the origin of the narrating voice is the intra-human geography of psyche and flesh. The human, conceptualized as a mine, is the terraqueous vessel containing that voice, which is itself the vocal figuration of the id, the human's consubstantial erotic force and life-giving inspiration. If we again compare "Mina" to Rima 5, we see that the ancestral "vaso"—the poet as vessel of the cosmic unknown—serves as the transformative basis for Aleixandre's particular conceptualization of hombre/tierra into mine, now a mineral vessel or site whose full potential is to be exploited through love, a human, nonethereal and carnal love crying ("clamando") in the instinctual wilderness. It bears adding that the "sol bajo tierra" verse succinctly juxtaposes inner and outer, a basic binary that organizes "Mina," including the textually made distinction between a false scene—an immense outer world of sea, firmament, and land propitious for Romantic pondering—and the scene referred to—the human underground.

The "tú," whose impertinent or futile question implicitly sets "Mina" into rhetorical motion, approximates the superego or the conscious mind impelled by the superego. This identity is suggested both by the questioning—an act of intellect—and by the misdirection of the same query, a search for truth, for the key to human destiny in the "más allá"—"el mundo en que tú vives"—not in the "más acá"—the psychosexual world indwelling within the human. The attempt at rationalizing the instinctual—namely, love itself—by appealing to the observable world or to internalized Romantic notions of it, is necessarily thwarted, a fact which desire, as narrator, makes clear in its initial reply to the "tú" addressee: "No soy el mar, no soy el cielo, / ni tampoco soy el mundo en que tú vives." As seen in "Sin luz" and in "Las águilas," the superego, whether figured as "milenaria columna" or as faux sky, is portrayed as internalized antagonist or barrier to full human realization, the latter being achievable only through sensual love. In "Mina," the "tú," like its psychic complement, the "yo"/id, is primarily conceived of as voice, though as an internalized voice whose Romantic quest for love in the beyond is at variance with the imperious voice of the libidinous narrator. It is important to keep in mind that the apparent duality of the I/you structure is but a grammatical and figurative illusion which, albeit in different narratological guise than that of the previously cited pieces, is designed to translate the same conception of the human: the human is first and foremost a lover, a Freudian era version of the eternal lover who now innately contains the mystery of love, an arcanum lying in a powerful psychosexual complex of id, ego and superego often at odds with itself. Similarly, the human (i.e., the amorous archetype) remains the poem's referential nucleus, and is, as it is throughout *La destrucción o el amor,* the structural tenor on which all figuration—including voice—ultimately rests.[4]

The present discussion of voice in "Mina" has so far concentrated on identifying speaker, addressee, and scene, which at once comprise the basic narratological ingredients of the poem and stand as the skeletal figurative components of the human subject, the poem's primary referent and tenor. There remains for further consideration the important structural and thematic role carried out by voice. Briefly, voice contextualizes "Mina"—including the parts played by narrator and addressee—as a specific event or discursive happening in the light of which the irrationality of the text assumes logic and coherence. To begin, a scrutiny of the structural role of voice. Reviewing the general conformation of "Mina," we see that the text, from the introit on, is discernibly organized by voicing. First and foremost, voice frames the entire poem as a reply, a reply given by the id to the off-stage query of the inquisitive "tú" or superego. Secondly, the response—the text proper—is itself visibly divided into two sections, each being neatly demarcated by the two speech acts performed by the libidinous narrator in reply to the addressee. The first speech act is that of the Bécquer-style self-definition expressed throughout the anaphoric "soy" series, that is, the first four stanzas. The second speech act, which could be considered Aleixandre's own addition to the already misread Rima 5, consists of the iterated exhortation "dejadme" and comprehends the final three strophes. Thus, despite the automatic style appropriate for representing the subconscious, there is at work in "Mina," even at first glance, an ordering principle intimately allied to voice. This principle, a rhetorical one, finds expression in verse 17, a transitional verse that specifies the logical relation between the two sections: "Dejadme entonces, comprendiendo que el hierro es la salud de vivir." Employing a "because, then" structure, the narrator establishes the enigmatic self-revelation of section one as the premise on which the remainder of the poem—the "dejadme" petition—is based. This is done by asserting that the "tú" addressee has understood that revelation, a piece of knowledge now summarized in the metaphorical formula, "el hierro es la salud de vivir." What is arresting—and of further structural significance—is the verse's noticeably didactic flavor, which is owed to its logical style and to the aphoristic sounding "el hierro es la salud de vivir." This formula indeed has a nonpoetic relative, the adage, "El que a hierro vive, a hierro muere" [He who lives by the sword, dies by the sword]. Owing to its key position in the poem, this markedly docent verse contextualizes the poem as a lesson, a rather well-ordered lesson set up as premise—the "because . . ."—(the first four strophes) and petition—the "then . . ."—(strophes 4–7). In view of this structure, we may discern a bit further the roles of narrator and addressee who, while figuring id and superego, also act as a teacher-student pair. The task of the teacher-like id is to deliver a lesson on life or love to the superego, the overly rational pupil whose mistaken query sets off the poem. The question, earlier gleaned from the opening response of the narrator as "¿Eres el cielo?, ¿el mar?, ¿el mundo?" or the simple "¿Quién eres?," can be paraphrased, in the amorous context of the poem, as "¿Eres el amor?" [Are you love?] or even "¿qué es el amor?" [What is love?]. The elaborate answer, which takes up the first four strophes, is summarized in "el hierro es la salud de vivir." As will become clearer, the aphoristic formula can be interpreted, for example, as "El amor es vida" [Love is life].

As asserted, the primary rhetorical function of section one (stanzas 1–4) is to set up the premise on which the lesson delivered by the id is based. The premise is set out by the id in a most orderly, even mathematical, fashion. The docent id does this via self-definition, precisely by employing four main analogues—"calor," "sol," "amenaza," and "brillo"—each placed at the beginning of the first four strophes. In tandem, these analogues make up the cluster of the id's minimal features; furthermore, each analogue generates a brief, antithetical inset or counter example. Thus viewed, stanzas 1–4 are presented as a set of complementary examples, a comparative pattern ideal for teaching. Before proceeding, it bears notice that the four seminal metaphors cloaking the libidinous narrator are all derived by association with "hierro." "Hierro," which appears most prominently in verse 17, is the primary structural vehicle of the id and is part of the poem's particular transformation of hombre/tierra into mine. Digressing for a moment longer, we see that the id is to the human what "hierro" is to a mine: the essential value contained in that vessel, which may either be exploited or left untapped. Aleixandre's choice of iron, rather than precious minerals such as gold or silver, is due to iron's potential for expressing amorous destruction, which it does as a metonym for "sword." The figurative elaboration of the premise, as we shall now see as each strophe is examined separately, is comprised of four sets of examples in which "hierro" or "amor" is contrasted with "no hierro," "desamor."

In stanza one, the metaphoric "calor" is derived associatively from the metallurgical phrase "hierro candente" [red-hot iron], the malleable stuff of which swords are made; "calor" itself, as mentioned, is also a popular analogue for eros and in "Mina" gives the clearest indication of the narrating persona's identity. The counter example produced by this mineral heat is a chilly maritime scene of abandoned love in which the floral—that is, nonmineral—human realizes that he or she was never "hierro," was never engaged in concrete, earthly love. In this instance, "soñando" emphasizes the illusory, and therefore futile, quality of the realization. The preterit "quedó" is an additional negative sign, marking the illusory love portrayed in the inset as a story of love past. The sketchy anecdote, with its "comprenden, soñando, que nunca fueron hierro," is a negative paraphrase of the transitional aphorism "comprendiendo que el hierro es la salud de vivir." The "sol" analogue of the second strophe derives from the luster typical of iron, specifically when, red-hot, it is hammered into an arm, a martial connotation actualized in the verb "pugna." At the same time, "sol," which implies open air, produces the antithetical incarceration inset, where the id, cast as mutinous and titanically forceful prisoner, fights single-handed in order to break out of its jail or shackles, "prisiones de hierro." The prison setting, that is, the human body or mineral vessel, is itself a re-elaboration of the time-honored body/jail trope, whereby the body is conceived of as the prison of the soul. Here we see a concrete instance of Aleixandre's redistribution of human ontology, the soul being replaced by the id, a secular version of the divine spirit or breath that gives life to the human clay. The "amenaza" metaphor of the third strophe, as well as other martial words in the poem ("avanza," pugna," "herir"), is directly produced from the common metonym, "hierro," for sword. Here, the id as willful menace is followed up by and set against a nocturnal firmament, the ethereal "cielos," an emblem of destiny, the pre-ordained order in the face of which human will is helpless. Reminiscent of the Duque de Rivas's Don Alvaro in *La fuerza del sino*, the id in Aleixandre defiantly faces destiny or, more precisely put, a conventionally received notion of what destiny is. Unlike the star-crossed lover don Alvaro, whose last word, "destrucción," seals his fate, the narrating id of "Mina" not only does not submit to convention but supersedes it by taking on the role of fate itself.[5] The id incarnates a new sort of destiny, an erotic destiny which, because of its concrete and therefore realizable nature, is a "sueño" standing in stark contrast to the ethereal and passive dreaming that was suggested in the first strophe. As we have seen in "Las águilas," the id-destiny pairing is a thematic constant in *La destrucción o el amor* and serves as the ideological and figurative premise informing the much anthologized "Soy el destino," a poem narratologically identical to "Mina."

Finally, we come to stanza four whose inset, a kind of "grand finale" of sexual repression, serves as a most dramatic counter example to the earth-bound love advocated by the narrator. Here, the "brillo" of

eros gives way to a "claroscuro," a nocturnal setting bathed in moonlight and set by the sea, a most propitious scene for bewailing unrequited love. The ethereal or nonmineral quality of the example is
carried most graphically in the stanza's penultimate verse, by the
dissolving eyes description, an emblem of Romantic longing, of
amorous glances futilely cast outward in solitude, toward lunar
glimmerings on the absorbent ocean surface. The sexual repression
associated with this sort of scene is iterated at every turn. In the syntactically complex and Gongorine opening verses, the repression
of the id—the true source of light or "brillo"—is expressed via two
artifacts, the fishnet and the mirror. The piscatorial first verse—which
reads, when straightened out a bit, "Soy el brillo de los peces que
una red de deseos finge sobre el agua"[I am the shimmering of fish
that a net of desires feigns on the water]—conceptualizes desire repressed as fish which, though glimmering on the ocean surface, find
themselves caught or restrained in a net. The verb "finge," a family
member of "mentir" of "Las águilas," is an anthropomorphic substitute for "cazar con red," that is, ensnare. With its connotation of will
or effort, "finge" suggests that the surfacing libidinous urges—the
glimmering fish—are held in check from within. The reason lies in
the fishing artefact—the subject of "finge"—which figures, like the
"milenaria columna" of "Sin luz," the superego, that censoring part
of the psyche which controls sexuality by transmitting learned social
mores. The mirror, which is both an artefact and a stereotypical description of the ocean's surface, is a mixed figuration of the superego. On one hand, the mirror iterates the superego's pejorative artificiality; as sea, on the other, "espejo" casts the superego as an
internalized destiny or fate. This fate, the cause of erotic death or
"non-life," is diametrically opposed to the amorous destiny incarnate
in the brilliant id which, by transmitting erotic emanations, melio-
ratively wreaks amorous death, that is, life. The personified "luna" who
gazes in that mirror is a complex and hyperbolic repetition of the instances of internalized repression that are embroidered throughout
the stanza. As landscape fixture, the moon and its necrophilous light
symbolize yearning for love impossible to attain. But "luna" is also a
lexical pun having the additional meaning of "looking glass." This
meaning, which is activated by the proximity of "luna" both to "espejo" and to the reflexive "se contempla," translates a mise-en-abyme
image of the superego-ridden and endlessly self-censoring human
who throughout the discourse of the first four strophes has served
as the antithesis of the human liberated by desire.[6] In the final
verses of this strophe, the ultimate consequence of erotic censorship
is relayed through the imagery of strangulation: the long-suffering

eyes of the lunar and spectral personage may dissolve in the clutches of darkness, the inverse of the liberating fist held up by the menacing and solar id.

The sense of the first four strophes, and of the counter examples contained therein, is synthesized by way of two logical words contained in verses 15 and 16: "pueden" and "cuando." When taken out of the rhetorical context of the poem, both words seem most anomalous or ungrammatical in the midst of the poem's irrationality. It may be recalled that such was also the case of the rational or bookish sounding opening of "Sin luz." However, when placed in the didactic frame of question and reply established by voice, the "pueden/cuando" pair expresses, in inverted form, a logical "if/then" formula ordering the rationale behind the lesson. By employing this formula, the didactic id wraps up the first section of its discursive presentation on a positive note. The exempla, since they are placed in the if/then context, are presented to the addressee as possibilities or options based on an amorous causality controllable by choice. To be chosen is either love or the repression of love, along with the consequences. The choices, illustrated in each of the first four strophes, can be summarized in retrospect as "calor o frío" [warmth or cold], "sol o cárcel" [sun or prision], "fuerza o inercia" [strength or inertia], "brillo directo o pálido reflejo" [direct shining or pallid reflection]. The four, it may be remembered, are variants of the structural "hierro o no hierro," itself translatable as "amor o destrucción," an almost literal rendering of *La destrucción o el amor.* The relation between the vocal act contextualizing "Mina" and the generative speech act behind the work as a whole will be treated below. The optative context established in the final verses of section one leads the poem to the synthetic transitional verse, "Dejadme entonces, comprendiendo que el hierro es la salud de vivir." Here, as already noted, we find the logical structure of "because/then," which, directly tied to the premise established via the definitory acts of section one, introduces the concluding petition.

At this juncture, the didactic energy of the poem is invested in the exhortation, "Dejadme." The id, the poem's arcane teacher and voice, repeatedly petitions that the option be made for erotic love, for the carnal knowledge—the sense of "comprendiendo"—that the id claims has been understood or sensed. The petitions made by the erotic narrator are as neatly ordered as the exemplary definitions of section one. The requests made in the three final stanzas follow an outer to inner progression. In stanza 5, the miner-like id requests that its pick be allowed to cleave the mineral surface, the flesh. In the sixth, that it penetrate the "boca o dientes," metonyms for the inquisitive and superego-driven "tú" whose query initiates the poem; by the attached, "que saltarán sin luna," the id also promises the destruction of the intellect, in particular that of the lunar superego. In the final strophe, the still-mining id asks that it be allowed to dig even deeper and ceaselessly, until it inters itself in a hot and nest-like flesh, an erotic and vital core or center. The recovery of this center, which is implicitly promised by the id, brings the poem full circle from the outwardly directed question of the "tú," to the core of the intra-terraqueous subconscious from whence the narrative voice hails. It is from this mineral locale, a region of mystery deep within the human vessel, that the teacher's voice seductively urges on its student, promising him or her nothing less than the completion of erotic destiny. That this core, an interior Eden in which the libidinous spirit dwells, is the site of human destiny, is an idea figuratively relayed both by voicing—the narrator being the very voice of destiny—and through other metaphorical raiment, namely the sun and the nest. The latter, like the wheel of fortune, symbolize destiny via the circle and thereby equate the id or love with destiny.

The exhortation delivered by the id is designed to persuade the poem's addressee to heed the libidinous voice and thereby to reclaim the innate patrimony for which he or she and indeed all of humankind is destined. This, the lofty mission of "Mina," is carried out by means of two rhetorical strategies. The first, and most visible, lies in the use of apostrophe. Apostrophe undergoes a noticeable formal shift, from the singular and colloquial formula, "Calla, calla," to the grander "vosotros" form of the anaphoric series, "Dejadme." At first glimpse, and in the context of both "Mina" and Aleixandre's surrealism in general, the "tú" to "vosotros" change may seem to be an instance of figurative mutability, the characteristic ease with which one thing abruptly turns into another. But upon reviewing the outstanding rhetorical and thematic characteristics of the text—its didactic structure, complex figuration, and engagement with human knowledge and destiny—we realize that the concluding "vosotros" apostrophes obey a generic rationale. "Mina," like the sublime and often didactic ode or elegy, uses the singular to plural shift to reinforce the universal scope and seriousness of its message. The shift, at least in the case of "Mina," is, in addition, but a surface transformation of an already collective being, the apostrophized "tú." An anonymous Everyman, the Aleixandrean "tú" is hampered on one hand by internalized social mores but, on the other, is bid by the equally universal id, the panerotic spirit, to choose freedom. Apostrophe, as noted in regard to "Las moscas," also places the poem and

its message in an atemporal frame—in an eternal here and now—
which reinforces the universality or timelessness of the poem's theme.

The second rhetorical strategy employed by the libidinous teacher
throughout the concluding stanzas of "Mina" is to contrast this petitionary section with the counter examples inset in the first four
strophes, a contrast which is intended to emphasize the virtues of
sexual freedom over the disadvantages of repression. To this end,
the martial ambience of section one—the armed strife between id
and superego—gives way to the highly positive scenario depicted in
part two, where the liberated id, as miner, sets about to exploit and
uncover the riches hidden in the human mine. In effect, the sword
of strife or sexual repression is beat into the plowshare—or the
"pico"—of amorous peace, a promise implicit in the metallurgy of
verse 24, "dejadme que se quiebre la luz sobre el acero." The id also
embellishes its petition by counterpoising the repressive darkness
of section one with the light of sexual freedom emphasized in the
second section. This is done by depicting the imminent release of
the "sol bajo tierra," the imprisonment of which accounts for the
dark and nocturnal figuration in the insets of section one. In contrast, the liberated sun of section two produces "el resplandor que
de sí mismo nace," "la luz sobre el acero," or "los amores de un día
cuando el sol luce fuera." In this way, the id promotes its argument
for erotic liberation by intimating that a new day will dawn, a high-
sounding commonplace encapsulated in the final statement of the
poem, "los amores de un día cuando el sol luce fuera."

There is one final note to be added on the particulars of voice in
"Mina." Voicing, as we saw in the much more accessible poem, "Las
moscas," constitutes the main event or plot of the poem and therefore answers the question of what happens. The plot of "Mina" can
be perceived in the same manner. Let us first review the action of
the poem in its figurative form. The figured plot consists of the narrator's discursive presentation; more particularly, the nuclear happening is construed as a lesson organized on the basis of three vocal
events. The first event is the implied question posed by the "curioso
impertinente" or superego as it attempts to rationalize love; this
sets the entire poem into motion. The second is the self-defining
discourse of the docent id whose offered wisdom functions as the
premise for the third and final happening or denouement. The denouement consists of the poem's exhortative calling. Here, the nar-
rator-protagonist, while holding out promises of amorous life, bids
that its voice be heeded, that humanity in general opt for instinctual
love and thereby resolve the eternal quest for amorous knowledge.
The non-figurative summary of the plot renders a head vs. heart

story much like those recounted via psycho-narration in "Sin luz" and "Las águilas." The happening, which is figuratively conceptualized as the elaborate locution outlined above, is, in its essentials, an account of the preverbal conflict between id and superego, which is spurred by the former's impingement on the body and mind of the human, the world or setting in which "Mina" takes place. The resolution of the plot depends on the relative strength of the psychosomatic components disguised as narrating persona and addressee. In "Mina," as in "Las águilas," the narrative casting of the conflict strongly suggests that the instinctual id will overcome the civilized superego. The chief technical device by which the triumph of the id is augured in "Mina" is voice. In particular, the sheer iteration and predominance of voice throughout both simulates the insistent and overpowering force of the id and foregrounds its imminent vanquishing of the rather silent superego. This resolution qualifies "Mina" as a highly positive piece and sets it into a complementary relationship to negative poems like "Sin luz," "La selva y el mar," or others in which the superego rather than the id is victorious. Such pieces portray the enchainment or repression of the id and the consequent nonlife or negative destruction diametrically opposed to the full life of meliorative destruction wrought by the force of the id.

Let us round out this discussion of voice by noting the particular usefulness of "Mina" toward understanding *La destrucción o el amor* in general. Although all voiced poems in the collection are not structurally identical to "Mina," the special enigmas it poses graphically serve to demonstrate the important role that narrative structure plays toward comprehending Aleixandre's surrealism. First and foremost, and together with the psycho-narrations discussed earlier, "Mina" provides concrete evidence that Aleixandre's surrealism is a well-wrought irrationality wherein narrative design serves as scaffolding for the poet's highly creative transcription of the human. More particularly, "Mina" illustrates the orientational usefulness of voice, which is directly tied to poetic basics, including the identity of speaking persona and addressee, the circumstantial fiction and the plot. In overview, then, voice organizes a text which, when not taken as a discursive event, may seem obscure or unfathomable. As has also been seen, voice is at the figurative core of the text; the happening and circumstances it creates constitute a fiction that gives lyric disguise both the primary referent of the poem and the thematic concerns of the poet. Lastly, the particular use of voice in "Mina" alerts us to the fact that specific modulations of voice may signal different intertextual relationships, either broad ones like genre or more specific ones such as Aleixandre's ancestral tie to Bécquer.

This brings the present discussion to its concluding point, and to the most compelling example of the structural role allotted voice in *La destrucción o el amor*. The optative speech act performed through voice in "Mina" is itself an echo of one of the chief structuring principles operant throughout the entire book. The principle, identical to the rhetorical kernel spawning "Mina," is based on the optative format of question and reply. The question—the same one posed by the imperious id in "Mina" as the schematized "hierro o no hierro" option—is most prominently displayed within the very title, *La destrucción o el amor*, where the ambiguous grammar word—the frequently cited "o" [or]—disjuncts destruction and love. Other interpretations of this richly ambiguous title will be deferred for later.[7] As a disjunctive, the "o" places destruction and love in a mutually exclusive relationship whereby the choice of one term precludes the other, as in the mundane question, "Coffee or tea?" Actually, the title, which was originally the more overtly optative *Destrucción o amor*, is thematically akin to Hamlet's celebrated "To be or not to be?," an existential question in which the disjunctive also counterpoises life and death, the termini of human destiny.[8] The answer side of the structural principle is to be found within the poems themselves. All, in one way or another, answer to the query posed by the title. There are several formal ways in which the liminal imperative is answered. The most overt manner of reply is voicing itself. For one thing, there is the highly vocal nature of the majority of the poems; approximately eighty percent echo the titular locution via their own voicing. Many of those poems, including "Mina," prominently display voicing in opening verses. But even more graphic evidence for the rhetorical structuring of the book comes by way of explicitly voiced titles, an unusual feature in poetry in general and a characteristic in Aleixandre nearly unique to *La destrucción o el amor*.[9] There are eight such titles: "No busques, no," "Ven siempre, ven," "Mañana no viviré," "Ven, ven tú," "A ti, viva," "Quiero saber," "Soy el destino," and "Quiero pisar." Of the eight, all but "Mañana no viviré" and "Soy el destino" directly respond to the optative speech act posed by the main title. These subtitles either reject destruction—the illusionary love referred to in the negative injunction "No busques, no"—or choose love, the instinctual and corporeal love championed by Aleixandre. Even at that, "Soy el destino" answers the destruction or love query but does so by taking the question not as optative but as interrogative—"¿[Eres] la destrucción o el amor?," the type of question triggering "Mina," a poem with which "Soy el destino" demonstrates a marked narratological affinity.

Whether the response to the titular query is textually prominent or not, all poems make answer to the erotic imperative. They do so in one of two ways: the poems either portray the acceptance of "el amor"—be it realized or imminent—or record the rejection of love, equivalent to "la destrucción" of the disjunctive title. In this way, the poems fall into two thematic clusters determined by their response to the optative speech act performed by the title: a positive cluster of poems based on accepting love and a negative grouping of poems based on the rejection of love. Of the examples we have seen, "Sin luz" belongs to the negative cluster while "Las águilas" and "Mina" fit into the positive group. Others that poeticize the refusal of love, and thus fall into the negative cluster, are "La selva y el mar," "Unidad en ella," "Noche sinfónica," "Vida," "Humana voz," "Corazón negro," and "El escarabajo." Reflective of their negative orientation, these poems, like "Sin luz," tend to have a rather dark atmosphere and tone. Examples from the positive cluster include "Soy el destino," "La luz," "Canción a una muchacha muerta," "La muerte," "A ti, viva," and "La dicha." In contrast to the poems of "desamor," these are typically dynamic and vital in tone; several, for example "La luz" and "Soy el destino," are paeans to earthly love in which the erotic imperative of the id is most joyously celebrated. Metapoems, such as "La dicha" and "El escarabajo," make it quite clear that the choice between "amor" and "desamor" is one of Aleixandre's major formal and thematic concerns. In "La dicha," the poet, after launching a rejection of art that mortiferously congeals eros in its artistic creation, concludes by defining his personal "arte poética" as a choice for erotic love, the reality or carnal knowledge in the service of which his poetry stands: "Canto el cielo feliz, el azul que despunta, / . . . [la] amorosa presencia de un día que sé existe" (*La destrucción* 180) [I sing the happy sky, the dawning azure, the amorous presence of a day that I know exists]. As may be seen in "El escarabajo," Aleixandre's commitment to singing instinctual love does not preclude poeticizing its complement, the nonlife or "destrucción" of love repressed. On the contrary, this option produces counter examples like those seen in the insets of "Mina." It is to this structuring principle that the "también" of the opening verse of "El escarabajo" [The Scarab] refers. Here is the first strophe:

He aquí que por fin llega al verbo también el pequeño escarabajo, tristísimo minuto,

lento rodar del día miserable,
diminuto captor de lo que nunca puede aspirar al vuelo.

(*La destrucción* 206)

[Behold, at last to the word has also arrived the little scarab,
A sad minute,
The slow turning of the miserable day,
The diminutive captor of that which can never aspire to flight.]

As the above may have suggested, *La destrucción o el amor* has a sizable investment in voice, specifically in its apostrophic modulations. Owing to the atemporal aspect of apostrophe, *La destrucción o el amor,* from the title and throughout, is framed within a forever now and assumes overall coherence as a self-contained event, a rhetorical happening whereby the book both asks, and answers, its own question. Similarly, the voicing that saturates the text stands as one of the principle means of transmitting the work's ideological mission.[10] *La destrucción o el amor* is designed both to vindicate the irrational and to exhort humanity to reclaim that subconscious patrimony. The marked vitality of the book—its impassioned and immediate tone—is at once an effect created by voice and a reflection of the eminently optimistic message that voice relays. Human destiny is not beyond human control. Rather, as the title advertises, human destiny—an essentially amorous fate—is achievable by choice: one may either elect "la destrucción," a destiny falsely predicated on received notions of love, or one may choose "el amor," the psychosomatic circle of destiny whose beginning, center, and end are intrinsically bound within the essentially terraqueous, and essentially erotic, human vessel.

The vindication of the irrational, and the exhortation to reclaim the subconscious, both define Aleixandre's surrealist thematics and mark out the place that *La destrucción o el amor* occupies in the poet's artistic career. As all three narrative examples have demonstrated, *La destrucción o el amor*—a work engaged in the portrayal and meliorative treatment of the subconscious—falls squarely in line with the aesthetic tenets of the surrealist movement headed by Breton. Voice, in particular the exhortative modulation of voice that frames *La destrucción o el amor,* further reinforces Aleixandre's link to the surrealist movement. The publicly directed call for sexual freedom—a call inscribed in the title, the most public of textual places—concords with surrealism's social program, a revolutionary program intended to free humanity from the restraints imposed upon it by the habits of rationality. Breton, in the 1924 Manifesto, describes the civilization vs. subconscious conflict in this manner: "Under the pretense of civilization and progress, we have managed to banish from the mind everything that may rightly or wrongly be termed superstition, or fancy; forbidden is any kind of search for truth which is not in conformance with accepted practices. . . . The imagination is perhaps on the point of reasserting itself, of reclaiming its rights. If the depths of our mind contain within it [sic] strange forces . . . there is every reason to seize them."[11] Within the scope of Aleixandre's extensive lyric output, *La destrucción o el amor* not only stands as the poet's most refined expression of surrealism; it is also unique among all his works for its impassioned tone and ebullient verve. Again, this distinction is owed to the poet's highly optimistic view of human life and to the modulations of voice through which that view is delivered. In a sense, *La destrucción o el amor* is a book of youth in which Aleixandre transmits the discovery of love as the discovery of a universal truth. The erotic epiphany gives way, in the three following books, to the nostalgic and often melancholy sense of love lost. In marked contrast to *La destrucción o el amor,* the verbal modulation of *Mundo a solas, Sombra del paraíso,* and the already cited "Como el vilano" section of *Historia del corazón* is systematically indicative rather than imperative. The voicing of the later books, which is dominantly cast in past tenses, repeatedly points back to the atemporal moment captured in *La destrucción o el amor.*[12] Here is but one example, verses from "Nacimiento del amor" *(Sombra del paraíso):*

> Eras tú, amor, destino, final amor luciente,
> nacimiento penúltimo hacia la muerte acaso.
>
> .   .   .   .
>
> En mi alma nacía el día. Brillando
> estaba de ti; tu alma en mí estaba.
> Sentí dentro, en mi boca, el sabor a la aurora.
> Mis ojos dieron su dorada verdad. Sentí a los pájaros
> en mi frente piar, ensordeciendo
> mi corazón. Miré por dentro
> los ramos, las cañadas luminosas, las alas variantes,
> y un vuelo de plumajes de color, de encendidos
> presentes me embriagó, mientras todo mi ser a un mediodía,
> raudo, loco, creciente se incendiaba
> y mi sangre ruidosa se despeñaba en gozos
> de amor, de luz, de plenitud, de espuma.
>
> (*OC* 1:497)

> [It was you, love, destiny, last shining love,
> Penultimate birth toward death perhaps.

. . . .

In my soul the day was dawning. It was shining
With you; your soul was in me.
I sensed within, in my mouth, the taste of dawn.
My eyes gave up their golden truth. I could hear in my brow
The chirping of birds, which deafened
My heart. I looked among
The branches, the shining streams, the variable wings,
And a flight of colored plumage, of brilliant
Presents, intoxicated me while, at the noon of the day, my whole being
In a mad growing rush was blazing
And the din of my blood was overflowing with ecstasies
Of love, of light, of fullness, of foam.]

To conclude this discussion of voice and mood, the "qué es aquello" question might again be posed. In retrospect, a relatively
schematic reply may be made: from a narrative point of view, *La destrucción o el amor* is a story of love discovered; the focal character
and narrator are one and the same, an amorous Everyman; the plot
is an allegory in which false love and true love vie with one another
in determining human destiny; the didactic and illocutionary aim
of the story is to move the reader to choose true love over false love.
Typically, the story and its narrative presentation are textually ob-
scured. Perception of both is complicated by Aleixandre's innovative treatment of narrative structure and by the complex figurative
boscage overgrowing the text. As we now move to a discussion of
genre, we face the last question regarding Aleixandre's discursive
structure, which concerns the family membership of his poetry. The
information accrued from the study of narrative structure will be
most helpful in this endeavor.

5

La Razón de la Sinrazón:
The Logic of Genre

¿Qué firme arquitectura se levanta del paisaje . . . ?
[What solid architecture rises from the landscape . . . ?]
—Aleixandre

"Sɪɴ ʟᴜᴢ," "Lᴀꜱ Áɢᴜɪʟᴀꜱ," ᴀɴᴅ "Mɪɴᴀ" ʜᴀᴠᴇ ᴀꜰꜰᴏʀᴅᴇᴅ ᴀ ɢᴏᴏᴅ
deal of experience with the obscurity and the poetic rationale operant in Aleixandre's surrealism. In the process of examining the nar-
ratology of these pieces, several generic signals have been received
which orient *La destrucción o el amor* and this study of genre in three
cardinal directions: toward odic poetry, including the elegy; toward
the love lyric; and in the direction of self-aware poems or metapoetry. The Aleixandrean affinity with odic poetry is manifest in several
appreciable features, including the very length of the poems, their
grand thematic scope, figurative complexity, and didactic intention,
the latter frequently being carried out via voice. The love lyric tends
to develop as a much more intimate and personal type than the ode
or elegy. The affiliation of Aleixandre's poetry with this genre is most
overtly signaled via the title of *La destrucción o el amor,* itself a kind of
contract with other poetry engaged in this ancient tradition. Other
specific traces of this generic connection can be seen, for example,
in the lover-before-the-beloved scene from which pieces like "Sin
luz" or "Soy el destino" develop, despite their narratological differences. Aleixandre's affinity with the metapoem is signaled in two
general ways: by means of explicit statements on art or on his own
poetry like those cited in reference to "La dicha" and "El escarabajo"; or more covertly by alluding to literary or plastic arts, though
without explicit commentary. Such allusions are quite frequent
throughout *La destrucción o el amor* and may be seen, for instance, in
"Aurora insumisa," wherein the lyric description of a woman is an
ekphrasis of pictorial representations of the birth of Venus. This
transposition of art links the poem to other metapoetry—such as
Salinas's "Don de la materia"—that, by thematizing art within art, calls

attention to its own aesthetic concerns. In particular, "Aurora insumisa" conveys Aleixandre's preoccupation with idealized or artificial love, and with art that reproduces and promulgates amorous fallacy.

Having taken this panoramic view of genre in *La destrucción o el amor*, let us now attend to three specific examples: "Unidad en ella," a love poem; "No busques, no," an ode; and "La dicha," the metapoem already cited in passing. First "Unidad en ella":

Cuerpo feliz que fluye entre mis manos,
rostro amado donde contemplo el mundo,
donde graciosos pájaros se copian fugitivos,
volando a la región donde nada se olvida.

Tu forma externa, diamante o rubí duro,   5
brillo de un sol que entre mis manos deslumbra,
cráter que me convoca con su música íntima,
con esa indescifrable llamada de tus dientes.

Muero porque me arrojo, porque quiero morir,
porque quiero vivir en el fuego porque este aire de fuera   10
no es mío, sino el caliente aliento
que si me acerco quema y dora mis labios desde un fondo.

Deja, deja que mire, teñido del amor,
enrojecido el rostro por tu purpúrea vida,
deja que mire el hondo clamor de tus entrañas   15
donde muero y renuncio a vivir para siempre.

Quiero amor o la muerte, quiero morir del todo,
quiero ser tú, tu sangre, esa lava rugiente
que regando encerrada bellos miembros extremos
siente así los hermosos límites de la vida.   20

Este beso en tus labios como una lenta espina,
como un mar que voló hecho un espejo,
como el brillo de un ala,
es todavía unas manos, un repasar de tu crujiente pelo,
un crepitar de la luz vengadora,   25
luz o espada mortal que sobre mi cuello amenaza,
pero que nunca podrá destruir la unidad de este mundo.
                              (*La destrucción* 126–27)

[Oh happy body that flows through my hands
Beloved countenance in which I contemplate the earth,
Where graceful birds fleetingly multiply,
Flying off to the place where nothing is forgotten.

Your outer form, diamond or hard ruby,   5
Flash of a sun that shines in my hands,
Crater that summons me with its intimate music,
With that indecipherable call of your teeth.

I die because I throw myself in, because I want to die,
Because I want to live in the fire because this air outside   10
Is not mine, but only your warm breathing
Which, if I draw near, will from its depths burn and color my lips.

Let me, let me see, tinged with love and
With my face reddened by your mauve life,
Let me see the deep clamor of your depths   15
Where I die and give up life forever.

I want love or death, I want to die completely,
I want to be you, your blood, that roaring lava
That as it nourishes fair extremities from within
Thus sets the beautiful boundaries of life.   20

This kiss on your lips like a slow thorn,
Like a sea that, turned into a mirror, took flight,
Like the shining of a wing,
Is still only hands, only a glimpse of your sparking hair,
A crackling of avenging light,   25
Of the light or deadly sword that above my neck threatens,
But that will never be able to destroy the unity of this world.

"Unidad en ella" seems to be a rather straightforward love poem,
at least insofar as Aleixandre's surrealism is concerned. Its overall
design, based on the "yo"-"tú," lover-before-beloved situational kernel, is most conventional in amorous verse and is presented quite
clearly. Similarly, the structural metaphor—beloved/geography—is
relatively accessible, as is its volcano variant. The title and the text
appear to describe love completed or imminent, a thematics that
would place "Unidad en ella" in the positive cluster of poems responding to the destruction or love option posed by the main title,
La destrucción o el amor. As to the difficulties of the text, they appear
to be local rather than general and include the always boggling
destruction/love conceit and the arbitrary flavor of images such as
"beso como una lenta espina." In brief, "Unidad en ella" appears to
be a relatively accessible sample of Aleixandre's surrealist treatment
of love.

Nonetheless, Aleixandre's poems consistently prove that appearances can be deceiving, and such is the case of "Unidad en ella." The

textual clarity that I have sketched out results from a failure to perceive one of the poem's decisive generic signals, even after no few readings.[1] This signal, which is emitted throughout more than half of the text (strophes 3–6), is the invitation-to-love, an ultra conventional structural motif in amatory poetry and the nuclear speech act of "Unidad en ella." Before considering how receiving the signal affects the sense of the poem, consider why the transmission of the signal is blocked. First, the title, which in combination with the clarity of the lover-contemplating-the-beloved scene, leads one to expect that the text recounts the optimistic fiction of love fulfilled, a frequent anecdote in *La destrucción o el amor*. It is also tempting to naturalize the titular "ella" as female lover through whom "unidad" is accomplished. Such an interpretation is logical in light of the poem's genre, even though there is no compelling textual evidence for this exclusive reading. A rule of thumb for reading Aleixandre is that premature closure should be avoided, created ambiguity being a quintessential Aleixandrean device, as the title of the collection eloquently bears out. Second, the introductory verse of the amorous petition proper—"Muero porque me arrojo, porque quiero morir,"—*seems* to place the poem, and the amorous destruction, in the time frame of a present process ("I am dying because I am casting myself, because I want to die"). There is no sound grammatical or contextual reason for this temporal interpretation either. "Quiero," together with the "deja" imperatives, are instead key to the temporal modality that frames the poem. That is, "Unidad en ella," like "Mina," first and foremost relays a petition and is set, therefore, in an atemporal mode. It bears remembering that, as Jonathan Culler has pointed out, readers generally tend to ignore verbal mood—apostrophe in particular—and thereby reduce many a poem to a descriptive account instead of seeing it as an atemporal happening, be it one of volition or option, and so on. This said, let us examine how the sense of this particular Aleixandrean love lyric is significantly shifted, and enhanced, by taking its more complete generic horizon into account.

Briefly put, picking up both, rather than only one, of the poem's generic signals provides the point of departure for evaluating the piece's basic elements, including its overall structure, image, and theme. Of immediate note is the seminal organizational role that the invitation-to-love plays in "Unidad en ella." Whereas the situational kernel—the "yo" lover before the "tú" beloved—suggests the poem's backdrop, the amorous invitation or volitional mode organizes the poem as a story of attempted seduction. The plot of the story is simple, and quite conventional in this sort of love lyric: the narrating lover, through the force of rhetoric, endeavors to bed the fictive addressee; the resolution of the plot—the addressee's acceptance or refusal of the invitation—is to be gleaned from the speech of the amorously aflame narrator as the poetic seduction reaches its conclusion. It is on the basis of this petitionary scheme that "Unidad en ella" is organized, as we shall now see.

The first two strophes invoke and describe the beloved and function to express the narrator's acute attraction to that object of desire. The reason for the attraction lies in the addressee's beauty, a beauty which hardly seems conventional, to say the least. Words like "cuerpo," "forma externa," and the dissonant "cráter" fall well outside poetry's standard lexicon for physical perfection. Even so, "Unidad en ella" retains generically determined traces of that lexicon for describing the "tú," the stereotypical beloved on which Aleixandre's "tú" is based. Among such remains, there are the Petrarchan eyes-like-suns, the lips or "boca" like roses, which are manifest, respectively, in the "brillo de un sol," part of the face description seen in verse 6, and in "Este beso en tus labios como una lenta espina" of verse 21. The latter is Aleixandre's reworking of a mouth/rose variant—the thorn beneath the rose—an analogy that conceptualizes the dangers immanent in love. For its part, the harsh "cráter" hails from Romantic love poetry, being a variant of the hyperbolic passion/volcano metaphor. In "Unidad en ella" this figurative elaboration of the terraqueous vessel makes restricted reference to the mouth, a logical choice since "cráter" is the "boca del volcán" [mouth of the volcano]. Splicing together the two buccal vehicles—rose and crater—we see that Aleixandre, in figuring the anonymous beauty of "Unidad en ella," has scattered and slightly varied another Romantic cliche, the flower that grows on the edge of the abyss, an additional expression of love's danger.[2] In overview, the first two strophes, and the poem on the whole, do their conventional job of expressing beauty and the fatal attraction immanent therein.

This expressed attraction leads the way to the poem's main discursive event, the invitation-to-love, which takes up strophes 3 to 6. Reflective of its seductive purpose, the amorous invitation is couched in a most hyperbolic and "conceptista" language, a style generically appropriate for this end. The inflamed tone of the invitation is intended to leave no doubt as to the depth of the passionate feelings that the beloved has inspired in the amorous narrator. Most notable are the contortions of the meliorative love/death conceit, which comes to Aleixandre by way of the Mystics. Indeed, San Juan's "Llama de amor viva"—the fatal flame of love that through destruction delivers the moth-poet to everlasting life—is present in the figurative amalgam of the text. The intertext is signaled not only in the igneous version of the love/death conceit but is also in confluence with the volcanic figuration of the human vessel whose senses or instincts, in San Juan, are caverns illuminated by the light of divine love.[3] Other fragments indicating that the Mystic love lyric is in play in "Unidad en ella" are the joined "rostro" and "amado" of verse 2 which, though rare in Aleixandre, are common lexical choices in the Saint; lastly, the titular "unidad" recalls the Mystic—and not Romantic—notion of love, the eminently accessible "via unitiva," the unitary path. At any rate, and in the generic context of "Unidad en ella," the use of the Romantic and Mystic languages of love can be naturalized as the narrator's stylistic embellishment of his amatory petition, the end of which is to gain the favor of the beautiful addressee.

The most significant contortion of the love/death conceit is to be found in the striking introductory verse of the invitation-to-love section: "Muero porque me arrojo, porque quiero morir." A close reading of this bothersome verse is crucial to understanding the poem; in it lies some rather troubling information concerning the personality of the poem's amorous "yo," the narrative source to whose perspective the text is restricted. As mentioned, the verb "quiero" sets this introductory verse—and indeed the whole poem—in the volitional rather than indicative mode, a fact which is emphasized throughout the invitational section, both through the iterated "deja" and again by means of "quiero," repeated in strophe 5, at the close of the narrator's impassioned invitation. Upon further scrutiny, it may also be noticed that the verb "quiero," besides its petitionary function, creates an ambiguity, a situational ambiguity which both puts into doubt the veracity of the invitation itself and troubles the seemingly flesh and blood ontology of the "tú," the fiery receptor of the amorous petition. The ambiguity is created syntactically, by qualifying "Muero porque me arrojo" of the first hemistich of verse 9 with the two volitional paraphrases immediately adjoining it, "porque quiero morir," and "porque quiero vivir en el fuego." Condensing the verses a bit, we have, "Muero porque . . . quiero morir" [I die because I want to die] or "Muero porque . . . quiero vivir" [I die because I want to live], both paraphraseable as "Amo porque . . . quiero amar" [I love because I want to love]. The semantic disparity—and the faulty logic—owes to the modal difference between the indicative "Muero" and the volitional "quiero morir," phrases which are placed in a causal relationship by the conjunctive, "porque." In the light of quotidian logic, wanting to die and actually dying do not necessarily follow nor, in any case, are they equivalent.[4] In other words, the anomaly activated in the verse lies in the difference between reality and wish, an unevenness like that advertised in the title of Cernuda's *La realidad y el deseo*. In the context of *La destrucción o el amor*, the reality vs. fantasy dichotomy is at the anecdotal core of the book, a book which recounts the struggle between heart and head, between the force of instinctual love and the superego's repressive powers, which are often manifest as longings for an idealized and therefore impossible love, as has been seen.

The reality-fantasy disparity created by this verse puts us in a quandary regarding the situational particulars and thematic orientation of "Unidad en ella." We must wonder whether the illogic of "Muero porque me arrojo, porque quiero morir," indicates that the invitation to love and the "tú" to whom it is directed are phantasmagorical, the product of the amorous narrator's overheated imagination. In this case, the poem is to be taken as an interior monologue voiced by a solitary and frustrated narrator. Or it is also possible that the irrationality of the phrase—and of the poem in general—both reflects the amorous persona's erotic state and is as well an impassioned language of seduction meant to bring the emotions of the volcanic addressee to full eruption. In this case, "Unidad en ella" may be considered a highly positive poem in which love's realization is imminent. In either event, the associative flow of the verses, the unstable and illogical flavor of the imagery suggest that the invitation to love is impelled by the irrational force of the id as it impinges on, and somewhat muddles, the mind of the narrator.

The reality versus fantasy quandary outlined above is resolved in the final stanza, where the outcome of the narrator's petitionary efforts contextualizes the invitation-to-love as a vain one, as an imaginary act of seduction directed to an ephemeral creature of the mind. Here, deictics play an incisive role in determining the significance of the closing verses. Noticeably absent now are the volitional "quiero" and "deja," which saturate the invitation-to-love proper contained in the preceding three stanzas. Instead, these give way to one main verb, the static "es" of verse 24, whose nominative is the opening "Este beso en tus labios." The demonstrative "este" brings the amatory discourse of the poem back to its circumstantial origin, where the amorous narrator beholds and addresses the volcanic beloved; "este beso" would also seem to draw the lovers close together and to augur their imminent lovemaking. Nevertheless, this amorous destiny is contradicted in each of the three similes qualifying the kiss. The first—"como una lenta espina"—makes the kiss on the roselike lips of the beloved a slow and dangerously reluctant one. The second analogy—"como un mar que voló hecho un espejo"—suggests the fleeting and illusory nature of the kiss, a pejorative qualification emphasized by the preterit "voló." "Como el brillo de un ala," the

third simile, is an ornithological version of the former, whose re-
fractory and aerial character is here repeated in diminished form;
underlying both similes lies "el amor vuela" [love flies], itself the
amorous equivalent of the ancient aphorism, "tempus fugit." Added
up, the three similes cast the beloved's kiss and the happy erotic denouement that the kiss seems to promise as an elusive destiny. This
particular thematics is transmitted by the circle implicit in "espina,"
a synecdoche for the round rose; by "mar" the alpha and omega
of life; by means of "brillo," a diminished form of "luz," itself an
Aleixandrean shorthand for erotic destiny, the symbolic value of
which is prominent in "Sin luz" and "Las águilas," for example. The
symbolic function of light is examined in relation to Fray Luis in
chapter 6.

That the kiss, and the beloved on whose lips it rests, are indeed
illusory is iterated throughout the remainder of the concluding
verses. Having been qualified by the three analogues, the imagina-
tion-inspired "Este beso" now joins "es todavía," the centrally located
main verb phrase whose adverbial, "todavía" [still]—and not "ya"
[already]—qualifies the kiss as unrealized. The imprecise ontology
of the beloved is bolstered by the triad of indefinite articles, which
stand in marked contrast to the apparent concreteness of the initial
"este." That is to say, the narrator's beloved is anything but "las
manos," "el repasar," or "el crepitar de la luz vengadora." Rather, the
indefinite deictics suggest that the narrator's invitation is directed to
an impalpable though yearned for lover not unlike the "tú" so often
addressed by Bécquer, for example, in Rima 15, the last strophe of
which reads:

> ¡Yo, que a tus ojos, en mi agonía,
> los ojos vuelvo de noche y día;
> yo, que incansable corro y demente
> tras una sombra, tras la hija ardiente
>   de una ilusión![5]

> [I who in my suffering turn
> My eyes to yours by night and by day;
> I who madly and without rest pursue
> A shadow, the ardent offspring
>   Of an illusion!]

In the final two verses of Aleixandre's poem, the love/death conceit appears in one last variant, the "luz o espada mortal." Here, the
heat of passion and the light emanating from it are combined with
a hyperbolic form of the "espina" [thorn] metonym, the synthesis of

which produces the sword. This poetic amalgam summarizes the disparity wrought by imaginary love: this love is a sword that threatens but does not strike, an ineffectual instrument of destruction not unlike the pointed protuberance of the "pez espada"; this imagined eros is an "espada mortal" [mortal sword] because it brings about not meliorative death (i.e., life) but rather the non-life or "destrucción" caused by the phantasmagorical misdirection of erotic instinct. In the final verse, the narrator sums up what he has learned from inviting the mortal sword of imaginary love. While such love does threaten, it will not be able to destroy "la unidad de este mundo," a phrase with which the futilely enamored narrator punningly alludes to himself and to his actual circumstance. "Unidad" does not refer to the union of lover and beloved but, on the contrary, to the narrator's "oneness," or unitary solitude.[6] Similarly, "este mundo" designates not the world in its expansive sense, but rather the narrator himself who, divorced from reality, pines for love alone, in the limited sphere of his imaginary world, the ambit in which the poem takes place. The narrator is not bounded or touched by tangible love, the "hermosos límites de la vida," to which verse 20 alludes. Rather, he is the prisoner of his own mind, most especially of received and internalized notions of love. In the light of the closing verses, the sense of the title now becomes clear. The "unidad" that the title heralds is not amorous union but erotic and vital segregation. The immediate referent of the equally ambiguous "ella" is, strictly speaking, "luz o espada mortal," the imaginary and false instrument causing the affective death and unitary solitude of the narrator. A grammatical pun, "ella" also makes reference to other associated personages, certainly to the stereotypical "tú" conjured up in the mind of the well-versed narrator, and to "Ella," to "la Muerte," who on the basis of grammatical gender is figuratively garbed as a woman.[7]

In the light of the psychic ambience in which the poem takes place, the preceding elements of the poem assume referential coherence. Notice, for example, the first strophe. The liquid and mirrorlike "cuerpo feliz" that the narrator contemplates and that flows through his hands is the very image of illusory love. The vaporous quality of the specter is signaled at every descriptive turn, being carried not only by the verb "fluye"—here effectively a synonym of "escapa"—but also by means of the fleeting birds, which are of the same thematic feather as the erotically segregated "azul pájaro o pluma" of "La selva y el mar." The alliterative use of "f" in "cuerpo feliz que fluye," "pájaros fugitivos," and "forma externa" phonetically simulates the fugitive quality of the poem's referent. As to the destination and point of origin of these birds and of the flowing body in which they are reflected—"la región donde nada se olvida"—it is, as the cognitive verb suggests, the overly civilized mind of the narrating persona. He cannot forget or shake off received notions of love like those behind the traditional language of love that thickly interweaves the text of the poem. The same amorous ideology, as we have seen, is the cause of the solitary unity portrayed in "Sin luz." In the context of *La destrucción o el amor* as a whole, "Unidad en ella" falls within the cluster of negative poems which respond to the optative of the main title by portraying emotional "destrucción," the nonlife of "desamor." Like poems such as "Mina," "Unidad en ella" not only responds to the title of the collection, but also structurally echoes its optative speech act, which the present example does in the invitation-to-love, its main generic event.

To sum up, "Unidad en ella" is a love lyric whose basic significance depends on two factors. The first is genre, which plays a primordial role in structuring the poem and in determining its diction and figurative ornaments. The second factor is Aleixandre's surrealist engagement with poetic type and the conventions associated with it. As witnessed here and in other examples, Aleixandre reelaborates and interprets poetic conventions by recasting them as elements expressive of the subconscious mind and its dynamics. In "Unidad en ella," the automatic flavor of the text and its gaps in logic lead one to naturalize the work as the product of a dimly conscious or somewhat altered mind. Further scrutiny confirms that the narrating perspective is eminently psychic, specifically, that the poem takes place in, and ultimately refers to, the largely self-deceptive and deluded mind of the persona, itself an ethereal region where, paraphrasing Bécquer's Rima 66, "[no] habite el olvido" [forgetfulness does not dwell]. It is in this mental context that genre assumes its thematic role in Aleixandre. This love poem is presented as an illusory invitation-to-love limited to the workings of the narrating mind, a mind construed as a storehouse of amatory lore, a collection of commonplaces accumulated most notably from literature. And it is due to this world of internalized fiction with its attendant notions that a real amorous invitation is impossible. The psychological twist that Aleixandre gives to a conventional sort of poem stands as a concrete example of the poet's extraordinary talent for combining the old with the new to produce a highly original art. The psychic recasting of the love lyric also constitutes the poet's personal response to this particular genre and to the amorous ideology therein espoused through time. In "Unidad en ella," the citation of Mystic and Romantic language and the appearance of the archetypal "tú" are qualified here as phantasmagoria, as specters of inculturation threatening love, the realization of the human through eros.

Let us now attend to "No busques, no" [Do Not Seek, No], a hybrid form of the ode, a generic type with which Aleixandre shows great affinity, as previous examples may have suggested.

Yo te he querido como nunca.
Eras azul como noche que acaba,
eras la impenetrable caparazón del galápago
que se oculta bajo la roca de la amorosa llegada de la luz.

Eras la sombra torpe   5
que cuaja entre los dedos cuando en tierra dormimos solitarios.

De nada serviría besar tu oscura encrucijada de sangre alterna,
donde de pronto el pulso navegaba
y de pronto faltaba como un mar que desprecia a la arena.

La sequedad viviente de unos ojos marchitos,   10
de los que yo veía a través de las lágrimas,
era una caricia para herir las pupilas,
sin que siquiera el párpado se cerrase en defensa.

Cuán amorosa forma
la del suelo las noches del verano   15
cuando echado en la tierra se acaricia este mundo que rueda,
la sequedad obscura,
la sordera profunda,
la cerrazón a todo,
que transcurre como lo más ajeno a un sollozo.   20

Tú, pobre hombre que duermes
sin notar esa luna trunca
que gemebunda apenas si te roza;
tú, que viajas postrero
con la corteza seca que rueda entre tus brazos,   25
no beses el silencio sin falla por donde nunca
a la sangre se espía,
por donde será inútil la busca del calor
que por los labios se bebe
y hace fulgir el cuerpo como con una luz azul si la noche   30
   es de plomo.

No, no busques esa gota pequeñita,
ese mundo reducido o sangre mínima,

esa lágrima que ha latido
y en la que apoyar la mejilla descansa.

(La destrucción 120–21)

[I have loved you as never before.
You were azure like the waning night,
You were the impenetrable shell of the tortoise
That beneath the rock hides from the amorous advent of light.

You were the uneasy shadow   5
That congeals between the fingers when, on earth, we sleep alone.

It would have been futile to kiss the dark intersection of your
    alternating blood,
Where suddenly your pulse was sailing
And just as suddenly it would disappear like a sea averse to sand.

The living dryness of those withered eyes,   10
Of those eyes I used to see drowned in tears,
Was a caress to wound those pupils,
Without the eyelid closing even in defense.

How amorous a shape
That of the earth on summer nights   15
When in earthly repose the turning world is caressed,
The dark dryness,
The deep silence,
The total oblivion
That happens like the farthest thing from a sob.   20

You, poor human who slumbers
Without heeding the waning moon
That, as it groans, barely grazes you;
You who straggles behind
With the dry crust that turns between your shoulders,   25
Do not kiss that absolute silence wherein
No trace of blood can be seen,
Where futile will be the quest for the warmth
That through the lips is drunk,
Making the body resplendent as with a blue light   30
    on a lead-dark night.

No, do not seek that little drop,
That diminished world or bit of blood,
That throbbing tear
That rests on a resigned cheek.]

"No busques, no" is markedly different in tone and structural clarity from the other poems examined so far. It lacks the soporific atmosphere and the breathless "versículos" of "Sin luz"; absent is the dramatic flavor of "Las águilas" or the intense and pulsating apostrophes of "Mina"; gone too is the frantic and hallucinatory ambit of "Unidad en ella." Instead, the tone of "No busques no" is contemplative and relatively reposed. The tonal difference can most immediately be explained in light of the subject undertaken by the poem, which is the very positive portrayal of love fulfilled. This is announced in the "in medias res" opening, a favorite Aleixandrean means of introit. "Yo te he querido como nunca" establishes a highly positive circumstantial fiction as poetic point of departure, identical to that set by "Sí, te he querido como nunca," of "Soy el destino." The perfect tense indicates that the poem is born as a post love-making address of lover to beloved, a standard sort of situation in the circumstantial repertoire of the amatory lyric. In this way, the reposed tone of the text may justifiably be taken as a simulacrum of the sense of well-being and balance that love has brought to the poem's narrator. Well over half of the text—stanzas 1–5—clearly develops on the basis of this kernel. What is more, here there are none of the narrative "engaños" such as those seen in each poem so far examined. There is, for example, no identificational enigma like that seen in "Mina." In "No busques, no" both the narrator and addressees— the beloved "tú" of strophes 1–5 and the collective "tú," the "pobre hombre" of 6–7—are clearly defined. Likewise, there is no textual indication leading us to naturalize the poem as taking place in the imaginary and deluded world of the narrator's mind, as in "Unidad en ella." "No busques, no" refers us without great ado to the conventional scene announced in the opening verse.

What seems to trouble the text is its discursive structure. To be specific, the intimate love poem of strophes 1–5 appears to have little relation to the remaining two stanzas, a publicly directed and notably odic conclusion. Not only does the transition—"Tú, pobre hombre que duermes"—seem unprepared for; the balance of the text would seem to be an addendum, an add-on at organic odds with the preceding strophes, which could well stand on their own as an independent love lyric. The abrupt transition and the structural irregularity might be written off as an instance of the automatism effect, which is created in Aleixandre in order to simulate love's irrational nature. However, this justification is rather weak, "No busques, no" being one of the least irrational and most lucidly presented poems in *La destrucción o el amor*. The solution to this particular textual problem lies in genre itself, which in this poem is signaled most clearly via specific intertextualities. Before identifying those intertexts, consider first an abstract of the love lyric contained in stanzas 1–5, which may serve to suggest the generic integrity of this section.

The amatory poem is neatly arranged in two parts, each developing from the situational kernel established in verse one. The first part, which is coextensive with stanzas 1–4, or roughly half of the entire text of "No busques, no," is an anecdotal digression in which the love story of narrator and addressee is summed up. In his exposition, the narrator both describes the pre-amatory condition of the beloved ("Eras azul como noche que acaba," etc.) and, in strophe 4, suggests the invitation-to-love precipitating the erotic denouement. The latter is gloriously celebrated in stanza 5, a sort of paean to love. Outstanding in the first four stanzas is the use of the imperfect in main clauses, a tense sparingly used in *La destrucción o el amor* and a feature contributing to the soft and measured tone of the love poem. The second and final section of the love poem is contained in the fifth stanza. Here, the narrator both records the ecstatic union of lovers and praises the virtues of love. The timelessness and ecstasy of the experience is transmitted both through the elision of main verbs and via the atemporals of the subordinate clauses. In brief, the five strophes are generically complete in that they supply a self-contained causality, and a closure, for the amorous topos taken up therein.

The intertextualities that are key to the generic rationale behind "No busques, no" are most clearly signaled in the love poem section. Here, Aleixandre invokes two Mystic ancestors, San Juan de la Cruz and Fray Luis de León. The loudest signal of this ancestry is emitted by the peculiarly Mystic description of love fulfilled, most notably by portraying amorous union as an ecstasy, as a suspension of the senses through which the self is effectively annihilated. The connection between Aleixandre and the Mystics is bolstered through an intertextual pastiche of diction, syntax, and meter, which specifically orients "No busques, no" toward San Juan de la Cruz and Fray Luis de León. Most outstanding in this amalgam are verses 14–15, which introduce the ecstatic closure of Aleixandre's love lyric: "Cuán amorosa forma / la del suelo las noches del verano." Here, spliced together in their respective verses, are two recognizable fragments, the first from San Juan, the second from Fray Luis. Let us consider each separately for now. The first—"Cuán amorosa forma"—evokes the saint's well-known "Llama de amor viva" [The Living Flame of Love], a love poem "a lo divino," that is, imbued with religious significance. Aleixandre's verse not only paraphrases a specific line from the ancestral poem—"¡Cuán manso y amoroso / recuerdas en mi pecho" [How gentle and lovingly you awake in my breast]—; it also clearly mimics the model by means of metrical and positional repetition. Like San Juan's verse, Aleixandre's is both a heptasyllable and is the liminal verse of the concluding amatory strophe. This specific poetic ancestry can be seen in other textual fragments. From the first verses of "Llama de amor viva"—"¡Oh llama de amor viva, / que tiernamente hieres / de mi alma en el más profundo centro!"[8] [Oh living flame of love, that so tenderly hurts in the deepest center of my soul]—comes the verb "herir" of Aleixandre's verse 12, "era una caricia para herir las pupilas." In Aleixandre, the tender hurt paradox of the Mystic's flame of love figuratively maps the exchange of glances between lover and beloved, an eyes-meet-eyes story which, narrated in the fourth stanza, sparks the happy amatory denouement. Finally, it could also be guessed that San Juan's deep "centro del alma" is transformed into Aleixandre's caressed "este mundo que rueda," an hombre / tierra variant emphasizing exterior carnality rather than soul but which retains in its verb the circularity implicit in the Mystic "centro," itself a symbol of destiny.

Fray Luis is incorporated into the Aleixandre poem in a similar fashion, although he is more extensively assimilated than the saint. This same pattern of ancestral absorption holds true throughout *La destrucción o el amor* and is discussed in detail in the next chapter. Fray Luis is most openly cited in the second verse of the amatory closure—"Cuán amorosa forma, / la del suelo las noches del verano,"—where Aleixandre paraphrases the third verse from "Noche serena [Serene Night]." Here are the first two "liras":

> Cuando contemplo el cielo
> de innumerables luces adornado,
> y miro hacia el suelo,
> de noche rodeado,
> en sueño y en olvido sepultado:
>   el amor y la pena
> despiertan en mi pecho un ansia ardiente;
> despiden larga vena
> los ojos hechos fuente;
> la lengua dice al fin con voz doliente:[9]

> [When I contemplate the heavens
> Adorned with countless lights,
> And I look toward the ground,
> Surrounded in night,
> In dream, and forgetfulness:
>   Love and pain

Waken in my breast a burning desire;
Sending forth a long stream,
My eyes are become a font;
At last my tongue in plaintive tone says:]

Aleixandre's object of contemplation or "tú"—variously, the "amorosa forma" and nocturnal "suelo," the ground spinning under a summer night's sky—is a figurative mixture, and transformation, of fragments from the specific poems of San Juan and Fray Luis. As might be expected, the Luisinian landscape cloaking Aleixandre's beloved is not limited to strophe five but is scattered throughout the poem. An example of this further transformation may be seen in the description of the beloved in verses 5 and 6, where Aleixandre's "sombra torpe" is a condensation of Fray Luis's "suelo . . . en sueño y en olvido sepultado." Here, "sombra" economically synthesizes the ancestral sleep, forgetfulness, and death trio; the adjective "torpe"— as well as other phrases such as "encrucijada de sangre alterna"— connotatively adds vacillation to the "sombra" in order to explain that the beloved's once spectral existence or nonlife was due to hesitating when invited to love. The Luisinian "sueño" motif is reemployed in the opening verses of the odic section (stanzas 6–7) where the Everyman "tú" is "pobre" because he effectively sleeps in forgetfulness of love. He does not notice that time goes on, that he now barely hears the whimpering of the waning moon, the Romantic emblem of forlorn love.

Aleixandre's incorporation of these Mystic intertexts obeys a discernible pattern whereby the various ancestral elements are effectively spliced together. This transformative strategy is most patent in verses 14–15, where two memorable fragments from model poems are joined and prominently displayed. The poetic rationale that affects the seemingly inorganic appearance of "No busques, no"— what Riffaterre would call an ungrammaticality—is to be found in the light of the same intertextual strategy. The generic hybrid that is "No busques, no" is the result of Aleixandre's combining the love lyric of the saint with the odic form of Fray Luis. By means of this generic recombination Aleixandre achieves two things. The first is to reinforce the Mystic pedigree of his poem, which, though already quite discernible in citation, is reconfirmed by retaining the generic types of the ancestral models. The connection with both ancestors and with the Renaissance tradition in which they wrote is also strengthened via the metrical containment of "No busques, no," whose verses tend toward the seven- and eleven-syllable length characteristic of the "lira," a strophic form favored by San Juan and Fray Luis.

Aleixandre's stanza five, it might be noticed, is but a slightly expanded and unrhymed "lira" which, in a very "lira"-like manner, comes to a "rest" upon arriving at the longer last verse. The second thing Aleixandre achieves through generic recombination is to recontextualize the love lyric by placing it in the odic frame, a formal strategy which, as we shall see, is directly in line with the mission of Aleixandre's poetry. In effect, Aleixandre makes San Juan's love lyric part of the materia prima of Fray Luis's Horatian ode. The generic recasting may be most clearly appreciated in view of the title and the addendum—stanzas 6–7—which literally surround the five strophe love lyric and signal the all encompassing odic horizon via apostrophe, one of the ode's salient generic features. To be considered at this juncture are the effects of generic hybridization and the question of how the integration of generic types produces an organic whole.

The overall effect realized by generically recontextualizing the love lyric with the ode is to redefine the poetic role of the amatory poem. Under the aegis of the ode, the amatory poem is no longer a self-contained and intimate form but an exemplum subordinated to the thematic concerns expressed by the odist. The generic role shift may be most clearly appreciated in the light of speech acts. The nuclear speech act of "No busques, no" is not an invitation-to-love like that of "Unidad en ella"; nor is it the praise of a mistress, nor the celebrating of love fulfilled, which are all typical in the love lyric's vocal repertoire. The definitive speech act of the poem is the quintessential odic act of exhortation advertised in the title and carried out in the closing stanzas. In this light, the Mystic, and very positive, love poem attains its functional significance by supplying the exemplary circumstance on which the odist bases his concluding admonishment. If we compare "No busques, no" to Aleixandre's other odic poems, we can see that the love lyric inscribed here is an especially expanded, single exemplum akin in function to the baroquely interwoven miniatures found in "Sin luz" or "Mina."[10] The generic recontextualization of this particularly extensive and generically complete example serves to underline one of ode's outstanding characteristics. The ode effectively ensures that the poetic material that it absorbs—be this material a brief inset, a swordfish, an urn, a person or an otherwise generically complete poem like the Bécquerian arcanum poem taken up in "Mina"—transcends a potentially local significance. The ode conventionally broadens the import of assimilated material by overtly stipulating its significance, an odic trait which can be appreciated most clearly in anti-odes like Pablo Neruda's witty Odas elementales, in which we are told that the transcendental meaning of an artichoke, for example, lies in the vegetable's very down-to-earth alimentary value.

In "No busques, no," the thematic horizons of the typically local and intimate love lyric are vastly broadened both by increasing the scope of the addressee and by stipulating the exemplary significance of the entire love poem. The addressed "tú" becomes much more than the amatory beloved. Rather, this entity is a collective "tú," an all-encompassing and timeless being to whom countless odes, including those of Fray Luis, make their apostrophic turn. The love poem is given transcendent value as a didactic exemplum precisely in order to illustrate a lesson on amorous "vanitas," like the one delivered, though in a much less explicit manner, in "Sin luz." In the final stanzas of the present example, the collective "tú" is admonished not to search for incorporeal love, "por donde será inútil la busca del calor"; the dreamy Everyman is advised in particular not to search for unrequited love past, which is variously figured as "luna trunca," "silencio," "gota pequeñita," "ese mundo reducido o sangre mínima." These appellations of unrequited love are thematic motifs which repeat in summary form the pre-love exposition of the first three strophes and which, in this way, organically enmesh the amatory and odic sections of the text. This summary is also part of the odist's rhetorical strategy by which he underlines, via iteration, the exemplary significance of the previous amatory verses. Additional reason for the odist's repetition—and for generically recontextualizing the love lyric—lies in the personality of the poem's public addressee, an overly mental Everyman akin to the "tú" of "Mina." As the exhortative odic section closes, the narrator supplies a brief sketch of the addressee who, tear-stained cheek resting in hand, is the very image of the resignation and passivity against which the poem is directed. For his part, the narrating odist of this poem, like the docent id of "Mina," is a figure of authority or wisdom whose lesson on amorous "vanitas" is based on the experience recounted in the first section, where the narrator recalls the beloved's once wavering response to his amorous invitation: "De nada serviría besar tu oscura encrucijada de sangre alterna, / donde de pronto el pulso navegaba / y de pronto faltaba como un mar que desprecia a la arena." The odist of "No busques, no" is not, to be exact, the voice of desire but rather the voice of experience, a role conventionally in line with the didactic function assumed by many odic personae. As the present discussion may have served to demonstrate, the generic recontextualization at work in "No busques, no" explains the poem's seemingly inorganic appearance. The generic recasting of the love poem as odic exemplum also serves as a further instance of the over-arching mission of *La destrucción o el amor,* which is to define and advocate Aleixandre's surrealist notion of love.

In overview, the generic crossing illustrated by "No busques, no," is symptomatic of the generic tradition with which Aleixandre's book is most engaged. On one hand, *La destrucción o el amor* has a very hefty investment in the love lyric, and is, among all of Aleixandre's books, the most celebratory expression of love. On the other hand, this book is also profoundly anchored in the tradition of the ode, a fact that is demonstrable in the conformation of a great many poems. This particular generic horizon is signaled in open adver-tisement—in the generic subtitle of section 3 of the book, "Elegías y poemas elegíacos"—and in the title, *La destrucción o el amor,* whose latent apostrophic character qualifies it as a sign of the ode. As "No busques, no," graphically serves to illustrate, the love lyric and the ode are at the heart of Aleixandre's discursive logic, a logic whereby *La destrucción o el amor* serves as a surrealist "libro de buen amor," an odic book of good love based on amatory examples of true vs. false love. Finally, "No busques, no" is suggestive of the particular relation between Aleixandre and his Mystic ancestors. Aleixandre not only assimilates specific poems from Fray Luis and San Juan as basis for his generic reconfiguration of the love lyric. The poet's assimilation and reworking of the ancestral poems also constitutes a Bloomian response to them through which he defines his own amorous ideol-ogy. Suffice it to say for now that Aleixandre's sense of what love is—love is an immanent and accessible human destiny—places the poet in direct thematic line with these Mystics. Aleixandre's nondivine version of Mystic love also places the poet at odds with the Roman-ticism of Bécquer, whose presence is also felt at every turn in this book, as there has been opportunity to see. For Bécquer, love, though sought and partially visible, is neither immanent nor accessible but lies beyond the poet's grasp. In "No busques, no" Aleixandre's the-matic juxtaposition of Mysticism and Romanticism is noticeable in the unrequited-love motifs such as "luna trunca," which contrast with the Mystic love-fulfilled exemplum from which the poem de-parts. The Mystic-Romantic contrast is also very much a part of the particular formula with which the odic narrator petitions his ad-dressee not to choose ethereal love but rather that of the "amorosa forma." The petitionary "no busques, no" directly recalls Bécquer who, in Rima 11, makes as amorous choice the "vano fantasma de niebla y luz" [illusory specter of mist and light] while rejecting the apparently tangible and raven-haired beauty, to whose query—"¿A mí me buscas?" [Is it me who you seek?]—the poet responds, "No es a ti, no" [No, it is not you]. Aleixandre's convocation of ancestry will be the subject of the following two chapters.

To end the discussion of discursive structure and of genre in particular is "La dicha," an example of metapoetry in *La destrucción o el amor*. All Aleixandre pieces so far examined have provided instances of implicit self-consciousness wherein specific intertextualities effectively intimate that Aleixandre's poetry is to a great extent spawned by and refers to other poetry rather than the world per se. Notwithstanding this metapoetic dimension, none of those texts explicitly foregrounds Aleixandre's own "arte poética," a textual feature that distinguishes the surrealist's poems from the Salinas and Machado pieces studied in chapter 2. However, like the latter poems, "La dicha" is expressly engineered to define Aleixandre's poetry and to voice the poet's concerns with his own work. As will also be seen, this poem, akin to so many other Aleixandrean works, is an ode. Following is the text of "La dicha" [Bliss].

No. ¡Basta!
Basta siempre.
Escapad, escapad; sólo quiero,
sólo quiero tu muerte cotidiana.

El busto erguido, la terrible columna,   5
el cuello febricente, la convocación de los robles,
las manos que son piedra, luna de piedra sorda
y el vientre que es el sol, el único extinto sol.

¡Hierba seas! Hierba reseca, apretadas raíces,
follaje entre los muslos donde ni gusanos ya viven,   10
porque la tierra no puede ni ser grata a los labios,
a esos que fueron, sí, caracoles de lo húmedo.

Matarte a ti, pie inmenso, yeso escupido,
pie masticado días y días cuando los ojos sueñan,
cuando hacen un paisaje azul cándido y nuevo   15
donde una niña entera se baña sin espuma.

Matarte a ti, cuajarón redondo, forma o montículo,
materia vil, vomitadura o escarnio,
palabra que pendiente de unos labios morados
ha colgado en la muerte putrefacta o el beso.   20

No. ¡No!
Tenerte aquí, corazón que latiste entre mis dientes larguísimos,
en mis dientes o clavos amorosos o dardos,

o temblor de tu carne cuando yacía inerte
como el vivaz lagarto que se besa y se besa.   25

Tu mentira catarata de números,
catarata de manos de mujer con sortijas,
catarata de dijes donde pelos se guardan,
donde ópalos u ojos están en terciopelos,
donde las mismas uñas se guardan con encajes.   30

Muere, muere como el clamor de la tierra estéril,
como la tortuga machacada por un pie desnudo,
pie herido cuya sangre, sangre fresca y novísima,
quiere correr y ser como un río naciente.

Canto el cielo feliz, el azul que despunta,   35
canto la dicha de amar dulces criaturas,
de amar a lo que nace bajo las piedras limpias,
agua, flor, hoja, sed, lámina, río o viento,
amorosa presencia de un día que sé existe.
                              (*La destrucción* 179–80)

[No. Enough!
Enough forever.
Escape, escape. I only want,
I only want your quotidian death.

The erected bust, the terrible column,   5
The feverish neck, the convocation of oaks,
Hands made of stone, the moon of deaf stone
And the womb that is the sun, the only extinct sun.

May you be grass! Dry grass, crowded roots,
Foliage between the thighs where even worms no longer live, 10
Because even the soil cannot be pleasing to those lips,
To those that were, yes, snails of what was humid.

To kill you, immense foot, spit-out plaster,
Foot chewed for days on end when eyes dream,
When they imagine a new and innocent azure landscape   15
Where an entire girl bathes without foam.

To kill you, round coagulation, form or pile,
Vile material, contemptuous regurgitation,
Word that, dangling from mauve lips,
Has hung on putrefied death or the kiss.   20

No. No!
To have you here, heart that beat, in my teeth so long,

In my teeth or amorous nails or darts,
Or the trembling of your flesh when it used to lie inert
Like the lively lizard that endlessly kisses itself.   25

Your feigned cataract of numbers,
Cataract of hands of a bejewelled woman,
Cataract of baubles where locks of hair are kept,
Where opals or eyes are covered in satin,
Where even the fingernails themselves are stored in lace.   30

Die, die like the cry of the sterile earth,
Like the turtle crushed beneath the foot,
A wounded foot whose fresh and most innocent blood
Tries to run and be like a nascent river.

I sing the happy sky, the dawning azure,   ·   35
I sing the bliss of loving sweet creatures,
Of loving that which is born under pure stones,
Water, flower, leaf, thirst, lamina, river or wind,
The amorous presence of a day that I know exists.]

The particular problem involved in approaching "La dicha" is
not that its self-conscious horizon is not clearly signaled. On the
contrary, the metapoetic filiation of this piece is announced quite
audibly, in fact much more so than in the other metapoems of *La
destrucción o el amor*.[11] We are alerted to this generic information in
the relatively limpid final stanza where the prominently placed and
twice repeated verb, "canto" [I sing]—an ancient metonym for poetic activity—engages the poem in the tradition of metapoetry and
instructs us to read it accordingly. In brief, "La dicha" is to be taken
as a statement on poetry in general and on Aleixandre's in particular. Recall that Machado employs a variant of "cantar" in "Las
moscas," wherein "no tendréis digno cantor" [you likely haven't a
worthy singer] not only refers to the poem within the odic tradition
but also brings to the fore the author's specific concern with his
own art as "la palabra en el tiempo" [the word in time]. In the final
stanza of Aleixandre's poem, "canto," a clear generic signal in and
of itself, introduces a most lucid synthesis of what Aleixandre's poetry aspires to be. The poet, as other poems passionately indicate,
sings the human who is—or can potentially be—an "amorosa presencia," an instinctual and concrete world anchored in the present,
in "un día que sé existe."
    The problem—a problem similar to that of "No busques, no"—is
that the preceding balance of the poem, or roughly 90 percent, obviously seems divorced from the closure. Whereas the closure is char-

acterized by its generic clarity, lucid diction and celebratory tone, the first eight stanzas are maddeningly automatic and hallucinatory in flavor and could handily serve as a specimen of surrealism at its most obscure and disorienting. This part of the text is saturated with indications of the irrational, which are patent in such images as the remarkably random "muslos donde ni gusanos ya viven," or "pie masticado días y días." As to the intended addressee or addressees of the poem's imperatives, they seem to shift mysteriously by the verse. The receiver of the opening "¡Basta!" is a "tú" who is subsequently referred to as "pie inmenso," "palabra," and "corazón que latiste." Not to go unnoticed either are the maledictions directed to this obscure personage by the narrator, "¡Hierba seas!," and "Muere." For its part, the "vosotros" form of the double "escapad" of verse 3 makes but this one brief textual incursion, not to be heard again. One must wonder who is bid to escape and from what. Finally, all apostrophic forms completely disappear as the text arrives at its limpid closure where "canto" seems to issue forth as if from poetic spontaneous generation, no direct allusion to song having been made throughout the entirety of the previous text. Indeed, the greater part of the poem simulates an involuntary psychic expulsion, a rhetorical purging suggested in verses 18 and 19 where "vomitadura" and "palabra" are placed in equivalence. In this way, then, the circumstantial nucleus of all but the final strophe would seem to be first and foremost the narrator's overwrought and phantasmagorical mental world, a world not unlike that seen in "Unidad en ella." Summarizing the present lyric dilemma, "La dicha" coquettishly troubles reception of the text by simultaneously revealing and veiling its discursive shape, in particular the outlines of its full generic profile.

Perhaps the most direct and economical strategy toward fathoming the shadows cast by "La dicha" is to examine first the generic information that the poem does not hold back. For this purpose, consider the last stanza, where the generic signal, "canto" overtly points to the poem's metapoetic horizon. To be taken into account are both the strategic position of this generic signaling and the additional discursive information that can be gleaned from the passage. Given that the poem's statement of self-consciousness is also its closure, we may assume that the contents introduced by "canto" are somehow both a synthesis and a consequence of the preceding poetic narration. A preliminary indication of the last stanza's synthetic function may be seen in the concluding blue sky and landscape motifs, which have counterparts in the anterior herbal references and in the "paisaje azul." Of greater overall utility is the self-defining activity of this section itself, which here and in other metapoems constitutes the nuclear speech act or main discursive plot through which a poem establishes its particular identity. In this generic light, it may be guessed that the self-defining closure of "Mina" is the resolution of its discursive plot, a drama of self-identity played out in the mind of the poet-narrator. For its part, and up to the placid closure, the narrative psyche appears to have undergone a tumultuous crisis of identity, as stanzas 1–8 forcefully suggest. The metapoetic closure affords an additional discursive clue which, together with the information already gleaned, leads a step further toward perceiving the overall design of "La dicha." Bearing in mind the either/or optative principle that organizes *La destrucción o el amor* on the whole, it may be justifiably suspected that the text preceding the closure acts as an antithetical counter example of what the poet does not choose to sing, of what he explicitly rejects as the material of his own poetics. In other words, the discursive plot of the poem consists, first, of an instigating event that moves the narrator to effectively voice a "No canto," the denial of a poetic other; this reaction is indeed audible in the curt and firmly negative stance voiced in the first apostrophe, "No. ¡Basta!" Second, this same act of antithetical self-definition leads to the self-aware and affirmative lyric denouement, the "Canto," where the narrator's poetic identity crisis is resolved or at least averted, a thematic resolution which accounts for the clarity and measured tone of the poem as it comes to its rest. As we now turn our attention to the first eight strophes, we will see that "La dicha" indeed follows this self-conscious outline, a scheme that can be fleshed out by recovering additional generic signals covertly inscribed in the eight-stanza counter example.

The generic signals hidden therein repeat the self-conscious filiation already announced quite explicitly in the closure; what is more, they orient the poem in the direction of the ode. The most important signals are buried in the circumstantial nucleus or scene of the text, to which close attention will presently be lent. But because the setting is fragmented and strewn about the text's first eight stanzas, a bit of referential archeology is necessary in order to reconstruct those fragments. The first object of value is a statue, a shattered sculpture whose pieces include "el busto erguido," "la terrible columna," "las manos que son piedra," "los muslos donde ni gusanos ya viven," and "yeso escupido." There are yet other situational elements to be gathered up, including flora—"los robles," "hierba," "raíces," "follaje"—and temporal references, principally the presence of "luna," and the concurrent extinction of the sun. Having reassembled these remnants, the setting of Aleixandre's poem seems to be a neoclassical garden scene, such as those depicted in eighteenth-century paintings. Elements of this sort of setting might include classical statuary set in a bower, perhaps a handsome Adonis, a chaste Diana, a shapely Venus, or the lusty pursuit of satyrs quickening in on nymphs.

Additional textual remnants scattered in "La dicha" help to more precisely reconstruct the outlines of the garden and in fact to locate it in the Modernista sphere of Rubén Darío, who himself, in "Era un aire suave . . ." (*Prosas profanas*), reinterprets the neoclassical landscape according to his own Versaillesque vision. In the aforementioned poem, the Nicaraguan poet bathes his highly manicured garden in moonlight and sets it as a scene against which the courtly evasion of love is played out. The Daríoesque site of "La dicha" is suggested by the description of the garden as a "paisaje azul," an allusion to Darío that is strengthened by the exquisite refinement of the garden and additionally bolstered via the gemological and costume references of stanza 7—"manos de mujer con sortijas," "dijes donde pelos se guardan," "ópulos," "terciopelos," "encajes." The situation from which "La dicha" departs and to which the poet-narrator refers is therefore a literary object, a poem which itself depicts the sort of garden scene referred to above. For the moment, and for generic purposes, the exact outlines of the poetic object that has been reassembled matter less than the orientational function that the object serves toward comprehending "La dicha." Now visible is that Aleixandre's poem is engaged in the time-honored tradition of countless metapoems whose self-defining point of departure is another object of art, be it a poem, a painting, a statue, or a "naturaleza muerta," a still life as in Salinas's "Don de la materia." It may be surmised that the presence of this aesthetic other is what instigates the discursive plot of the poem, most notably the repeated apostrophizing in which the poet-narrator both invokes and scathingly rejects that object of art. By the same token, the addressed "tú"—that object of art—is the antithesis against which the poet's own "cantar" will be defined and stand out. Together with the traditional meditation-on-art motif, the repeated apostrophizing serves to further fill out the generic profile of "La dicha." Not only is the work a specific type of metapoem; it is also an ode, a type often signaled by apostrophe. As the discussion continues, the odic horizon of "La dicha" will prove most useful toward discerning its discursive design. At any rate, that the generic conformation of "La dicha" is odic as well as self-aware aligns the poem with a traditional kind of lyric.

For the present purpose of scrutinizing the generic composure of "La dicha," a brief digression is necessitated in which the contours of Aleixandre's poem will be further delineated by comparing it to Keats's "Ode on a Grecian Urn," a prototypical odic metapoem.

These seemingly unrelated poems have a great deal in common, a communality which is explicable in the light of their close generic kinship. To begin, both poems are spawned in identical manner, issuing from a situational kernel in which the poet meditates on an object of art, be it a Greek urn or a Modernista poem. On the basis of this starting point, both poems ostensibly set about describing that object and, in so doing, perform the nuclear speech act of the metapoem, which is to define itself and to express the author's poetic credo. The latter is discussed, both in "Ode on a Grecian Urn" and in "La dicha," in terms of the relation between art and life, a theme to be considered shortly. It bears adding that each poem supplies the story of its own genesis—the poet sees an object of art and meditates on it—though to one extent or another this is true of all poetry. But in line with metapoetry, both the Romantic and surrealist odes are presented, to be precise, as a poetic autobiography, a story of genesis in which both the poem's becoming, or process of growth, and its poetic identity are of primary importance, as are the poet's vital and aesthetic concerns thereby expressed. This schematic comparison, as so far laid out, could also apply to Salinas's "Don de la materia," a self-aware poem whose nascence is also attributable to the poet's confrontation with an object of art, the "naturaleza muerta" of "jarrón" and "mesa." But, oriented in odic direction, the Keats and Aleixandre metapoems depart from Salinas's piece, which is hybridized in mock epic form. Unlike the latter, the odes not only make ostensible display of apostrophe but also, by this very means, express a public and even didactic purpose, like that voiced in "Mina" or in "No busques, no." Another generic similarity between Keats's ode and Aleixandre's is architectural, specifically the tripartite structure that these pieces and many other traditional odes exhibit. This formal distribution, which is commonly referred to as "strophe," "antistrophe," and "epode," coincides with the establishment of the situational nucleus, an expansion on that nucleus, and closure. Later discussion of "La dicha," particularly of the structuring of its poetic exempla, will be facilitated by evoking this odic design. But first, a brief account of the differences between the two generic family members.

For all of their similarities—both structural and thematic—"La dicha" and "Ode on a Grecian Urn" quite obviously diverge, a contrast which could be explained in view of Romantic and surrealist aesthetics. But the differences that interest this discussion are those which are attributable to the poems' reaction to genre, a reaction by which each establishes its own poetic identity. In "Ode on a Grecian Urn," Keats expresses a profound faith in poetry, especially insofar as poetry, like other art, can both redeem and illuminate life by eternalizing that fleeting existence in beautiful form. This theme is iterated in all Keatsian miniatures, which consist of brief anecdotes based on stereotypical scenes common to ancient Greek art, including vases, statuary, and paintings. In tandem, these insets not only simulate the apocryphal urn to which the title makes reference but, more importantly, act as the metaphorical vehicle through which the poem refers to itself. In particular, the poetry/art metaphor is employed so as to cast Keats's work as a paradoxical "still life," as a perennial freeze-frame whose mission it is to monumentalize life, the latter being a significant but necessarily fading image. Indeed, the pictorial phrase, "still life," which designates a traditional genre of painting, is a hypogram that informs each miniature of Keats's poem. Half of the phrase surfaces in the opening verse—"Thou still unravished bride of quietness"—where "still" is grammatically ambiguous and feasibly can be taken as either an adverb or adjective. At any rate, Keats's art—and specifically his ode—is designed to carry out a transcendent task, a fact made patent in traditional odic fashion as the poem reaches its closure. Here, Keats's poet-narrator makes an apostrophic turn, now facing away from the addressed "thou"—the urn—and, thus, from his artistic self-absorption. The ode now gazes toward humankind, the human collectivity referred to as "ye." To this anonymous being the odic persona offers an aphorism, a pithy bit of wisdom intended to encapsulate Keats's poetic credo and to underline that the ode is itself exemplary of that poetic ideal. Below, the closure of Keats's ode.

> When old age shall this generation waste,
>   Thou shalt remain, in midst of other woe
> Than ours, a friend to man, to whom thou say'st
> "Beauty is truth, truth beauty,"—that is all
>   Ye know on earth, and all ye need to know.[12]

While maintaining the exact self-conscious design and the associated literary topos of Keats's metapoem, "La dicha" absorbs its poetic other—the Darío poem—in a manner diametrically opposed to the reception of the ancient urn by its English relative. Most visibly, "La dicha" engages in a savage invective against the object of its meditation. Indeed, Aleixandre's self-conscious odist appears to dismember or shred the Darío piece, as the necessitated archaeological reconstruction of its fragments makes patent. The unusually fierce quality of the attack is iterated throughout the poem, for example in the maledictions, "¡Hierba seas!" and "Muere." For its part, the hallucinatory style with which that art is reinterpreted—a far cry from the understated beauty of Keats's verses—suggests that the internalization of that art by the mind produces a kind of nightmare in which the regurgitated or "masticada" "materia vil" resurfaces. The motivation for the attack is intimated in two of the opening verses, "Basta siempre" and "sólo quiero tu muerte cotidiana." The key phrases—"siempre" and "muerte cotidiana"—set Aleixandre's poem into direct opposition to the long metapoetic tradition in which, as in Keats's ode, Machado's "Las moscas" or Darío's "Era un aire suave . . . ," the poet celebrates the eternalizing power of art. Aleixandre's poet-narrator begins his discourse by squarely rejecting this topos, which he expresses in the stern "No," in the repeated "basta" referring to "siempre," and in "muerte." In this, we may recall Salinas's "Don de la materia" where, in the "nostalgia" series, the poem similarly rejects topoi associated with Romanticism. In "La dicha" the choice is made instead for the "muerte cotidiana," the living death of real love, which is necessarily noneternal, being instead the "amorosa presencia de un día que sé existe." Aleixandre's aesthetic, while squarely rejecting the artistic "naturaleza muerta" [still life, literally, "dead nature"], embraces the ideal of a "naturaleza viva," the artistic hypogram at play in "La dicha." This conception of poetry is plainly antithetical to other poetic ideals which, like that of Keats, place faith in the eternalizing value of the word. For Aleixandre, love-made-art is tantamount to "amor muerto," which, as will be seen, is the thematics expressed throughout the entire counter example of "La dicha."

Despite his innovative treatment of the metapoem, Aleixandre incorporates into his text traditional self-reflective material, most notably the meditation on an invoked artistic object, which functions as the situational kernel giving rise to the poem. "La dicha" also transmits clear odic signals, which include, most eminently, apostrophe but also the very girth of the poem and its all-encompassing closure. As mentioned, the odic architecture of "La dicha" lies in its tripartite conformation, which proves to be of utility in appreciating the poem's discursive organization. The trinal structure of "strophe," "antistrophe," and "epode" is discernibly delineated by voicing and is roughly coextensive with the establishment of 1) the situational kernel, announced by "No. ¡Basta!" 2) an elaboration departing from that kernel marked by "No. ¡No!" and 3) closure, heralded by "Canto." In overview, the odic distribution of the poem is the following: stanzas 1–5 (strophe); 6–8 (antistrophe); 9 (epode). Let us consider each part of this distribution in order to see how odic conformation organizes the act of surrealist self-definition portrayed in "La dicha."

The opening apostrophes, which demarcate the strophe, establish the poet-before-art circumstance out of which the poem is to arise. Here, and throughout the majority of the poem, the style of the odist's voicing is an important means of creating the noticeable psychic ambience. In particular, "No. ¡Basta! / Basta siempre" simultaneously invokes and rejects Darío's poem, a delicate and beautiful minstrel's song—"un aire suave" [a gentle air]—which Aleixandre remodulates as the mad babbling of his poet-narrator. Together with the total absence of conjugated main verbs and the rapid succession of nightmarish images, the thick reiteration of imperatives moves us to naturalize the odist's personality as obsessive, if not deranged. This psychic effect is translated by means of the repeated "basta" and "no," as has already been mentioned; the use of imperatives in infinitive form—the anaphoric "Matarte a ti," and "Tenerte aquí"— also simulates the mental ambience of the text, being syntactic representations of still unformed or preverbal language issuing from the mind, in this case a mind maddened, rather than lifted, by the ingestion of literature. The anomalous incursion of the "vosotros" imperative—"Escapad, escapad"—is certainly another vocal sign of the poem's psychic perspective. However, not unlike other instances of voicing—no matter how disquieting they are—the plural imperative is very much part of the ode. Like the "ye" of Keats's ode and the "dejadme" of "Mina," this plural form is directed to the poem's public receiver—humankind—who is exhorted to flee, to reject love-made-artifice, of which the invoked Daríoesque "aire suave" is exemplary.[13] This collective apostrophe, which is an integral generic feature, is defamiliarized. For one thing, it is placed at the beginning rather than in the closure, where an odist usually makes public apostrophes; for another, and at least upon initial reception, the overall discursive structure of the poem is unclear. With respect to the ode, this particular instance of apostrophe could be considered as a generic trace, as the surfacing remnant of the tradition in which "La dicha" most unconventionally takes part.

While the point of departure established in the strophic section of "La dicha"—again, stanzas 1–5—is the Darío poem, this fact is less than obvious. As noted, the ancestral poem lies scattered throughout the entire text, having been savagely fragmented by the focal perspective of the narrator. Here, the presence of the exemplary model is unavailable because the Aleixandrean odist largely limits his deranged meditation to one selected component, Darío's statuary motif, which is itself subject to referential dismemberment. Below is the fourth quatrain of "Era un aire suave . . .":

Cerca, coronado con hojas de viña,
reía en su máscara Término barbudo
y, como un efebo que fuese una niña,
mostraba una Diana su mármol desnudo.[14]

[Close by, and crowned in grape leaves,
Bearded Terminus was laughing behind his mask,
And, like an ephebe who might have been a girl,
Diana was displaying her bare marble.]

Aleixandre's defamiliarization of the model is carried out by circumlocuting the sculptural referent, which is never explicitly named. Instead, the maddened odist alludes to a cluster of statuary features—"busto," "columna," "cuello," "manos," "piedra," "muslos," "pie"—which in turn serve as the basis for further poetic expansion. In the fourth stanza, for example, the statuary foot, described as an ingested and now regurgitated material, gives way to a complex inset of sexual repression, a much favored Aleixandrean maneuver. In the run-on syntax of these verses, Aleixandre qualifies the statue with time ("cuando") and place ("donde") by which he responds to Darío who claims about the setting of "Era un aire suave . . ." that, "Yo el tiempo y el día y el país ignoro"[15] [The time and the day and the country I do not know]. The "días y días," adverbial, a variant of the rejected "siempre" of verse two, transmits the tedium evoked by the artistic "forever," specifically by the created illusion of an azure and nonexistent landscape. The adjectives qualifying that scene—"cándido y nuevo"—both underscore, and ironize, the naive character of that Modernista ambit. The "niña," the present occupant of the region of Modernista art, has an especially complex poetic genealogy. First, she is associatively born of the preceding "ojos," "niña" meaning ocular "pupil" as well as "girl," themselves diminished forms of "ojos" and "mujer." In the ocular sense, the ironic "niña entera" is attached to those eyes that dreamily gaze towards the azure never-never land, an illusory and necessarily diminished and mistaken vision. This girl-pupil bathes "sin espuma" in the azure "locus amoenus" of poetry, which is a dry place, as the malediction, "hierba reseca," intimates. The specifically artistic context of "La dicha" offers additional territory for explaining the textual "Nacimiento de la niña" [Birth of the Girl]. She is described as an ocular "niña entera" because she is a metonym for "estatua clásica," a classical statue whose eye is a featureless "all pupil" and to which Aleixandre's description refers, despite its convolutions. The word "espuma" calls to mind the sea, particularly Venus's birth from its foam; in this way, "niña sin espuma" is a diminished Venus who, without "espuma," is without her

oceanic birth place and thus without amorous destiny.[16] Aleixandre's baroque play on "niña" is set into motion by the object of art
upon which his poem meditates, this being Rubén Darío's "Era un
aire suave. . . ." Notice that "niña," a very unusual word in *La destrucción o el amor,* can be seen in the Darío statue description cited above,
in which "niña" refers to a statue of the forever chaste goddess of the
moon, Diana. In the Darío poem, the word "niña" and the androg-
ynous description of the goddess as having ephebe-like thighs suggests that art, the eternal incarnation of youth and sensuality, has
the power to create an illusion as teasing as the sonorous laughter
of la marquesa Eulalia, the femme fatale of "Era un aire suave. . . ."

As indicated, Aleixandre's narrator subverts the art-as-eternity topos
by passionately assailing the object of his meditation. By means of
this attack he responds to the ancestor poem by inverting its elements and thematics, now converting Darío's beautiful Versaillesque
vision into a surrealist nightmare, which is to serve as counter example of the explicitly self-defining conclusion. The theme of poetry
itself is specified in verse 19, where the epithet, "palabra," prepares
"La dicha" to launch the antistrophe. The appearance of "palabra"
seems arbitrary or unprepared for because all preceding poetry
appellations—"busto erguido," "pie inmenso," "cuajarón redondo,"
and so on—would seem to refer to something solid, not linguistic.
Even recognizing that the immediate referent is a piece of statuary
would not explain "palabra." This metonym for poetry only makes
full sense once the Darío intertext has been salvaged, that is, once we
realize that all textual elements, no matter how wildly they stray from
Darío's "aire suave," ultimately refer to this poetic other. Similarly,
the Daríoesque "tú" serves as the premise on which Aleixandre's
self-conscious poem establishes its identity. Considering the poem as
a whole, one may discern an entire poetry paradigm related to "palabra" and to the concluding "canto." Included therein are the apostrophes themselves, the digestion lexicon, which is related to "boca"
and "labios," "dientes larguísimos," and of course "números," of
verse 26, a shorthand for meter and poetry. Not to be overlooked either is the ambivalent title, where "dicha" not only means "bliss" but,
also related to "decir," signifies the lyrically uttered word, "la palabra
dicha." Even in clearer self-conscious odes such as that of Keats it is
easy to lose sight of the fact that the object on which the poem meditates becomes, in its poeticized form, the self-defining poem itself.
Thus, just as Keats's poem is the "urn," so "La dicha," though in highly
transmuted form, is Darío's "Era un aire suave. . . ." It is this ontological ambivalence that sparks the self-defining plot of "La dicha,"
which traces a fiction in which the poet-narrator attempts to purge

himself of his ancestor, and by so doing, to cast off the poetic superego. The artistic superego, an inherited memory that through artifice sublimates the connatural force of desire, is succinctly defined
in the closure of "El desnudo" [The Nude], a metapoem much like
"La dicha." Here is the last strophe of that poem:

> La muerte es el vestido.
> Es la acumulación de los siglos que nunca se olvidan,
> es la memoria de los hombres sobre un cuerpo único,
> trapo palpable sobre el que un pecho solloza
> mientras busca imposible un amor o el desnudo.
> (La destrucción 226)

> [Death is the piece of clothing.
> It is the accumulation of never-forgotten centuries,
> It is the memory of humanity on our collective body,
> A palpable cloth over which a breast weeps
> While impossibly seeking a love or the nude.]

The antistrophe—stanzas 6–8—is marked by the apostrophe, "No.
¡No!," which brings the poem back to its vocal starting point, "No.
¡Basta!" Here, Aleixandre's odist turns from the Darío sculpture
motif as the focus of his narration, now concentrating on another
metonym for the Darío poem, this time the femme fatale, who serves
as the addressed "tú." "She"—the Darío poem—is described as a
past love (stanza 6), and as a "mentira," a bejeweled receptacle of
artifice (stanza 7).[17] In the penultimate stanza, the narrator casts a
final malediction—"Muere, muere"—while "sangre"—the antithesis
of the "tierra estéril"—prepares the poetic discourse for its final odic
turn, which is heralded by "Canto," the introductory element of the
epode. The antistrophe contains a twist to the self-defining plot. The
wishful "Tenerte aquí, corazón que latiste entre mis dientes larguísimos" describes the Aleixandre-Darío relationship as a love affair, as
the memory of love past which, though reviled, is still yearned for,
as if in a moment of weakness. The vampire-like image, "dientes
larguísimos," is one of the metonyms for poetic voice and for Aleixandre's "poética" in particular. The long teeth intimate that the self-
defining odist yearns for his lyric youth, for a time now past in which
he was tempted—or seduced—by Darío's beautiful Modernismo.
The latter is a self-contained poetry that, like the "lagarto," is suffi-
cient unto itself, thus forming a hermetic circle of false amorous
destiny. The sixth stanza can be naturalized in its totality as a mixed
reaction or second thought regarding the Darío "urn." This vacillation—a reflection of the optative principle at work in La destrucción

o el amor—is resolved in stanzas 7 and 8 where the narrator, now decisively banishing the aesthetic melancholy from his mind, both delivers the final invective—"Muere, muere"—and resolutely turns to life and to his own song, the denouement of this story of self-definition.

In the epode, Aleixandre's choice is the antithesis of the refined poetics of the Modernista ancestor: the younger poet celebrates not the artificial albeit seductive "paisaje azul" of Darío's beautiful moon-lit world but rather the dawning azure of desire, of a concrete "amorosa presencia." The penultimate verse—"agua, flor, hoja, sed, lámina, río o viento"—is both a paradigm of the primordial human world sung by Aleixandre throughout *La destrucción o el amor* and a summary of the relationship between the poet's work and that world. The relationship is suggested by means of the syntactically buried and anomalous "lámina," an artistic sign which, while a metonym for Aleixandre's poetry, literally refers to either a plate used in etching or to an illustrative image commonly found in books. The syntactical interment of "lámina" in the verse, together with its associated value as reflective image, serves to express that Aleixandre's art is intimately bound up in human reality and that this art is a lyric mimesis of the human. The concluding verse of "La dicha," which emphatically portrays Aleixandre's poetry as the transmitter of an eminently attainable amorous knowledge—the "amorosa presencia de un día que sé existe"—makes a last direct response to "Era un aire suave. . . ." In the closure of the model poem, Darío encapsulates the sense of his work by stating that what he knows is that the mocking love incarnate in the laughing beauty Eulalia is still and ever beyond human reach. Here is the final "serventesio" of that poem:

> ¿Fue acaso en el Norte o en el Mediodía?
> Yo el tiempo y el día y el país ignoro;
> pero sé que Eulalia ríe todavía,
> ¡y es cruel y eterna su risa de oro![18]

> [Could it have been in the North or the South?
> The time and the day and the country I do not know;
> But I do know that Eulalia laughs still,
> And her golden laugh is cruel and eternal!]

Through his final paraphrase of Darío, Aleixandre not only defines his own poetics but also repeats the exemplary significance of the forebear to whom he owes, as "La dicha" intimates, his poetic identity, or at least a share thereof.

We have seen that Aleixandre's response to Darío is a complex one. On one hand, the aesthetics of the great Modernista poet is employed as a counter example by which Aleixandre works out what his own poetry is, the poetic point of arrival and denouement of the self-defining plot of his metapoem. On the other hand, "La dicha" portrays an internal struggle in which the self-conscious younger poet attempts to overcome the poetic strength of the elder master for whom he feels a mixture of admiration and repulsion.[19] This fiction of self-consciousness and inner identity crisis is a plot well suited to surrealism and to the Freudian ambit in which surrealism has its roots. Harold Bloom, whose theory of poetic generation is based on psychoanalytic theory, describes exactly the psychoartistic conflict played out in "La dicha," which he calls "apophrades," a process whereby a new poet overcomes the strength of his lyric father by introjecting him, by transumptively taking over the elder in order to establish his own strong identity.[20] Finally, we may look at "La dicha" from a slightly different angle. That is, this poem, like so many other pieces in *La destrucción o el amor*, is a head vs. heart story but one in which an aesthetic conflict is acted out. Here, amorous knowledge—the "presencia de un día" in the service of which Aleixandre's poetry is enlisted—is pitted against poetic sentiment—the admiration for a beautiful though artificial poetry, a late Romanticism that propagates false amorous ideology. The resolution of the aesthetic head vs. heart story comes about both by advocating carnal knowledge and by doing so in a language assimilated from the admired though mistaken forebear.

Summing up the present discussion of "La dicha" and of genre, we have seen that Aleixandre employs traditional generic types in a very unconventional manner, to say the least. This he does by remodeling familiar kinds of poems—specifically, the love lyric, the ode, and the metapoem—which are now presented as psychic happenings. Despite the significant textual obscurity consequent with Aleixandre's surrealist treatment of genre, it is nonetheless possible to recover traces of the conventional structure which point us toward this poetry's generic horizon and toward its figurational and thematic significance. "La dicha," the final example of genre in Aleixandre, most teasingly presents its generic signal, which it does by clearly announcing itself as metapoem in its closure while obscuring throughout the great majority of the text the archconventional premise on which it develops, the object of art, or the Daríoesque "urn." In its odic conformation, "La dicha" repeats the Aleixandrean proclivity to direct publicly his amorous thematics, a discursive move in line with the transcendent mission of his poetry. In this particular generic context, Darío's "Era un aire suave . . ." carries out the same, though thematically inverted, exemplary function as the Mystic love lyric in "No busques, no." These examples, together with the markedly Bécquerian "Mina," also suggest the seminal role played by specific poetic forebears in Aleixandre's surrealist conceptualization of love, the subject to which *La destrucción o el amor* is most passionately committed. Attention will be given shortly to the question of Aleixandre's specific ancestry, and to the seminal role that model poets play in his book.

But first, a brief recapitulation of Aleixandre's discursive logic, the subject that has occupied this and the preceding two chapters. There has been some pause to appreciate that *La destrucción o el amor* is a book of poetry engaged in the task of simulating the working of the subconscious mind. This mind, a sentient and preverbal human construct theorized scientifically by Freud, constitutes the surrealist "Mystery," as Breton in majuscule refers to the revolutionary discovery of the Viennese. Aleixandre poetically maps this arcanum and the human in which it is contained as a panerotic world, a strictly human world upon which he imposes a discursive and figurative order. The rhetorical scaffolding on which Aleixandre has organized that world is itself made up of a poetic materia prima taken from the collective source known as "poetry." That material includes narratological and generic structures, as well as metaphor, anaphora, syllepsis, and specific ancestral intertexts. The reader's task, which is to make sense out of Aleixandre's surrealism, can be greatly hindered if the standard critical analogy, "world," is taken literally. In this event, one remains befuddled in the face of the Aleixandrean text, and is unable to begin to account for its many penumbral ungrammaticalities. While Aleixandre is deeply committed to human reality—specifically to the vindication of humankind's natal erotic condition—the language and structures with which he mediates that reality pertain to the realm of poetry, the ambit in which, as the previous discussion of discursive structure may have served to suggest, the poet's revolutionary art reveals its logic.[21]

6
Luz No Usada

Influence, in the deep sense, is a
never ending process.

—Harold Bloom

Esa llegada de la luz que descansa en la frente.
¿De dónde llegas, de dónde vienes?

[That dawning of light that reposes on the brow.
From where do you come, from where do you hail?]

—Aleixandre

THIS AND THE FOLLOWING CHAPTER EXAMINE ALEIXANDRE'S POETIC
ancestry, principally the poet's relation to two specific forebears,
Fray Luis de León and Gustavo Adolfo Bécquer, the model poets
whose voices are most audible in *La destrucción o el amor*. The question of what motivates Aleixandre to allot the major generative role
to these poets rather than to others who are also present therein
serves as introduction to both chapters. The theories of Harold
Bloom and Michael Riffaterre, which were discussed in chapter 1,
prove to be most useful for this purpose. But before considering the
logic of Aleixandre's choice of ancestry in the light of intertextual
theory, a brief note on the formative historical and aesthetic circumstances that impinge on Aleixandre's lyric personality.

Like other poets of the "Generación del 27"—Lorca, Alberti, Diego,
Alonso, Cernuda, Salinas, Guillén, or Prados—Aleixandre was actively
engaged in reviving and vindicating Spain's literary past, in particular the Golden Age and Romanticism. Perfectly in step with his contemporaries, Aleixandre paid homage to his lyrical ancestors most
explicitly, both in poems dedicated to those poets and in speeches
delivered on various occasions.[1] Given the poet's keen awareness and
interest in his lyric patrimony, it should come as no surprise that he
engages Golden Age and Romantic poets in lyric dialogue, including in his apparently most "untraditional" poetry, that is, in his surrealism. Likewise, Aleixandre's effacement of ancestors is motivated

as much by the nature of his poetic task as it is by the Bloomian "anxiety of influence" per se. That is, Aleixandre's tradition affords him a repertoire of formal and thematic possibilities, an exemplary language on which he draws and which he transumptively manipulates in order to conceptualize his surrealist notion of love and his poetic world. Aleixandre's engagement with his ancestry, which is often quite prominently signaled, is also a means of transcending a potentially local significance. By invoking his forebears, Aleixandre becomes a participant in an on-going lyric dialogue in which, by virtue of his similarity to or difference from the progenitors, he marks out his place and sense of poetic identity in that tradition. Bloom, though here referring to poems rather than poets, explains the dialectic of poetic identity in this way: "No poem rejoices in its own solitary inscape, any more than we can do so. . . . To say that a poem is about itself is killing, but to say that it is about another poem is to go out into the world where we live."[2] In concluding these introductory remarks this point will be addressed anew.

Notwithstanding such formative historical and aesthetic circumstances, Aleixandre's selection of Fray Luis and Bécquer as seminal ancestors in *La destrucción o el amor* is ultimately determined by a common matrix, Riffaterre's primordial stuff of significance and seal of intertextual kinship between text and intertext. Tailoring the critic's concept to the present purpose, the matrix affiliating Aleixandre with the Mystic and the Romantic is a shared expressive field that might be called "transcendence." The transcendence matrix manifests itself in two basic and quite visible textual traits, which all three poets share. The first trait is a common thematics whereby each poet addresses questions of interest not only to himself or to a select few but to the whole of humanity. As previously noted, Aleixandre himself terms such poets "poetas radicales." The second trait is formal and stylistic and has to do with the discursive presentation of that thematics. In particular, the poet presents the question of human interest that concerns him in a way that explicitly reinforces its transcendent scope. To clarify what has been said about the transcendence matrix shared by Aleixandre, Fray Luis, and Bécquer, consider a brief example from each.

In Aleixandre, the transcendence matrix could be neatly summarized as "destiny," a key thematic concept behind the mission of his poetry, as expressed in the poet's aphorism, "Hay muchos modos de tener conciencia de un destino común: uno de ellos es la poesía" (*OC* 2:663) [There are many ways of being conscious of a common destiny: one of them is poetry]. One of the outstanding instances of the transcendence matrix is "Soy el destino," the grand-scale revelation poem in which the voice of destiny—the connate force of eros or the id—inveighs humankind to recover its erotic patrimony and thus its authentic nature, through love. Like the discursive presentation of "Mina," that of "Soy el destino" is patterned on the enigma design of Bécquer's Rima 5, a seminal intertext wherein the narrator is the voice of the enigma revealing itself. In Fray Luis, the transcendence matrix is thematically manifest in the Augustinian's preoccupation with mankind's divine destiny, a destiny that can be realized only by uniting oneself with God. This union is to be achieved either by renouncing the world and its vain folly or through the suspension of earthly senses, as illustrated in Fray Luis's well-known ode, "A Francisco Salinas." Here, the "son divino," the divine sound inherent in Salinas's music, awakens the soul, which is transported to its Platonic "origen primera esclarecida" [primal luminous origin]. The formal manifestation of the transcendence matrix is actualized via genre, in particular via the ode, the Renaissance writer's preferred lyric vehicle. As seen in the discussion of Aleixandre's markedly Luisinian "No busques, no," the ode, typically by means of apostrophizing, stipulates the transcendent value of its contents. In "A Francisco Salinas," the most important Luisinian model poem or hypotext in *La destrucción o el amor,* the poet makes an apostrophic turn to humankind, whom he invites to enjoy Salinas's music, a harmony which transports the soul of the listener from the worldly "bajo y vil sentido" [low and vile senses] to its celestial and harmonic origin, "un mar de dulzura" [a sea of sweetness].

In Bécquer, the thematic manifestation of the transcendence matrix is clearly enunciated in Rima 1, where the goal of the poet's work is advertised. Bécquer, who himself reworks and reinterprets the Luisinian music of the spheres, defines his poetry as an effort, though a necessarily thwarted one, to capture "cadencias" [cadences] of "un himno gigante y extraño" [a strange and immense hymn], an ineffable song that, to the contrary of Fray Luis's "son divino," eludes complete human perception. The transcendence matrix is formally actualized throughout Bécquer in the characteristic length of his rimas, in their all-encompassing imagery and in narrative design. Such, for instance, is applicable to Rima 5, the Bécquerian model for Aleixandre's "Mina." The mysterious narrator, who is the voice of the cosmic enigma eluding human comprehension, is poetically conceptualized as "indefinible esencia" [indefinable essence] or "la ignota escala / que el cielo une a la tierra" [the unknown scale joining heaven to earth].

In ancestors of less seminal impact in *La destrucción o el amor*—San Juan or Darío, for example—one of the traits commensurate with the transcendence matrix, either the thematic one or the formal one, is absent or less apparent. As a textual consequence, these model poets tend to assume a subordinate role in Aleixandre. Recall, for example, the part played by San Juan in "No busques, no," where the saint's love lyric is subsumed by Fray Luis's odic form. San Juan, whose Mystic thematics of divine union is essentially identical to that of Fray Luis, uses a much more personal and less public lyrical vehicle for expressing the ineffable experience of union with God, the Mystic death that gives life. Rather than using the transcendence-ensuring ode typical of Fray Luis, San Juan, as noted in discussing "No busques, no," is a writer of love lyrics, an ostensibly personal or nonpublic form of poetry. Examples include intimate love poems like "Llama de amor viva," or lengthier narrative types, such as the exquisite "Canto espiritual," a pastoral lament "a lo divino." Darío, the great Modernista poet to whom Aleixandre responds quite frequently, also plays a lesser generative role than Bécquer or Fray Luis. While the Nicaraguan habitually ponders human destiny, the narrative premise on which much of his poetry is built stems from either a highly personal situation, as in the confessional poems of *Cantos de vida y esperanza*, or from a refined disengagement, a stance implicit in such sumptuous poetic narratives as "Sonatina" or "Era un aire suave . . ." *(Prosas profanas)*.

There is one additional factor that determines or at least predisposes Aleixandre's particular choice of Fray Luis and Bécquer as seminal ancestor poets. As suggested earlier, these ancestors, as they are received by Aleixandre, are themselves engaged in a preestablished intertextual relationship. Such may be seen in Bécquer's Rima 1, where the younger poet reinterprets Fray Luis's ode, "A Francisco Salinas"; similarly, Rima 8 transumptively responds to "Noche serena." Aleixandre's "A ti, viva," whose first verses simultaneously allude to both of the latter ancestor poems, is emblematic of the intertextual confluence of the Mystic and Romantic poets in *La destrucción o el amor*. Here are the opening verses from each of the three poems: "Cuando contemplo el cielo / de innumerables luces adornado / y miro hacia el suelo" [When I contemplate the heavens adorned with innumerable lights and look toward the earth] (Fray Luis); "Cuando miro el azul horizonte / perderse a lo lejos / al través de una gasa de polvo" [When I see the blue horizon become lost in the distance, behind a gauze of dust] (Bécquer); "Cuando contemplo tu cuerpo extendido / como un río que nunca acaba de pasar, /

como un claro espejo donde cantan las aves" [When I see your reclining body like a ceaselessly flowing river, like a mirror where birds
sing] (Aleixandre). By invoking both forebears, the Aleixandrean
text establishes through similarity and difference both its own identity and its place in a pre-established tradition, a tradition spawned
of the transcendence matrix. Most striking in "A ti, viva" is the atmospheric change of focus from the sky—the site of destiny common
to the ancestors—to the terraqueous human whose amorous presence is mapped, as is the firmament of both predecessors, as a font
emanating light and music. It is worth repeating Bloom's assertion
that such interpoetic communication is at the heart of tradition:
"Literary tradition begins when a fresh author is simultaneously cognizant not only of his own struggle against the forms and presence
of a precursor, but is compelled also to a sense of the precursor's
place in regard to what came before *him*."[3]

The presence of Fray Luis in *La destrucción o el amor* is one of the
essential keys to the formal and semantic texture of this book. Indeed, to a great extent *La destrucción o el amor* is about Fray Luis and
his poetics of transcendence; it is also about other ancestors who,
in tandem with this poetic forebear, are defined and evaluated by
Aleixandre. The presence of Fray Luis is signaled in two ways. The
first, encapsulated in the "morir es vivir" [to die is to live] conceit,
evokes Fray Luis and the Mystic tradition in general. Fray Luis's presence is also advertised via specific citational fragments such as "Allá
por las remotas / luces o aceros aún no usados" of "La selva y el
mar," which echo the ancestral "El aire se serena / y viste de hermosura y luz no usada," of "A Francisco Salinas."

The most prominently placed evidence of Aleixandre's intertextual communication with Fray Luis and the Mystic tradition is to be
found in the title of *La destrucción o el amor,* where the "o," read as
conjunctive, makes the destruction/love pair a variant of the traditional trope, "morir es vivir." I label this figure "Mystic conceit" because of the meliorative sense that this conventional and otherwise
negative paradox has in Mystic poetry and in Aleixandre alike. This
is the feature that distinguishes them from the vast majority of writers who have taken up this literary topos.[4] Under the pen of Mystic
writers—not Fray Luis exclusively but also Santa Teresa and San
Juan—the conceit encapsulates the culmination of the Mystic experience. The individual, in self-annihilating amorous union with God,
simultaneously dies and lives, joined now in spiritual rebirth with the
divine destiny to which he or she was born. Following is a well-known
example of the conceit, a secular "copla" that both Santa Teresa and
San Juan were to rewrite "a lo divino," giving it a sacred sense.

Vivo sin vivir en mí,
y tan alta vida espero,
que muero porque no muero.[5]

[I live without living in myself,
And so lofty is the life that I await,
That I die because I do not die.]

In the Luisinian ode, "A Francisco Salinas," the conceit is visibly displayed and likewise serves to expresses the happy annihilation of the self in divine love:

¡Oh, desmayo dichoso!
¡Oh, muerte que das vida! ¡Oh dulce olvido!
Durase en tu reposo,
sin ser restituido
jamás a aqueste bajo y vil sentido![6]

[Oh blissful swoon!
Oh death that gives life! Oh sweet oblivion!
Could I but remain in your repose
Without ever being restored
To these low and vile senses!]

In *La destrucción o el amor*, Aleixandre internalizes the mystic paradox in order to conceptualize the consummation of human love as the ecstasy of erotic instinct, as a psychosomatic ecstasy whereby humanity may recover the amorous destiny to which it was born. Recall, for example, "Unidad en ella," in which the self-deceived narrator only imaginatively realizes amorous destruction: "Muero porque me arrojo, porque quiero morir, / porque quiero vivir en el fuego" [I die because I throw myself, because I want to die, because I want to live in the fire]. Other of the numerous instances of Aleixandre's treatment of the Mystic conceit may be seen in "Las águilas"—"Aguilas de metal sonorísimo, . . . / cantan la ira de amar los corazones, / amarlos con las garras estrujando su muerte" [Eagles of most resonant metal, . . . Sing the ire of loving hearts, Of taloned love squeezing out death]—or in "A ti, viva"—"Cuando miro tus ojos, profunda muerte o vida que me llama" [When I look into your eyes, a deep death or life calls to me].

Further evidence of the conceit's strength as intertextual signal is registered in the critical reception of *La destrucción o el amor*. While many of the traditional intertexts underlying this book have largely gone unnoticed, the Mystic spirit of Aleixandre's book has received frequent mention. In fact, in one of the early reviews of *La destrucción o el amor*, the intuitive poet-critic Dámaso Alonso incisively qualified Aleixandre's surrealism as "panteísmo místico" [Mystic pantheism], a phrase that has become an established critical motif in Aleixandre studies.[7] In light of the human rather than deific ontology of Aleixandre's poetic world, Alonso's phrase might be qualified as "Mystic paneroticism." This formulation suggests Aleixandre's internalization of Mysticism, and his lyric apotheosis of desire, the spirit infusing his anonymous telluric human.

For the purpose of illustrating the nuclear role played by Fray Luis throughout *La destrucción o el amor*, I have selected "La selva y el mar," one of Aleixandre's most intricate, and most markedly Luisinian poems. To begin, a word about the strategic placement and overall appearance of this key text. The book's first piece, "La selva y el mar" is given an eminent position among the book's poems, a situational status that is enhanced by its panoramic character. The vast scape of jungle, sea, and bestiary portrayed therein casts "La selva y el mar" in an introductory role whereby this text appears to afford an aerial vista of the poetic world. Indeed, most of the poems to follow confirm this impression. The animal poems—for example, "Sin luz," "Las águilas," "Tristeza o pájaro," "El escarabajo," or "Cobra"—seem to be particularized treatments of the inhabitants of the universe displayed in the liminal work. Likewise, many other pieces appear to portray different atmospheric components of that universe; among such examples are "La luz," "Noche sinfónica," "Paisaje," "Mar en la tierra," "El frío," "La luna es una ausencia," or "La noche." While the critical analogy, "poetic world," would thus seem to be a justifiable and even a useful means of referring to Aleixandre's poetry, it bears keeping in mind, however, that this comparison is not to be taken literally since "world" or "cosmos" is an expanded form of Aleixandre's nuclear trope, hombre/tierra. In this light, "La selva y el mar" maps out in its lyric geomorphology the human condition that *La destrucción o el amor* undertakes to address. Below, the text of "La selva y el mar" [The Jungle and the Sea]:

Allá por las remotas
luces o aceros aún no usados,
tigres del tamaño del odio,
leones como un corazón hirsuto,
sangre como la tristeza aplacada,   5
se baten con la hiena amarilla que toma la forma del poniente insaciable.

Largas cadenas que surten de los lutos,
de lo que nunca existe,

atan el aire como una vena, como un grito, como un
  reloj que se para
cuando se estrangula algún cuello descuidado.   10

Oh la blancura súbita,
las ojeras violáceas de unos ojos marchitos,
cuando las fieras muestran sus espadas o dientes
como latidos de un corazón que casi todo lo ignora,
menos el amor,   15
al descubierto en los cuellos allá donde la arteria golpea,
donde no se sabe si es el amor o el odio
lo que reluce en los blancos colmillos.

Acariciar la fosca melena
mientras se siente la poderosa garra en la tierra,   20
mientras las raíces de los árboles, temblorosas,
sienten las uñas profundas
como un amor que así invade.

Mirar esos ojos que sólo de noche fulgen,
donde todavía un cervatillo ya devorado   25
luce su diminuta imagen de oro nocturno,
un adiós que centellea de póstuma ternura.

El tigre, el león cazador, el elefante que en sus colmillos
  lleva algún suave collar,
la cobra que se parece al amor más ardiente,
el águila que acaricia a la roca como los sesos duros,   30
el pequeño escorpión que con sus pinzas sólo
  aspira a oprimir un instante la vida,
la menguada presencia de un cuerpo de hombre que
  jamás podrá ser confundido con una selva,
ese piso feliz por el que viborillas perspicaces
  hacen su nido en la axila del musgo;
mientras la pulcra coccinela
se evade de una hoja de magnolia sedosa . . .   35
Todo suena cuando el rumor del bosque siempre virgen
se levanta como dos alas de oro,
élitros, bronce o caracol rotundo,
frente a un mar que jamás confundirá sus espumas
  con las ramillas tiernas.

La espera sosegada,   40
esa esperanza siempre verde,
pájaro, paraíso, fasto de plumas no tocadas,
inventa los ramajes más altos,
donde los colmillos de música,

donde las garras poderosas, el amor que se clava,   45
la sangre ardiente que brota de la herida,
no alcanzará, por más que los pechos entreabiertos en tierra
proyecten su dolor o su avidez a los cielos azules.

Pájaro de la dicha,
azul pájaro o pluma,   50
sobre un sordo rumor de fieras solitarias,
del amor o castigo contra los troncos estériles,
frente al mar remotísimo que como la luz se retira.

                                           (*La destrucción* 117–19)

[Beyond, along the distant
Lights or steels yet unused,
Tigers the size of hate,
Lions like a hirsute heart,
Blood like placated sadness,   5
Vie with the yellow hyena that takes on the form of the
     insatiable setting sun.

Long chains that gush forth from mourning,
Out of what never exists,
Bind the air like a vein, like a scream, like a clock that halts
When some careless throat is strangled.   10

Oh the sudden pallor,
The mauve circles under wilted eyes,
When the beasts bare their swords or teeth
Like the beating of a heart that is unaware of almost everything,
Except for love,   15
Exposed on the distant throats, in the beyond where the artery throbs,
Where what shines on the white fangs is indistinguishable
From love or hate.

To caress the rough mane
While the powerful paw is felt in the earth,   20
While the trembling tree roots
Feel the long claws
Like a love that so invades.

To look into those eyes that only burn at night,
Where a lately devoured fawn   25
Emits its tiny image of nocturnal gold,
A farewell that shines with posthumous tenderness.

The tiger, the prowling lion, the elephant that in its tusks carries
     some soft necklace,
The cobra that looks like love most ardent,

The eagle that caresses rocks like hard brains,   30
The little scorpion that with its claws aspires but for an instant
    to grasp life,
The diminished presence of a human body that will never be able
    to be confused with a jungle,
That happy ground where sharp-eyed vipers make their nest
    in the axilla of moss;
While the immaculate coccinellida
Avoids a silky magnolia leaf . . .   35
Everything resounds when the murmur of the ever-virgin forest
Rises like two golden wings,
Elytron, bronze or round shell,
In the face of an ocean that will never confuse its foam with
    tender little branches.

The serene vigil,   40
That ever-verdant hope,
Bird, paradise, luxuriance of untouched plumage,
Invents the highest branches,
Where the musical fangs,
Where the powerful clutches, love that digs in,   45
The burning blood that spurts forth from the wound,
Will not reach, no matter how long breasts, open ajar on the earth,
Project their pain or their yearning into the azure heavens.

Bird of happiness,
Azure bird or feather   ,50
Above the muffled murmur of solitary beasts,
Of love or the scourge of sterile trunks,
Looking out over the most remote sea that, like the light, is ebbing.]

"La selva y el mar" poses a familiar Aleixandrean problem. The poem, like "No busques, no" or "La dicha," at once reveals and withholds its major orientational intertext. The intertextual signal is sounded via citation in the first verses, which are no less than the first verses of *La destrucción o el amor*. As previously noted, "Allá por las remotas / luces o aceros aún no usados"—points, or would seem to point, to Fray Luis's famous ode, "A Francisco Salinas." Again, here is the first stanza from that piece:

> El aire se serena
> y viste de hermosura y luz no usada,
> Salinas, cuando suena
> la música extremada,
> por vuestra sabia mano gobernada.[8]

[The air becomes serene
And dresses in beauty and light unused,
Salinas, when resounds
The extraordinary music
Governed by your sage hand.]

As mentioned in chapter 1, the closeness of this poetic kinship is confirmed not only by Aleixandre's citational paraphrase of the Augustinian's opening verses but also by positional and metrical repetition. In Aleixandre, as in Fray Luis, the phrase "luz no usada" appears in the second verse and with its three elements in identical order; also resounding in Aleixandre's first two verses is ancestral meter, the seven- and eleven-syllable verses that make up Fray Luis's "liras." The citational communication between the two poems continues and, though buried among the verses of "La selva y el mar," is again visible in Aleixandre, but only some thirty lines later, where Fray Luis's subordinate clause, "cuando suena," reappears, its syntax inverted, in "Todo suena cuando el rumor" (verse 36). Together with the lexical similarity between the modern and the model verses, the placement of this phrase, like that of the previously cited "luces o aceros aún no usados," intimates that Aleixandre's poem is somehow modulated on the ancestral ode. The latter verse stands out because of its collocation at the beginning of the second part of the poem. The division is formally marked by the "puntos suspensivos," or ellipses, of the immediately preceding transitional verses, "mientras la pulcra coccinela / se evade de una hoja de magnolia sedosa. . . ." Here, the selvatic bestiary description that abruptly began in verse three comes to its conclusion, a conclusion that the typographical device may lead us to read as the closing of parentheses or, in the psychic context suggested by the automatic flavor of the text, as a momentary pause in the associative meanders of the narration of "La selva y el mar." In overview, the joined Luisinian fragments—"Allá por las remotas/ luces o aceros aún no usados . . . Todo suena cuando el rumor"—which are quotes from an ode to music, suggest that "La selva y el mar" is a remodulation of the ancestral poem whose key phrasing now returns in jungle song variation. The radical internalization of the ancestor poem that the above suggests is indeed operant both in "La selva y el mar" and throughout *La destrucción el amor.*

Before pursuing Aleixandre's relation to Fray Luis, the complexity of "La selva y el mar" necessitates a rather lengthy digression. To be considered are two additional but basic textual features of "La selva y el mar." These features, which are decisive in fully defining

Fray Luis's lyric role in Aleixandre, are the poem's narrative structure and the intertextual presence of Rubén Darío.

"La selva y el mar," like "Sin luz" and "Las águilas," is a psycho-
narration, a narrative form in which the otherwise hidden psychic
life of a focal character is mediated by an omniscient narrator. "La
selva y el mar" is also similar to the other two poems in that the psychosexual inner life of the focal human is lyrically conceptualized in
the guise of a vast landscape. The latter, a metaphorical boscage or
"arborización" as Bousoño aptly characterizes Aleixandre's figurative
process, effectively inters the primary human referent of the poem.
As in other poems of *La destrucción o el amor,* the poetic basis for the
overgrowth is the hombre/tierra metonym, the metaphoric sub-
stratum below Aleixandre's world. While that landscape covers the
human, it also offers via textual ungrammaticalities—in particular,
the intense anthropomorphic saturation of the ostensibly natural
world—important clues toward disinterring the human referent. One
such example is the cobra. Certainly not a zoological specimen to
be found in the pages of *National Geographic,* this lyric reptile is one
of the erotic members of the poem's bestiary paradigm. Dangerously
armed, this inhabitant—"la cobra que se parece al amor más ardiente"—is a fanged phallus poised erect and ready to eject its fatal
but life-giving venom. Like the other "espada"-bearing beasts, the
cobra acts as an emblem of the id which, indwelling in the focal
character, promises positive amorous annihilation.

Other clues to the base tenor/vehicle conformation of the poem
may be picked up by attending to analogies such as "como latidos de
un corazón que casi todo lo ignora, / menos el amor" (verses 14–15),
"como un amor que así invade" (verse 23) or "donde las garras
poderosas, el amor que se clava" (verse 45). These phrases, which
follow strings of selvatic animal descriptions, both act as figurative
summaries of those descriptions and stipulate the amorous theme
and the human source of the poem. Characteristic of Aleixandre's
surrealism, the human referent to which these analogies refer is
largely invisible, this owing in part to the inverted metaphorical
syntax of these formulae—"selva como amor" and not "amor como
selva." This inversion foregrounds, as does the entire text, the vehicle rather than the tenor. In any case, the intensely anthropomorphic nature of the landscape as well as the analogies pointed out
above should dispel any illusion that the poem refers to the natural
world per se.

Apart from the signs of human affect that pervade the geographic
description, the single most important clue to the poem's narrative
structure and to the identity of its human subject is to be found in

the apostrophe that heads the third stanza, "Oh la blancura súbita, / las ojeras violáceas de unos ojos marchitos, / cuando las fieras muestran sus espadas o dientes." These verses, like the vocalization "Escapad, escapad" of "La dicha," anomalously stand out from the poem's general narrative pattern. Their strangeness is owed to the unprepared for and brief incursion of voice, which is sounded via "Oh." This apostrophe alters the otherwise systematic design of internally focalized psycho-narration, the modal point of view to which the greater part of the text is restricted.[9] The apostrophic alteration is most important toward discerning the poem's narrative design, especially insofar as it affords a brief though telling outer image of the poem's focalizer, the human whose inner preverbal world, in the guise of a selvatic wilderness, is mediated by an omniscient narrator. The description of the human focalizer is rapidly sketched by way of two features: a sudden pallor—"la blancura súbita"—and bedraggled eyes—"las ojeras violáceas de unos ojos marchitos." The roundness, color, and wilted appearance make these eyes comparable to moribund roses. As in "Las águilas," the narrative rationale for selecting the eyes as the sole external image of the focal character lies in the notion that the eye is the window of the soul, or the threshold of the subconscious as in the present case. Although withheld until the third strophe, the invoked eyes intimate the poem's situational nucleus. It may be imagined that the unobtrusive narrating persona contemplates the addressee, an unnamed "tú," a conventional point of departure in love poetry.

The same eye description—namely the sudden pallor and the mortiferously colored "ojeras"—suggestively rounds out the personality of the anonymous focal character and the inner happening or psychic plot that is recounted in "La selva y el mar." The constitution of the invoked personage, like that of a delicate rose, is somewhat less than robust. In fact, this being appears to be prone to swoons or fainting spells, the latter intimated in particular by "blancura súbita." The cause of this sudden pallor is explained in the text surrounding the ocular description. The immediately following verses indicate that the fainting is a sudden psychosomatic reaction brought on when the instinctual "fieras" of desire—the id—become active, threatening the delicate and civilized sensibility—the superego—of the focalizer. The latter strives at all costs to repress those unacceptable and nearly overwhelming animal urges—"el amor." The repressive force of the superego is lyrically chronicled in stanza two where, as if from a font in the carnal boscage—later the fountain-like heart of verses 46–47—the chains of internalized self-censorship gush forth—"surten"—to strangle or civilize the untamed erotic species afoot in the recesses—the Edenic "allá"—of the focal character's pre-verbal world. Nonetheless, the same libidinous beasts, armed with instruments of positive amorous destruction—"aceros aún no usa-dos"—still—"aún"—lie in waiting, an immanence tied to the innate erotic condition of the focal character.

The strife between these antagonistic psychic forces within the lyric focalizer is intimated throughout "La selva y el mar," most generally via the jungle-in-upheaval figuration, such as that seen in the previously cited examples. But perhaps more telling of the particulars of the psychic plot—a head vs. heart story common in *La destrucción o el amor*—are the cognitive verbs that surface subsequent to the ocular description of stanza three. These verbs include, in order, "saber" ("no se sabe si es el amor o el odio," [verse 17]), "sentir" ("se siente la poderosa garra en la tierra," [verse 20]) and "inventar," a synonym of "imaginar," ("inventa los ramajes más altos," [verse 43]). Taken together with the ocular description that they follow, these verbs outline the particulars of the head vs. heart story that unfolds within the selvatic focalizer. "No se sabe si" refers to the state of mental confusion or indecision into which the blanching "tú" is thrown as surfacing libidinous urges vie with the powerful superego; "se siente la poderosa garra en la tierra" conceptualizes the sharp pangs of erotic instinct which have instigated the inner turmoil and which have set off the hysterical swooning reaction; "inventa" seals the conflict, suggesting that the erotic crisis suffered by the focal character has been averted, at least temporarily, this owing to an escape from erotic reality.

The escape—the denouement of the psychic plot—is carried out as the mind takes flight on the wings of the imagination, a noticeably artificial imagination metaphorically feathered in the final strophes as "azul pájaro." The ornithological hegira, which leads to the closure of "La selva y el mar," constitutes a sublimation of eros, a psychological defense mechanism which has been triggered in order to suppress the "sordo rumor" of the id, whose erotic emanations are now rendered palatable as longing for an ideal and eternal love—"esa esperanza siempre verde"—a sort of fable acceptable to the threatened ego of the well-bred and delicate focal character. The latter's sublimation of eros is indicated both in strophe 7, where the roar within the ever-virgin jungle is metamorphosed into a strange winged creature, and at the end of the penultimate strophe where the topos, suffering-for-love-to-come, is cast as psychic projection: "la sangre ardiente que brota de la herida, / no alcanzará por más que los pechos entreabiertos en tierra / proyecten su dolor o su avidez a los cielos azules." Thanks to the "pájaro" of the imagination, the mind of the focalizer of "La selva y el mar" remains aloof and un-touched, hovering in a faux "paraíso," the illusory ether or "cielos azules" to which the opening "Allá" now refers. There is, however, an ironic twist to the resolution of this head vs. heart story. The final strophes suggest that the psychic placation of libidinous instinct is both temporary and futile. The erotic denizens of the jungle—the id—are an insatiable and connate element of the focalizer's human ontology. As such, this erotic force is immanent and exercises a strong gravitational pull on the imagination, the "azul pájaro o pluma," a rather insubstantial savior from erotic destruction. By the same token, the refuge which the ornithological imagination has built for itself is a rather flimsy perch. It is located among the in-vented, and therefore unreal and incorporeal "ramajes más altos," a place in which the frightened self will have but a short-lived respite from the "sordo rumor" below. The ebbing of the sea and the asso-ciated dimming of light of the final verses—"el mar remotísimo que como la luz se retira"—symbolically recapitulate the anecdote of erotic repression. The withdrawal of sea and light, which are at-mospheric emblems of destiny in Aleixandre, cast the suppression of the id as the loss of human destiny. Nevertheless—and this is symptomatic of the optimistic spirit which infuses *La destrucción o el amor* on the whole—the loss of erotic destiny is neither sealed nor hopeless, a thematic feature that is carried by the cyclical connota-tions of these particular symbols of fate. That is, eros, and the op-portunity to opt for amorous destruction or life will, like the flow of the sea and the waning of light, make their natural eternal return.

On the basis of its narratological design and figuration alone, "La selva y el mar" is comparable to some of the most intricate of Aleixandre's surrealist texts. However, and again like other psycho-narrations such as "Sin luz" or "Las águilas," this poem grows out of the svelte psychosomatic binary of id and superego whose struggle makes up the local happening of the text. In this poem, the psychic binary and the associated inner conflict serve as the scaffolding on which the ancestral intertexts are to rest. To wit, the id/superego struggle is mirrored by a coextensive ancestral clash which, staged by Aleixandre, is played out between Fray Luis and Rubén Darío. The poem, which may be read in this way, throws into relief the themat-ics of love incarnated in each of these forebears. Specifically, Darío is allotted the antagonistic or superego role of the text while Fray Luis is allied with the id, the positive force of love. Therefore, dis-cerning the role of either poet necessarily entails defining that of the other. Let us first examine the part of Darío in the poem.

Darío's antagonistic role in "La selva y el mar" is suggested in the trappings and action of the superego, which are intimately bound to a Daríoesque pastiche and to a specific model poem. The pastiche of Darío citations orients Aleixandre's poem toward several ancestral texts. The clearest intertextual signal may be found in the transitional verses of stanza 6—"mientras la pulcra coccinela se evade / de una hoja de magnolia sedosa. . . ." The transitional function is marked via pause—the semicolon and the ellipses that frame the verses—and by the noticeable stylistic variance of this passage with the entirety of the preceding text, that is, the jungle description proper. The pair of verses, which lead into the psychic denouement, emit two sorts of Darío signals: the first, transmitted by the phrase "pulcra coccinela," consists of a lexical mimesis of Daríoesque vocabulary; the second, given off by "se evade de una hoja de magnolia sedosa . . . ," is paraphrastic of a particular Darío poem, "Era un aire suave . . . ," the poem internalized in "La dicha." The phrase "pulcra coccinela" recalls Darío's penchant for choosing rarified or exotic words such as "bouquet," "Sport," "kaolín," "papemores," or "bulbules." The present example, a double Latinism for the everyday "mariquita" or "ladybug," stands out in Aleixandre's poem because it is much at odds with the plain generic names given to the erotically charged beasts of the preceding jungle description, primitive beings with which this pleasure-avoiding insect thematically contrasts. Other such lexical signs of Darío's presence are the "esdrújulas" [words stressed on the antepenultimate syllable], acoustic favorites of the ancestor which are recalled in "violáceas," "súbita," "élitros," in the repetition of "pájaro," and in "estériles" and "remotísimo." With the significant exception of "violáceas" and "súbita," which in Daríoesque accent outline the eyes of the focal character, the concentration of "esdrújulas" is to be found in the concluding section of "La selva y el mar," which recounts the focalizer's withdrawal from eros on the wings of the imagination, an evasion from the seething jungle below.

The second of the transitional verses—"se evade de una hoja de magnolia sedosa . . ."—describes the escape from pleasure of the "coccinela," herself an emblem of purity and, as such, a miniature of the superego. The pleasure avoided here is a sensual pleasure and is poeticized via image—the silk-like magnolia leaf, a botanical specificity rare in Aleixandre—and acoustically, through the internal o-a assonance of the three main elements making up the leaf description, "hoja," "magnolia," and "sedosa." These three elements, now rearranged in Aleixandre, come from the second strophe of "Era un aire suave . . ." where they also express sensuousness in a poem that recounts an evasion of love, that of the elusive marquesa

Eulalia as she coquettishly tempts two amorous rivals at once. Below is the second strophe:

> Sobre la terraza, junto a los ramajes,
> diríase un trémolo de liras eolias
> cuando acariciaban los sedosos trajes,
> sobre el tallo erguidas, las blancas magnolias.[10]

> [On the terrace, close to the thick branches,
> It was like a tremolo of Eolian harps
> When, erect on their stems, the white magnolia flowers
> Would caress the silken gowns.]

Given the Daríoesque atmosphere with which this section is charged, it can justifiably be assumed that the ellipses, a typographical device employed in two ancestral titles, in "Era un aire suave . . ." and in *Azul* . . . , are an additional remnant forming the intertextual collage. Indeed, the ellipses splice yet another intertextual fragment from Darío to those cited above. The points lead up to the lyric metamorphosis of the round and hard-winged "coccinela." Also called "caracol redondo" because of those two traits, the Latinate "mariquita," or ladybug, turns into "pájaro," and then "azul pájaro," a paraphrase of the Darío title, "El pájaro azul" (*Azul* . . .). Aleixandre's allusion to this piece—a prose poem in which the imagination, the "pájaro azul" [azure bird], causes the death of an idealistic and amorous young poet—iterates the theme of ideal, and therefore, unattainable love, a common Darío thematics and an amorous fatalism toward which Aleixandre takes an unambiguously negative stance.

Thus far, the scrutiny of the Darío intertextuality has yielded some basic orientational information. First, Aleixandre's focal character—specifically one of the psychic components of this personage—is an eminently literary creation formed out of the poet's reworking of other poetry.[11] Second, and endemic to this creative process, the poet's absorption of that other poetry constitutes an interpretation or misprision of it. In "La selva y el mar," the aesthetics and the amorous ideology of Darío are negatively qualified, having been installed in Aleixandre's focalizer as the figurative constituents of the repressive and life-inhibiting superego.

The specific model poem absorbed by Aleixandre is "El reino interior" [The Inner Realm] (*Prosas profanas*). The poet's reception of this piece reconfirms his negative stance toward Darío and reiterates the generative importance of the Modernista in "La selva y el mar."

The surrealist poem exhibits two particular features that seal its poetic kinship with "El reino interior." The first feature is the description and narrative function of the focal character's eyes. Those lifeless eyes, which are chromatically outlined with the Daríoesque "esdrújula," "violáceas," carry out the exact symbolic and narrative function in Aleixandre as they do in "El reino interior." Below, the second stanza of "El reino interior":

> Mi alma frágil se asoma a la ventana obscura
> de la torre terrible en que ha treinta años sueña.
> La gentil Primavera primavera le augura.
> La vida le sonríe rosada y halgüeña.
> Y ella exclama: "¡Oh fragante día! ¡Oh sublime día!
> Se diría que el mundo está en flor; se diría
> que el corazón sagrado de la tierra se mueve
> con un ritmo de dicha; luz brota, gracia llueve.
> ¡Yo soy la prisionera que sonríe y canta."
> Y las manos liliales agita, como infanta
> real en los balcones del palacio paterno.[12]

> [My delicate soul gazes out from the dark window
> Of the fearful tower where, for thirty years, she has been sleeping.
> To her, gentle Spring augers spring.
> Rose-colored and pleasurable, life smiles upon her.
> And she exclaims: "Oh sweet day! Oh sublime day!
> It could be said that all the world is in bloom; it could be said
> That the sacred heart of the earth moves
> In blissful rhythm; light shines forth, grace rains down.
> I am the captive that smiles and sings."
> And she waves her lily-white hands, like an infanta
> In the balconies of her father's palace.]

In both poems, the eyes are at once the "window to the soul" and the point of departure for narrating the inner happening of the focal character. There is only one difference between the two poems in their respective eye fenestration. In Aleixandre, explicit mention of the vehicle or "ventana" of the eye/window metaphor is suppressed whereas in Darío, it is the tenor or "ojo" that is elided. This may be seen in the first verses of Darío's stanza, "Mi alma frágil se asoma a la ventana obscura / de la torre terrible en que ha treinta años sueña." The second feature, and the characteristic that most strongly reinforces the Daríoesque genealogy for the superego, is the outline and nature of the interior plot shared by both texts. To wit, both works take as their basis an inner-world-in-conflict story which, markedly

allegorical in character, is resolved by the focal character's escape
or inaction. "La selva y el mar" chronicles a psychic dilemma protagonized by the opposing forces of id and superego, actors who, cloaked
in selvatic-Modernista trappings, schematically play out an inner
and universal human drama. The title itself—"La selva y el mar"—
heralds the text's allegory of love repressed, which it does by juxta-
posing via the disjunctive "y" two abstract nouns, one feminine, the
other masculine. In this, the title echoes legendary stories of frustrated love such as those of Polyphemus and Galatea, Hero and Le-
ander, or Apollo and Daphne.

The plot of Darío's poetic allegory traces the moral conflict of the
narrator's soul. In Gothic setting, the soul is portrayed as a maiden
imprisoned in her father's castle tower. She espies, from the ocular
"ventana oscura," the procession of the seven Virtues and the seven
Vices, groups to whom the fragile soul of the narrator is simultaneously drawn. The denouement of the conflict within the narrator is
affective paralysis: the spiritual infanta remains locked within the
tower of her father's castle where she has been dreaming for thirty
years. The reason for this oneiric nonlife in captivity is indecision,
the narrator's incapacity to choose between carnality and virtue, a
conflict resolved by withdrawing into fantasy. Following is the last
stanza of "El reino interior," which encapsulates the vital paralysis
in which the narrator, referring to his soul, finds himself:

> Y en sueño dice: "¡Oh dulces delicias de los cielos!
> ¡Oh tierra sonrosada que acarició mis ojos!
> —¡Princesas, envolvedme con vuestros blancos velos!
> —¡Príncipes, estrechadme con vuestros brazos rojos!"[13]

> [And dreaming she says: "Oh sweet heavenly pleasures!
> Oh rosy land that caressed my eyes!
> —Princesses, wind me in your white veils!
> —Princes, hold me close in your scarlet arms!"]

In addition to the eye motif and plot, Aleixandre internalizes
and transforms several other features of "El reino interior." The
most visible transformation is that of the ancestral first verse, "Una
selva suntuosa / en el azul celeste su rudo perfil calca," [The rough
outline of a sumptuous jungle stands out against the celestial azure],
which is expanded not into the sumptuousness characteristic of
the Modernista text but into a primeval "selva" populated with
amorously destructive beasts. Despite this divergence, Aleixandre's
text makes direct allusion to Darío's poetic "selva." The Modernista
jungle is ultimately figured as a sexually diminished locality, it is a

"bosque siempre virgen," a winged virginality safely delivered from erotic destiny. Lastly, "selva," the ambit of Darío's piece, acts as a key intertextual signal that in Aleixandre's title—"La selva y el mar"— metonymically stands for Darío's "El reino interior" and for the superego with which the text becomes closely associated. Aleixandre's negative interpretation of the ancestral poem is reconfirmed in the enchainment figuration of the second stanza. Translating the thematics of repression, the chains allude to "El reino interior" by way of this poem's Gothic setting, wherein the soul is a princess-captive-in-the-tower. Returning now in reduced form, the "cadenas" derive from the medieval prison tower, stereotypically outfitted with chains and other such equipment. Like the "milenaria columna" of "Sin luz," these chains and the prison tower poem from whence they ultimately issue are emblematic of the superego, a repressive and received artifice internalized in the focal character. Combining Aleixandre's two principal figures for the superego in "La selva y el mar"— the shackles and the escape on the wings of the imagination—we come up with a Darío-based paradox: escape or freedom on the wings of the imagination is an imprisonment, an imprisonment of the libidinous bestiary of love whose liberation, in contrast, is tantamount to the realization of humankind's inborn erotic destiny.

Recognizing the presence of Darío's "El reino interior" in "La selva y el mar" proves to be most illuminating toward deciphering the intertextual significance underlying the Aleixandrean "sombras." In particular, the recovered Darío poem reveals that the pragmatic or local referent of "La selva y el mar"—the poem's landscaped "tú"—is not only a "deshumanizado" or abstracted Everyman but is also identifiable with the soul in captivity of Darío's "El reino interior." Along with associated Darío texts, this spiritual model for Aleixandre's focalizer functions as the literary scaffolding on which the poet figuratively conceptualizes the superego and its influence on the human psyche. Associated in this way with the superego, Darío's exquisite and artificially wrought poetry is made to serve as an emblem of erotic repression, an interpretative recasting of the forebear similar to that seen in "La dicha," where Aleixandre demonstrates a mixed though ultimately negative stance toward his Nicaraguan ancestor. Lastly, the close association of the Darío poem with the superego leaves open the ancestral id role, that is, the "mar" of the poem's title. This space, as the paraphrase of the opening verses suggests, is filled by Fray Luis whose ode, "A Francisco Salinas" [To Francisco Salinas], plays opposite the Darío poem in an allegory of amorous ideology. Below is the Luisinian ode, which will be reviewed in preparation for analyzing Aleixandre's internalization of it.

El aire se serena
y viste de hermosura y luz no usada,
Salinas, cuando suena
la música extremada,
por vuestra sabia mano gobernada.   5
     A cuyo son divino
mi alma, que en olvido está sumida,
torna a cobrar el tino
y memoria perdida,
de su origen primera esclarecida.   10
     Y como se conoce,
en suerte y pensamientos se mejora;
el oro desconoce,
que el vulgo ciego adora,
la belleza caduca, engañadora.   15
     Traspasa el aire todo
hasta llegar a la más alta esfera,
y oye allí otro modo
de no perecedera
música, que es de todas la primera.   20
     Ve cómo el gran maestro,
aquesta inmensa cítara aplicado,
con movimiento diestro
produce el son sagrado,
con que este eterno templo es sustentado.   25
     Y como está compuesta
de números concordes, luego envía
consonante respuesta;
y entrambas a porfía
mezclan una dulcísima armonía.   30
     Aquí la alma navega,
por un mar de dulzura, y, finalmente
en él ansí se anega,
que ningún accidente
extraño y peregrino oye o siente.   35
     ¡Oh, desmayo dichoso!
¡Oh, muerte que das vida! ¡Oh, dulce olvido!
¡Durase en tu reposo,
sin ser restituido
jamás a aqueste bajo y vil sentido!   40
     A aqueste bien os llamo,
gloria del apolíneo sacro coro,
amigos a quien amo
sobre todo tesoro;
que todo lo demás es triste lloro.   45
     ¡Oh! suene de contino,
Salinas, vuestro son en mis oídos,

por quien al bien divino
despiertan los sentidos,
quedando a lo demás amortecidos.[14]   50

[The air becomes serene
And dresses in beauty and light unused,
Salinas, when resounds
The extraordinary music
Governed by your sage hand.   5
    At that divine sound,
My soul, who in forgetfulness is submerged,
Finds anew her direction
And the lost memory
Of her primal luminous origin.   10
    And since she now finds herself,
In fortune and thought does she improve;
Of gold is she forgetful,
That passing and deceptive beauty
Which the blind throngs adore.   15
    She rises up through all the air
Until she reaches the highest sphere,
Where she hears another mode
Of imperishable
Music, which of all music is the font.   20
    She sees how the Grand Musician,
Attentive to this great zither,
With dexterous movement
Produces the sacred sound
That sustains this eternal temple.   25
    And since she herself is composed
Of corresponding intervals, she thereupon sends
Consonant reply;
And the two sounds, as they intermingle,
Form a harmony most sweet.   30
    Here the soul sails
Upon a sea of sweetness and, finally,
So sinks in it
That no strange and foreign modulation
Does she hear or sense.   35
    Oh blissful swoon!
Oh death that gives life! Oh sweet oblivion!
Could I but remain in your repose
Without ever being restored
To these low and vile senses!   40
    To this heavenly delight I call you,
Glory of Apollo's sacred chorus,
Friends whom I love

Above all treasure;
For all else is but sad wailing.   45
   Oh may your music
Ever resound within me, Salinas,
Through whom the senses awake to
Divine delight,
Remaining deadened to all else.]   50

Fray Luis's ode to music, written in honor of his friend Francisco
Salinas, certainly seems far removed from its Aleixandrean relative,
"La selva y el mar." In overview, and in marked contrast to the surrealist poem, the outstanding features of the Renaissance ode include
its perfectly regular and contained formal arrangement into ten
"liras," and its controlled and svelte poetic diction. In a word, and
leaving aside both the Mystic spirit that permeates *La destrucción o el
amor* in general and the preliminary evidence for Fray Luis's role in
"La selva y el mar," this forebear appears to have little to do with
Aleixandre's poem but for the rather open citation. Nonetheless,
there are several features of the Luisinian ode that are of primary
generative importance to "La selva y el mar." These features include
the generic composure of the Luisinian poem, its symbology, thematics of spiritual destiny and, not least, the complex conceptual
play at work throughout.

Generically, Fray Luis's poem is a mixture of ode and allegory, a
hybrid form interpretatively reduplicated in Aleixandre. The primary
odic features displayed in "A Francisco Salinas" are apostrophe and
the conventional tripartite structuration. Apostrophe, which here
makes up the discursive nucleus of the text, carries out two types
of speech acts characteristic of this genre. The first is invocation, a
voicing through which the circumstantial fiction is created. The poet
addresses Francisco Salinas whose dexterously played music, when
heard by the poet, transports his soul to God and presumably inspires
him to write the ode. The poem appears to depart from this circumstantial kernel and returns to it in the final strophe where Fray
Luis addresses Salinas anew. The second apostrophic speech act is
exhortation, which functions to transmit the transcendental and
didactic mission of the poem. Fray Luis directs his exhortation to
the "apolíneo sacro coro" or, more humbly, to "amigos," both variants of humanity in general. The choral analogy reflects the spiritual
redemption/music metaphor that is elaborated throughout. This
figure emphasizes that all of humanity, like the poet, is essentially
musical. The communality owes to the soul which, in each human
being, is the eternal breath of God, himself the "maestro," the master

musician and composer of the human chorus. In odic fashion, Fray
Luis's widely broadcast exhortation stipulates that the intrinsic value
of Salinas's music, and of the spiritual autobiography that it inspires,
lies in the collective, rather than personal, nature of both.[15] In brief,
Fray Luis is not a writer of intimate verse but is, rather, a lyric transcendentalist or "poeta radical," as Aleixandre would have it.

The second odic trait that the Augustinian's work clearly exhibits
is triadic structure, a trait cited in the discussion of genre. This structure, traditionally referred to as "strophe," "antistrophe" and "epode,"
is intimately bound to voice. For its part, apostrophe symmetrically
frames the text, marking off both the strophe—"lira" 1—and the
epode—"liras" 9–10. In contrast, the antistrophe, the seven-"lira"
center of the poem, consists of a narrative dedicated to putting forth
the exumplum, the journey of the soul into the heavens. The plot—
the soul's transmigration to the celestial spheres—is based on the
Pythagorean conception of the universe and, subject to Fray Luis's
misprision, translates the Mystical experience of spiritual unity in
the love of God. Dámaso Alonso aptly describes the design of this
ode in spatial terms, observing that it follows a pattern of ascent and
descent.[16]

The allegorical character of this ode is patent in the spirit/music
analogy that enmeshes its three sections. The most explicit figuration
of the Pythagorean-inspired metaphor is to be found in stanzas 4–6.
This descriptive system explains one of the basic premises of the
poem, which is that music awakens the soul to its "origen primera
esclarecida," to its own originary or divine musical nature. The same
model also explains, but only partially so, the cluster of images
found in the two opening verses, an exquisite, sibilant-filled prelude
to the soul's textual entrance in verse 7. Here, the serene air, which
is garbed in extraordinary beauty and light, is associated with Fray
Luis's Pythagorean firmament, itself a system of spheres whose circularity, music, and shining stars embody human destiny.

In this allegorical ambit there is, however, one passage that stands
out, specifically because its figuration seems formally, though not
thematically, unconnected to the soul/music metaphor. This is the
seventh stanza where the soul's oblivion in God's celestial music is
now retroped as a shipwreck in which the spirit, traveling at sea,
sinks and thereby drowns in "un mar de dulzura," a happy fate ecstatically exclaimed upon in the Mystic conceit of verses 36–37. The
sea metaphor, though equivalent in meaning to the Pythagorean
trio—music, spheres, and light—hails from another allegorical system,
that of the spiritual shipwreck. Fray Luis employs this allegorical
topos in other poems, including "Descanso después de la tempestad,"

and "Vida retirada." In the latter, the story of maritime disaster functions as an exemplary inset that serves to illustrate the theme of "vanitas."[17]

In "A Francisco Salinas," a good portion of the shipwreck is implied rather than explicit. There are several textual clues pointing to the presence of this allegory. The first, and most general, is the discernible complementary pattern in which the images of this text are organized. Here, one component is matched with an analogue, a design coherent with the Neoplatonic intertext in which, for example, Salinas and his music are paralleled by the divine musician or the associated "luz no usada" is reflected in the divine stellar light, and so on. Seemingly absent from this reflective pattern of earthly elements and celestial counterparts is the worldly sea, the complement of the ethereal sea of stanza 7. The clue is held in the opening verses, which presuppose the earthly sea. The processive verb of the in medias res introit, "se serena," suggests the atmospheric conditions preceding the outset of the poem. Rather than the now calm air, beauty, and light, we can assume that there was a howling wind, driving rain and darkness, stereotypical elements of a storm at sea.

Further details of the shipwreck allegory can be gleaned from the following two stanzas. "Sumida," meaning submerged in water or entombed in earth, economically identifies the victim of the storm— the poet's soul—and her unlucky condition—she was drowning and was rendered unconscious, as repeated in "sin tino" and "memoria perdida." Likewise, "olvido" identifies the sea on which the spiritual wayfarer was traveling, the sea of forgetfulness or of human vanity; the vessel was unseaworthy because it was laden with gold, "que el vulgo ciego adora," a false god weighing down the ship and, with its dazzling glimmer, blinding the sea-faring soul to the guiding stars in the divine firmament. Such is the quandary in which the narrator's soul finds herself before the positive note of spiritual redemption is struck by Salinas. Salinas's significance in this allegory of redemption is suggested in verse 5 where his musical acuity is described with the adjective "gobernada," from "gobernar," a word conventionally meaning to steer a ship, not to play music. In the context of the shipwreck allegory, "gobernar" makes Salinas a sea captain or a sort of Christian Charon, a master who wisely—with "sabia mano"—sails his ship, that is, his music. This harmonic ship—itself an "aire," in the musical sense of the word—both revives the unconscious soul and carries her on her ethereal journey of redemption, which is to culminate in the "mar de dulzura," a baptism of spiritual renewal, the death that gives life.

By mixing the Pythagorean triad of light, music, and circle with the maritime allegory, Fray Luis at once fills out his plot of spiritual journey and significantly enriches the text's interpretative possibilities. In "conceptista" manner, the subtle intromission of the shipwreck allegory into the Pythagorean system creates a complex poetic punning, as the foregoing examples suggest. As an illustration of the complexity of Fray Luis's conceptual play, let us reconsider the opening verses—"El aire se serena / y viste de hermosura y luz no usada"—which Aleixandre paraphrases in the introit of "La selva y el mar." The initial sense of these verses is triggered by the musical context of the poem. They seem to refer to a concrete setting, perhaps to a chapel where Salinas's music fills the previously cacophonic ambit with serenity and with an extraordinary—"no usada" or divine—beauty and light. In this musical context, "aire," which also means melody, is a pun referring to the very music of Salinas. This music is an air that replaces an unnamed but spiritually discordant sound. The soul/music analogy of the poem suggests an additional music-based interpretation. The "aire" is also the soul itself, a musical air originating in the breath of God the musician. This meaning may be tested by replacing "aire" with "alma"—"El alma se serena / y viste de hermosura y luz no usada" [The soul becomes serene and dresses in beauty and light unused]—a substitution that encapsulates the spiritual denouement of the poem. The vestiary verb, "viste," both corroborates this personification and most economically suggests that the soul, having cast off the world, now dresses in celestial attire, an extraordinary vestment garbing her in spiritual serenity, light, and beauty. She is a vestal of the Christian church, "el eterno templo." The shipwreck allegory complicates and enriches the significance of the same verses. The soul, having been in the throes of spiritual death—drowning in the tempestuous sea of forgetfulness or human folly—is retrieved by Salinas's harmonic bark. The soul is revived by that "aire," and is given extraordinary—"no usada"— clothes, the lucent garb of salvation formerly unused or "no usada." Lastly, Fray Luis's spiritual allegory has a Christological underpinning. The plot motifs of maritime journey and of redemptive guiding light are tied to Christ, two of whose epithets are the "way" and the "light of the world."

The rich figurative ambiguity and the general conceptual play of which "morir es vivir" is emblematic are among the outstanding Luisinian features absorbed by Aleixandre in "La selva y el mar" and elsewhere in *La destrucción o el amor*. In "La selva y el mar" in particular, the poet not only garbs the id in "luz no usada" and in other metaphorical raiment of Luisinian origin but also recasts his poem in the ancestor's generic trappings. Fray Luis's ode affords compelling evidence for the poetic rationale behind Aleixandre's choice of ancestors in "La selva y el mar." The Fray Luis and Darío poems are variants of one story, the fate of the soul. The divergent outcomes given that story by the forebears—enchainment vs. liberation—make their texts ideal materia prima for representing both the psychic and the ancestral conflict in which Aleixandre casts Fray Luis and Darío. The lyric dichotomy is heralded in the title of "La selva y el mar" where just as "la selva" makes metonymic reference to "El reino interior," so "el mar" alludes to the Luisinian ode by citing one of its primary symbolic components. Yet even in the light of these concrete indications there is little overt evidence of Fray Luis's part in "La selva y el mar." This apparent lack of further intertextual communication owes to the thoroughness with which Aleixandre has absorbed the ancestral text. Fray Luis's ode, rather than appliqued, is tightly interwoven into the texture of "La selva y el mar." As the first step toward perceiving Aleixandre's internalization of the ancestor, the role of Fray Luis in Aleixandre's id/bestiary figuration is to be considered.

That Aleixandre has converted Fray Luis's ode into a coterie of dangerously armed beasts might seem highly unlikely if it were not for clues like those already cited. Specifically, and through the process of elimination, Fray Luis's role is suggested by that of Darío whose poetry serves as the guise for the superego, the diminished and fugitive fauna of the poem including "la pulcra coccinela" and "el azul pájaro o pluma." Aleixandre gives poetic form to the libidinous menagerie by transforming the Luisinian destiny cluster. This cluster, which consists of the symbols of light, music, circle, and sea, expresses spiritual destiny in the Augustinian's ode. Now spelling out amorous destiny in "La selva y el mar," the Luisinian quartet acts as a highly fecund hypogram which, like the human/earth formula, is a primary structural metaphor both here and throughout *La destrucción o el amor*. Aleixandre's absorption of the symbolic quartet is quite complex and includes two types of metaphoric transformations. In the first, the Luisinian symbols are subject to recombination. Through this process, any one of the four symbols may be combined with fellow cluster members. This mixing-up of ancestral symbolism is predetermined by the model poem itself, where light, music, circle, and sea are in an intimate causal relationship, being interchangeable emblems of destiny. In the second type of transformation, the ancestral cluster is hybridized. Here, non-Luisinian metaphors are spliced onto any or all of the four symbols. In this, Aleixandre repeats the example of his Renaissance forebear who in his ode retropes the Pythagorean triad—light, music, spheres—with the maritime allegory.

This figurative engineering is determined by the lyric nature of the spliced or donor metaphor which, as in Riffaterre's rule of intertextuality, must exhibit thematic and formal properties similar to those shared among the members of the Luisinian nucleus. The id's first Luisinian epithet, "luces o aceros aún no usados" will serve as the touchstone for discussing this intertextual figuration.

In positional imitation of the odic model, the Aleixandrean paraphrase of "hermosura y luz no usada" appears in the second verse, at which point the poem's jungle description abruptly ensues. With the brief exception of the apostrophe, the id/bestiary occupies the bulk of the first seven strophes, until the poem picks up the second paraphrase of the Luisinian introit, "todo suena cuando." The light motif reappears in the last verse—"mar remotísimo que como la luz se retira"—where it both assumes its original single form and is recombined with the Luisinian "mar," which gives title to Aleixandre's poem. The paraphrases of "luz" frame the surrealist poem and encapsulate its psychosexual denouement. That is, because the superego temporarily vanquishes the id, the light of desire—an extraordinary "luz no usada"—remains unused, being tantamount to "vida retirada," to life withdrawn. The Luisinian symmetry of "La selva y el mar" is also reflected in Aleixandre's ordering of the ancestral music motifs. Although paraphrased, the ancestral progression of "luz," "suena," "son," "música" y "son," is repeated in identical order in Aleixandre, where we read "luces," "suena," "rumor," "música," and "rumor." The significant difference, "rumor," an acoustically diminished variant of "son," reflects, as does the ebbing of sea and light, the poem's denouement. In either case, Aleixandre's iteration of the forebear reflects the primary generative role of the Luisinian ode in "La selva y el mar."

The immediate basis for outfitting the id as a coterie of dangerously armed beasts is the liminal Luisinian paraphrase, "luces o aceros." The combination of "luces" and "aceros"—the latter a metonym for swords—surfaces in the luminosity and shape of the libidinous fangs and claws, as in "no se sabe si es el amor o el odio / lo que reluce en los blancos colmillos." In stanza 5, Luisinian light is also recombined with the circle, making the eyes of the erotic predator and of its prey effulgent spheres, emblems of an erotic agape in which amorous destiny is realized. The final id/beast description likewise reflects Aleixandre's internalization of the Mystic's light. An additional version of the poem's psychic denouement, "fieras solitarias" (verse 51), is a pun on light—"sol"—and loneliness, the abandoned but still blazing and circular light of the id. This "soledad" or unhappy outcome is the result of choice, the focalizer's election of affective nonlife over amorous destruction. This "soledad" syllepsis, it may be recalled, is also found in "Unidad en ella" and "A ti, viva." Amorous annihilation or true human destiny is implicitly promised by the "luces o aceros" which, placed in the introit, are menacingly poised over the human wilderness whose psychic upheaval is the narrative core of "La selva y el mar."

While these examples demonstrate the immediate textual rationale behind the transformation of the Luisinian "luz" into "luces o aceros," this particular figurative metamorphosis is nonetheless puzzling and seems rather incongruous. Although the ancestral light and the addended swords share the traits of luminosity and annihilation, "aceros" ostensibly lacks the thematics of love, a primary semantic feature linking Aleixandre and Fray Luis. To a large extent, this ungrammaticality is resolved by locating the base metaphor that converts "luz" into the elongated and sharp weapons mapped onto the id/bestiary as teeth and claws. The metaphoric hypogram spliced onto Fray Luis's "luz no usada" is the Petrarchan conceit, "lips or mouth like roses." The "aceros" [steels], as well as the fanged and claw-bearing beast description, derive from the "espina" [thorn] or "sierpe" [serpent] lurking under that rose, a traditional figurative expansion that expresses the dangers immanent in love and beauty.[18] The most literal actualization of these thematic motifs is the "cobra que se parece al amor más ardiente," a phallic "sierpe de amor" ablaze with carnal desire. The logic behind this figurative engineering is based on thematic and formal features shared by Fray Luis's "hermosura y luz no usada" and the buccal rose. The thematic traits motivating the Luisinian cluster and rose pairing are beauty—"hermosura"—and the mortiferous nature of love, whether it be the positive annihilation in the love of God or the mortal destruction promised by the deceptive rose. The formal characteristics common to "luces" and "aceros" are circularity and sound, traits which are attached to both by association with their respective descriptive systems. "Luces," in that it is one of the components of Fray Luis's destiny cluster, is connected to the Pythagorean spheres and to the music that those circles produce. "Aceros"—hyperbolic thorns or fangs—are attached to the round form of the Petrarchan rose; sound comes by way of the human tenor—the mouth or lips of the beloved—who potentially speaks.

In general, this figurative amalgam is symptomatic of the rebus-like character of *La destrucción o el amor* on the whole. "La selva y el mar" is a prime example of the mysterious world of this book wherein poems simultaneously refer to a psychosexual geography and to a literary landscape. Much in the tradition of Renaissance "conceptismo," the perceptual refocusing of what this complex poem is or can be is brought about as different intertextual signals present themselves to our attention, which creates the impression that this is a poem in the constant flux of becoming rather than a stable linguistic object. The Fray Luis-rose hybrid makes possible this manner of figurative double vision. In view of this metaphorical hybrid, the id, in its suit of lights—"luces o aceros"—may plausibly be given several epithets. The id could be called the luminous thorn of desire, the light of erotic destiny, the blazing circle of eros, the universal and sonorous rose of love, and so on. Any number of combinations of the Luisinian destiny cluster and the rose metaphor would be appropriate. This figurative melange is applicable to all id metamorphoses and accordingly allows, if not necessitates, a reinterpretation of the psycho-narrative plot, which might be described in the following manner.

The id—the Luisinian "sierpe de amor"—lies in erotic ambush. Like a coterie of "fieras," or wild beasts, the libidinous being lurks, round eyes and thorny instruments of destruction effulgent with carnivorous lust. Moved by its innate hunger for flesh, the id sets the jungle aroar: "todo suena." The amorous "música de los colmillos" is in itself an extraordinary "luz no usada" emitted from the sonorous circle of amorous destiny—the fauces of the rosaceous id, the voice that cries in the instinctual wilderness. However, the intensity of that light and music diminishes, variously becoming "un sordo rumor de fieras solitarias" and the ebbing of the luminous sea, the "mar remotísimo que como la luz se retira." The immediate cause of this temporary loss of amorous vitality is the superego which, controlling the mind of the focalizer, instigates the latter to escape the circling and hungry beast of love. The hegira from instinctual reality is made on the wings of the Daríoesque "azul pájaro o pluma." This flight to freedom is a deluded one, since it enchains rather than liberates. The escape is only temporary since the libidinous light, and its imperious music or roar, will return full-volume, this owing to the natural and cyclical character of desire. With respect to the poem's ancestral allegory, the temporary defeat of the id is tantamount to the victory of Darío's refined and artificial poetry over the nature-based music of Fray Luis. The cause of this defeat stems from the rather simple logic that informs the spiritual plot of the Luisinian ode. This may be paraphrased as: when or if one heeds the "no perecedera," the imperishable, music of nature—God or the id—then one's innate essence—spiritual or instinctual—will be redeemed. If, on the other hand, one listens to the worldly or civilized cacophony of artifice—the Daríoesque "sonatina," "el aire suave"—

then one becomes deaf or insensitive to the song of nature, itself a
"canción . . . no aprendida," a song not learned, as described by Fray
Luis in "Vida retirada."

One of the most graphic examples of Aleixandre's metaphoric
alchemy in "La selva y el mar" is to be found in the apostrophic eye
description, "Oh la blancura súbita, / las ojeras violáceas de unos
ojos marchitos." The Daríoesque eyes, which serve both as access to
the human subject's inner world and as emblems of amorous repression, are retroped with fragments of the id's figurative attire.
Here, the Pythagorean circle-as-rose hybrid has its sole floral actualization within the poem. Easily displaced from mouth to eyes, the
floral circle is retroped as wilted eyes mortiferously outlined in vio-
let. In polar opposition to the brilliant and erect thorns—"luces o
aceros"—which, we can imagine, protrude from under the light-filled
rose of erotic destiny, these flaccid and thornless ocular roses emit
only a sudden pallor, in effect the non-light of sexual repression.
The function of the eyes as counter example is strongly bolstered via
the circularity concentrated in the eye description itself. The rosaceous orbs are not only relined with dark "ojeras violáceas" but also
contain and are surrounded by graphemes of destiny, by the iterated
"o's" that saturate the passage, most notably the apostrophic "Oh" itself. These wilted and dulled circles of amorous destiny unfulfilled
are the mirror image of the id in its hybridized Luisinian attire. The
full textual actualization of the latter is suppressed in "La selva y el
mar" but surfaces in "Soy el destino," another tour de force of Aleixandre's synthetic genius. In this latter piece, the id—"el destino"—
is figured as an amalgam of voice, music, light, circle, sea, and rose,
all primary elements of Aleixandre's Luisinian hybrid.[19] Below are
stanzas 7 and 8, which record the poem's epiphany:

> Soy la música que bajo tantos cabellos
> hace el mundo en su vuelo misterioso,
> pájaro de inocencia que con sangre en las alas
> va a morir en un pecho oprimido.
>
> Soy el destino que convoca a todos los que aman,
> mar único al que vendrán todos los radios amantes
> que buscan a su centro, rizados por el círculo
> que gira como la rosa rumorosa y total.
>
> (*La destrucción* 192)
>
> [I am the music that, beneath so many tresses,
> Is made by the earth in its mysterious flight,
> Bird of innocence that with blood on its wings
> Goes to die in an imprisoned breast.

I am the destiny that summons all who love,
The unitary sea to which will come all radiant lovers
Who, as they seek their center, are rippled by the circle
That, in gyres, turns like the sonorous and absolute rose.]

There remains yet another mystery regarding the figuration of the id as "luces o aceros." One may wonder what textual rationale motivates the "aceros" variant of the underlying thorn or serpent metaphor. What appears troubling about "aceros" as sword synonym is the word's possible connotation of manufacture or artificiality, which would be metaphorically inappropriate for the id, the eminently natural component of Aleixandre's human subject. In general, the transformation of the ethereal "luz" into concrete "luces o aceros" reflects Aleixandre's internalization of Fray Luis's mysticism, which the poet absorbs in order to express an analogous but human and unambiguously tangible notion of love. Given the erotic and Freudian context of Aleixandre's poetry, the long and erect form of "aceros" undoubtedly involves phallic symbolism. This dimension is visible in the aforementioned cobra—"la cobra que se parece al amor más ardiente." It may be surmised that phallic symbolism is part of the libidinous fangs and claws throughout the text. The factor motivating the sword trope in particular is the biblical intertext of *La destrucción o el amor*, of which the highly fecund hombre/tierra hypogram is a sign. The Edenic character of "La selva y el mar" is heralded in the first word—"Allá"—and is openly lexicalized in "paraíso" of the penultimate strophe. Indeed, this microcosmic text indicates that the world sung by Aleixandre is a carnal paradise, or at least potentially so. The placement of the luminous "espadas" at the textual entrance to the psychosomatic locus amoenus conjures up the geography of Eden at the entrance of which stands the flaming sword. Placed there by Jehovah after the expulsion of Adam and Eve, the flaming sword was to prevent the return of the first couple and of their descendants to the earthly garden of delight. Neatly inverting the sense and function of the biblical sword, Aleixandre's "luces o aceros" are the phalliform weapons of the id. Erect and aflame, the libidinous "aceros" both promise and provide access to an amorous paradise lost. The site of that erotic garden is to be found in the terraqueous "allá" of the carnal present, not in the mythological or personal past. In Luisinian paraphrase, paradise is "Aquí," it is where "la alma navega / por un mar de dulzura, y, finalmente, / en él ansí se anega." Thus seen, the liminal verses of the book—"Allá por las remotas luces o aceros aún no usados"—advertise the central mission of *La destrucción o el amor*, which is the reclamation of that instinctual paradise, that is, of humankind's natural destiny. On the other hand, the loss or expulsion from this erotic Eden will be Aleixandre's central concern in the later *Sombra del paraíso*.

Before pursuing Fray Luis' s figurative importance in other Aleixandre poems, consider briefly the genre-related role of this ancestor in "La selva y el mar" and in *La destrucción o el amor*. The ode, as noted on several occasions, is one of Aleixandre's preferred generic vehicles for his surrealist thematics of love. "No busques, no," provides clear evidence that Aleixandre's proclivity for the ode is closely aligned to his Mystic ancestor. "La selva y el mar," whose Luisinian model is the renowned "A Francisco Salinas," reconfirms the generic connection between Fray Luis and Aleixandre. The odic configuration of "La selva y el mar" may be observed in the text's tripartite structuration, which is marked off with Luisinian fragments. The first two stanzas—the "strophe"—are heralded by "luces o aceros aún no usados." This section presents a synthetic version of the entire text, including the psychic conflict played out therein. Occupying the bulk of the following four stanzas, the "antistrophe" is delineated by the apostrophe at one end—"Oh la blancura súbita"—and by the Luisinian paraphrase, "Todo suena cuando," at the other. The id/bestiary description is the main concern of this section, the most extensive of the poem. From this point, the poem is brought to its closure in the "epode," which is a bit over two stanzas in length. This section recounts the flight of the superego/"azul pájaro" and the psychic denouement of the poem.

The significant generic difference between Fray Luis's poem and Aleixandre's is apostrophe, which in the surrealist text is both reduced and defamiliarized. The sole instance of voicing is the rather fleeting apostrophic eye description, in which "Oh" invokes the human subject of the poem. Noticeably absent is the publicly directed apostrophe, the typically docent-flavored voicing that, as in Fray Luis's ode to Salinas or in "No busques, no," delivers the poem's lesson. The basis for that lesson in the model poem lies in the exemplariness of its subject—the music of Salinas—which the human chorus is inveighed to heed. The vocal divergence from the Luisinian intertext may be explained by the contrasting nature of the subject. Unlike the sublime music of Salinas or the story of love realized in "No busques, no," or even the apparently humble "moscas" of Machado, Aleixandre's focalizer, and the associated Darío poem, is presented by Aleixandre as a most disparate subject for the conventionally serious ode. The vocative—the high sounding "Oh"—is much at variance with the attached eye description, which is detailed as the melodramatic fainting spell of a delicate denizen of the salon. This element of parody, which is rare in *La destrucción o el amor*, targets both Darío and the bourgeois sense of propriety that promotes sexual repression. In this light, the suspension of the publicly directed apostrophe reflects the nonexemplary, indeed the trivial character of the poem's subject. In less covert form, this delicate soul would appear absurd or comical, and would make the poem openly parodic and less abstract. Like the rose of destiny image, the publicly directed apostrophe is suspended in "La selva y el mar," being reserved instead for other texts, including "No busques, no," "Soy el destino," or "Se querían."

In the second poem, the docent id puts forth clear and amorously edifying examples, the premise that inspires the apostrophic turn: "Soy el destino que convoca a todos los que aman, / mar único al que vendrán todos los radios amantes" [I am the destiny that summons all who love, the unitary sea to which will come all radiant lovers]. In "Se querían," the exempla consist of a collectivity of human lovers whose number and gender are left unspecified throughout. The positive value of the anonymous "mar redondo" [round sea] of amorous collectivity is succinctly specified in the voicing of the closing verse: "Se querían, sabedlo" [They loved each other, know this]. The odic structure absorbed from the ancestral "A Francisco Salinas" is one of Aleixandre's preferred generic vehicles, as evidenced in other poems including "No busques, no," "Sin luz," and "La dicha." The allegorical nature of Fray Luis's ode is also reflected throughout *La destrucción o el amor*, most notably in the abstracted representation of the human. All poems studied bear out that Aleixandre's amatory Everyman consists of a small nucleus of psychosomatic components that function as the basis of an equally schematic anecdote. Like Fray Luis's allegory of the soul, Aleixandre's story of earthly love hinges on the deliverance of the human. This salvation is possible and may be attained by recovering one's innate spirit, be it of divine or of instinctual origin. Liberating this spiritual immanence is then the key to transcendence, itself a destiny to be achieved in love whether divine or human. The culmination of love in Aleixandre, as in his Mystic forebear, is a "desmayo dichoso" [blissful swoon] or "muerte que da vida" [death that gives life]. In neither case is love disdainful, unachievable, or ideal. The impediment to love for both poets is the world, be it the vain cares of the court or the superego, that construct of life-inhibiting mores propagated by the artificial.

Perhaps the most important piece of information to be had from "La selva y el mar" is the close association between Fray Luis and the id, a pairing in line with Aleixandre's positive interpretation of Freud and of Fray Luis alike. Indeed, the Fray Luis–id link established in the liminal poem is systematic throughout *La destrucción o el amor,* where, again, the elements of the Luisinian destiny cluster—light, music, circle, and sea—are both recombined and hybridized and frequently produce antithetical complements.[20] Like the hombre/ tierra hypogram, the Luisinian destiny quartet functions as a master trope and, as such, is one of the seminal ingredients of Aleixandre's poetic world. Following are several samples of how the Luisinian cluster is absorbed and of how the functioning of this intertext affects the significance of *La destrucción o el amor.*

One such example of the ancestral part in Aleixandre's world building is "Las águilas," which was analyzed in chapter three in relation to mood. "Las águilas" is both a specific representation of Aleixandre's erotic fauna and an instance of how the Luisinian model can further illuminate the sense of an already familiar poem. This piece, it might be recalled, is a psycho-narration whose structural metaphor—id/eagles—emphasizes the positive and vital quality of erotic love. The human focalizer underlying the text is nearly reduced to the id and is further defamiliarized by the complex figurative expansion of the aquiline vehicle. The immediate elaboration of the latter involves a mixture of Golden Age intertexts including the Mystic "caza de amor" and Góngora's "Soledades." However, the master trope on which the poem is elaborated is the Luisinian destiny cluster, which acts as the figurative nucleus of the Renaissance melange. As in "La selva y el mar," the cluster functions in its roseaceous hybrid form and systematically infuses the text. One of the ways in which the functioning of the Luisinian hypogram is signaled is in the metallurgical and luminous traits of id/eagles, a flying variant of "luces o aceros." For example, the raptors of desire have "plumas de metal" [metal feathers] and "pico de hierro" [beak of iron] and are outfitted with powerful talons. The luminosity of the airborne "aceros" of amorous destruction is translated metonymically, the eagles being described as an ocular sun, as a "celeste ojo victorioso" [victorious celestial eye] or as "El sol que cuaja en las pupilas, / . . . es ave inmarcesible, vencedor de los pechos" [the sun that coagulates in the eyes is an everlasting bird]. The solar description of the taloned id, in effect a luminous circle, brings to bear the presence of the other elements of the Luisinian destiny cluster. The particular recombination of circle and light surfaces in the analogy, "ese deseo . . . como el azul radiante, corazón ya de afuera / en que la libertad se ha abierto para el mundo" [that urge like the radiant azure, the heart exposed, opening its freedom to the world]. Placed in equivalence, the heart—the circular emblem of love—and radiance—light in spherical form—are combined to actualize the id as the luminous circle of amorous destiny. The floral character of the Luisinian hybrid surfaces in the penultimate stanza where "sangre" [blood], a short-hand for passion, adds red to the circle of destiny, "la tierra como sangre que gira" [the earth as a gyre of blood]. For its part, the music associated with the luminous spheres of the ancestor is concentrated in the id/eagles description of the final strophe:

> Aguilas de metal sonorísimo
> arpas furiosas con su voz casi humana,
> cantan la ira de amar los corazones,
> amarlos con las garras estrujando su muerte.
> (*La destrucción* 217)

> [Eagles of most resonant metal,
> Furious harps with their almost human voice,
> Sing the ire of loving hearts,
> Of taloned love squeezing out death.]

"Las águilas" effectively closes with a variant of "todo suena," the music of the erotic spheres, a song which issues not from the "cítara" [zither] of the divine Musician but from the metallic and sharp strings of the "arpas furiosas" [furious harps], the sonorous id. "El mar," the remaining member of the destiny cluster, is the first Luisinian motif to appear in Aleixandre's text:

> El mundo encierra la verdad de la vida,
> aunque la sangre mienta melancólicamente
> cuando como mar sereno en la tarde
> siente arriba el batir de las águilas libres.
> (*La destrucción* 216)

> [Earth holds life's truth,
> Even though blood may sadly feign
> When, like a calm afternoon sea,
> It senses the narrowing swoop of free eagles.]

Employed to map the blood of the geomorphic human, the Luisinian origin of the "mar" is marked by "sereno," the adjective form of the ancestral "se serena," from "El aire se serena / y viste de luz y hermosura no usada" [The air becomes serene and dresses in light and beauty unused]. The adjective, and its specific ancestral connotation, is repeated once more, to qualify the air-borne id as "Las águilas serenas." Elsewhere described as "arpas furiosas" armed with "violentas alas," the raptors are only serene by lexical association with the ancestral intertext where "se serena" refers to the redemptive transformation of the soul, who is delivered to her destiny—the celestial sea—by the natural sound of Salinas's musical ship. In "Las águilas," the id, who is at once the sanguinary sea of passion and raptors circling above, is serene in the sense that it delivers the human to his or her natural destiny, love. As in "La selva y el mar," Aleixandre's complex figurative raiment of the id suggests several plausible epithets, a kind of surrealist "De los nombres del amor" [On the Names of Love]. In "Las águilas," the id's poetic onomastics could include such appellations as the sonorous raptor of love, the sanguinary gyre of passion, the winged portent of destiny, or the victorious sun of amorous destruction. In any case, what enables such paraphrasing is the figurative hybrid that underlies the id's metamorphosis into eagles. This hybrid is made up of the primary Luisinian destiny cluster, the metaphoric nucleus of the id, onto which Aleixandre has spliced Gongorine and Mystic figuration. The net effect is the noticeable Golden Age flavor of this poem. It also bears remembering that this complex figurative intertextuality is itself fused with the ever-present hombre/tierra trope, which lies beneath all of Aleixandre's poetic world. In summary, "Las águilas," like "La selva y el mar," involves the highly intricate lyric engineering characteristic of Aleixandre's surrealism, a dizzying process whereby the poet retropes a base metaphor with another trope which itself is again retroped, and so on.

The overall and perhaps most valuable lesson that "La selva y el mar" and "Las águilas" deliver is that Aleixandre's world is first and foremost a poetic world. The ecology of this universe is a system that depends to a large extent on the relationship between the poet and other poetry. Thoroughly integrated into this world, Fray Luis plays a primary role in figuring the id, the psychic trait of the human which acts as the protagonist of the amorous landscape of *La destrucción o el amor.* Lyrically polymorphous, the Zeus-like id assumes different metaphorical guises that at first sight may seem to simulate the natural universe. As seen, the id may be a coterie of beasts, the voice of a universal enigma or airborne raptors. Again, at the heart of such metamorphoses is Fray Luis's destiny cluster which, as it is subject to different mutations, makes possible and produces the id's many natural disguises.

One sort of disguise that has not been specifically pointed out is the environmental metaphor, whereby Aleixandre emphasizes the atmospheric character of the Luisinian cluster in cloaking the id.

The epitome of this type of Luisinian transformation is "La luz" [The Light], an exquisite and most moving piece in which the ancestral symbol of light, attended by other landscape features, serves as the structural vehicle for the id. Organized on a question-and-answer format, the poetic narrator ponders and supplies the origins of the instinctual illumination of the id as it impinges on his consciousness. Following is the poem's second stanza:

Esa llegada de la luz que descansa en la frente.
¿De dónde llegas, de dónde vienes, amorosa forma que siento respirar,
que siento como un pecho que encerrara una música,
que siento como el rumor de unas arpas angélicas,
ya casi cristalinas como el rumor de los mundos?

(La destrucción 161)

[That dawning of the light that reposes on the brow.
From where do you come, from where do you hail, amorous form whose
    breathing I hear,
That I hear like a breast containing a music,
That I hear like the murmur of angelic harps,
Now almost as crystalline as the murmur of the worlds?]

Appearing in the section of *La destrucción o el amor* subtitled "Elegías y poemas elegíacos" [Elegies and Elegaic Poems], "La luz" is concluded in amatory plaint. This conclusion is almost inevitable, given that the narrator's inquisitiveness, a rhetorical emblem of love intellectualized, is antithetical to Aleixandre's quite tangible and anti-rational view of love and life. Following are the final stanzas, a closure in which the origin of love, and the poetic persona's amatory complaint, are enunciated:

Oh tú, celeste luz temblorosa o deseo,
fervorosa esperanza de un pecho que no se extingue,
de un pecho que se lamenta como dos brazos largos
capaces de enlazar una cintura en la tierra.

¡Ay amorosa cadencia de los mundos remotos,
de los amantes que nunca dicen sus sufrimientos,
de los cuerpos que existen, de las almas que existen,
de los cielos infinitos que nos llegan con su silencio!

(La destrucción 162)

[Oh heavenly tremulous light or desire,
Burning hope of an inextinguishable breast,
Of a breast that laments like two long arms
Capable of encircling a waist on earth.

Oh amorous cadence of distant worlds,
Of lovers who never speak of suffering,
Of bodies that exist, of souls that exist,
Of the infinite heavens that reach us with their silence.]

In this poem, the Luisinian derivation of the amatory light is reflected both in the circumstantial premise—the poem begins as
the contemplation of the firmament—and in the recombination of
the Luisinian destiny cluster, which creates the many synesthesias,
an outstanding feature of this particular text. The circumstantial
point of departure of "La luz" recalls "Noche serena" rather than "A
Francisco Salinas." The former is a lament in which the poet, who is
in spiritual exile, yearns for the star-filled heavens, the Pythagorean
spheres where "el Amor sagrado" [Divine Love] dwells. As in "La
luz," the plaint is occasioned as the narrator contemplates and com-
pares heaven and earth:

Cuando contemplo el cielo
de innumerables luces adornado,
y miro hacia el suelo,
de noche rodeado,
en sueño y en olvido sepultado:
el amor y la pena
despiertan en mi pecho un ansia ardiente;[21]

[When I contemplate the heavens
Adorned with innumerable lights,
And I look to the ground
Surrounded in night,
In sleep and forgetfulness buried:
Love and pain
Awake within my breast an ardent desire;]

The libidinous light of "La luz," which kindles the hyperbolic "fuego
ardiente" in the lonely narrator, is principally refigured in combination with the music element of the Luisinian destiny cluster. The arresting synesthesias produced thereby include the luminous id as "el
rumor de unas arpas angélicas," "celeste túnica . . . con forma de
rayo luminoso" and "amorosa cadencia de los mundos remotos."
Coherent with Aleixandre's amorous credo and with the erotic referent, the synesthesias effectively solidify light and in so doing emphasize the tangible rather than ethereal nature of love. The Luisinian spheres, which are described in detail in "Noche serena," are
actualized in the verb "girar" of Aleixandre's fauna description:

Contemplando ahora mismo estos tiernos animalitos
que giran por tierra alrededor,
bañados por tu presencia o escala silenciosa,
revelados a su existencia, guardados por la mudez
en la que sólo se oye el batir de las sangres.
                                        (*La destrucción* 162)

[As I look at this moment upon these tender little animals
That, as they circle the earth,
Are bathed by your presence or silent scale,
Are open to existence and are protected by the silence
In which only the beating of blood may be heard.]

Appearing here without the rosaceous thorn or "espadas" hybrid, the id/fauna variant of "La luz" intimates, as does the poem's general atmosphere, a serene bucolic setting, a backdrop characteristic of several ancestral odes including "Vida retirada," "Noche serena," or "Morada del cielo."

As a final sample of Fray Luis's generative function in Aleixandre's amorous cosmos, consider the circle, the geometrical icon of destiny and the most abstract element of the Luisinian cluster. The circle, which like other Luisinian elements is subject to constant transformation, is a highly fecund source of imagery and of conceptual play in *La destrucción o el amor.* The preceding poems offer several examples of this icon's visual dimension including the rosaceous eyes of the focal character of "La selva y el mar," the great gyre of amorous destiny of "Soy el destino," the "celeste ojo victorioso," or ocular sun seen in "Las águilas." Following is but a handful of further examples. The first, from the third stanza of "El mar ligero" [The Swift Sea], illustrates in miniature the generative fecundity of the sphere.

El mar, encerrado en un dado,
desencadena su furia o gota prisionera,
corazón cuyos bordes inundarían al mundo
y sólo pueden contraerse con su sonrisa o límite.
                                        (*La destrucción* 128)

[The sea, captive within a die,
Unleashes its fury or imprisoned drop of water,
A heart whose banks would flood the world,
And can only contract with a smile or a boundary.]

The image of the sea confined within a die is a most implausible and seemingly random vision. The primary referent of this mixed gambling-maritime metaphor is the human whose repressed sexuality—the force of the id—is about to be unbound, as "desencadena" suggests. The quadrangular prison of the sea is produced antithetically, by geometrical contrast to the circle, a synonym of sea in the Luisinian destiny cluster.[22] Within this strophe, circularity is implicit in the round links of the chain verb, "desencadena," in the shape of the heart and in the buccal circle implicit in the cardiac "sonrisa" of the last verse. Aleixandre's particular choice of "dado" as the geometrical antithesis of the round sea is motivated by the manufactured or artificial connotation of the cube and by its thematic association with random luck. Together, these traits make the incarcerating die the image of the superego, the repressive and artificially imposed psychic component in conflict with the id. In the final strophe of "El mar ligero," the circular sea undergoes a floral metamorphosis, another actualization of the rosaceous hybrid of the Luisinian destiny nucleus. Exhibiting Daríoesque traces, the poem's maritime flower of eros is tied with an "adorno," the "cinta azulada":

> El mar acaso o ya el cabello,
> el adorno,
> el airón último,
> la flor que cabecea en una cinta azulada,
> de la que, si se desprende, volará como polen.
>> (*La destrucción* 129)

> [Perhaps the sea, or perhaps the lock of hair,
> The bauble,
> The last plume,
> The flower that nods in a bluish ribbon
> From which, if it is unleashed, it will fly like pollen.]

Another transformation of the Luisinian circle of amorous destiny can be seen in "Soy el destino," where its geometry goes into determining the exemplary icon of love placed in the final stanza:

> Nadie puede ignorar la presencia del que vive,
> del que en pie en medio de las flechas gritadas,
> muestra su pecho transparente que no impide mirar,
> que nunca será cristal a pesar de su claridad,
> porque si acercáis vuestras manos, podréis sentir la sangre.
>> (*La destrucción* 192)

> [No one can disregard the presence of he who lives,
> Of he who, standing in the midst of shouted arrows,

Exposes his transparent breast that does not halt the gaze,
That will never be glass despite its clarity,
Because if you draw your hands near, you will be able to feel the blood.]

The polar opposite of the mise-en-abyme of love repressed in "La selva y el mar"—"la menguada presencia de un cuerpo de hombre / que jamás podrá ser confundido con una selva"—this image incarnates love realized through erotic destruction. It also reflects Aleixandre's penchant for the visual and for the transposition of art as a technique of poetic creation. The image translated here is that of a reliquary, a common ecclesiastical artefact, often a statue inset with a round glass case that contains and displays a relic of the sculpted saint. The saint described in "Soy el destino" is Saint Sebastian, a third century Roman centurion martyred with bow-shots. Aleixandre's poetic interpretation of this popular church image is determined by formal and thematic factors. Two visual details of the Saint Sebastian reliquary—the round glass and the conventional arrow-covered representation of the saint—coincide with the circle of destiny and with the arrowlike thorn that potentially protrudes from under the amorous rose of destiny, the poem's central image. The anomalous adjective, "gritadas," is an intensified variant of the "música" produced by the luminous spheres of the rose of love. The insistence that the breast of the erect figure, though transparent, not be of glass emphatically expresses Aleixandre's thematics of life and love over art. The thematic tie between Saint Sebastian and "Soy el destino" comes by way of the love-death equivalence. According to pious legend, Saint Sebastian was ordered slain at the hands of his army comrades who, though they greatly loved him, were forced to martyr the saint with their bows while, bear-breasted, he faced them.

The most visibly placed circle in *La destrucción o el amor* is to be found in the book's title where the "o," like an icon flanked by miniatures of itself, stands framed between the twice stressed "o" of the lateral components, "destrucción" and "amor."[23] A grand lyric coup, this triptych of destiny advertises the human and ancestral allegory that is simultaneously played out in the book. In the light of Fray Luis, Aleixandre's Mystic ancestor, the titular icon suggests yet another reply to the "Qué es aquello" quandary facing the reader of Aleixandre's surrealism. One of the things that *La destrucción o el amor* is is a reply to an essentially medieval and highly optimistic conception of human ontology in which fate, God, and love are inextricably bound to mortal essence. Aleixandre's reply to Fray Luis involves a lyric metamorphosis whereby the human concerns and the poetic forms and language of the forebear become those of the younger poet. This transformation is manifest in the transcendent mission of Aleixandre's poetry, in its generic form and symbolism and, not least of all, in its complex conceptual play. A supreme example of the poetic pun, the title in its optative sense also invokes Bécquer, whose amorous choice becomes one of Aleixandre's central concerns. To Bécquer and to Aleixandre's intimate relation to this Romantic ancestor we now turn.

7

Ansia Perpetua

mientras haya un misterio para el hombre,
  ¡habrá poesía!
[As long as there is a mystery for man,
  There will be poetry!]
                                        —Bécquer

Desde lejos escucho tu voz
[From afar I hear your voice]
                                        —Aleixandre

AS THE CONNECTION BETWEEN ALEIXANDRE, FRAY LUIS, AND DARÍO
may have suggested, ancestral intertexts are instrumental toward fathoming Aleixandre's surrealism in *La destrucción o el amor*. This final chapter examines the intertextual importance of Gustavo Adolfo Bécquer therein and considers in what ways the sense of Aleixandre's work shifts and is enhanced when the presence of this precursor is taken into account. In the course of analyzing Aleixandre's poems in previous chapters, several clear Bécquerian signals have been picked up. A review and further consideration of these signals will serve as introduction to this chapter.

The most clearly sounded Bécquerian signals are to be found in the titles of several poems, namely "No busques, no," "Ven siempre, ven," "Ven, ven tú," and "A ti, viva." These titles advertise Bécquer by citing Rima 11 nearly verbatim.[1] This poem, it may be recalled, takes shape as an illusory dialogue between the poet and three amorous prototypes. Cited in its entirety below, Rima 11 is concluded as Bécquer elects the most ephemeral and thus least accessible of the three beings:

> "Yo soy ardiente, yo soy morena,
> yo soy el símbolo de la pasión;
> de ansia de goces mi alma está llena.
> ¿A mí me buscas?" "No es a ti, no."

"Mi frente es pálida; mis trenzas de oro;
puedo brindarte dichas sin fin;
yo de ternura guardo un tesoro.
¿A mí me llamas?" "No; no es a ti."

"Yo soy un sueño, un imposible,
vano fantasma de niebla y luz;
soy incorpórea, soy intangible;
no puedo amarte." "¡Oh, ven; ven tú!"[2]

["I am fiery, I am a raven-haired beauty,
I am the symbol of passion;
My soul is filled with longing for pleasure.
Is it me who you seek?" "No, it is not you."

"My brow is fair; my tresses are golden;
I can offer you endless delights;
I possess a wealth of tenderness.
Is it me who you beckon?" "No; it is not you."

"I am a dream, an impossible,
Illusive specter of mist and light;
I am formless, I am intangible;
I cannot love you." "Oh, come; do come."]

Besides quoting Rima 11, each of the Aleixandrean poems listed above makes reply to the elder poet by somehow inverting his fatal amorous choice. Following are a few samples of the poetic means used by Aleixandre in responding to Rima 11. Of the poems whose titles openly invoke Bécquer, perhaps "No busques, no," is the piece that seems least Bécquerian. This is due to its decidedly Mystic rather than Romantic flavor, a feature noted in chapter 5 in discussing genre. Nevertheless, the aim and discursive shape of the text are intimately tied to the Bécquerian option enunciated in Rima 11. The sway of the rima is explicitly brought to bear by way of the paraphrase, "no busques," which, placed in the title and closure, frames Aleixandre's poem in Bécquerian accent. The aim of the new poem, which is to admonish the somnolent addressee not to undertake the vane search for ideal love, is a mirror-image response to the definitive amatory choice made by Bécquer in Rima 11. Viewed against the horizon of Rima 11, "No busques, no" becomes a cautionary tale in which Aleixandre attempts to orient the addressee—including Bécquer's reading audience—away from the precursor's amorous misdirection. The placement of this poem in *La destrucción o el amor* also bears comment. "No busques, no," the second of the book's poems, follows the liminal "La selva y el mar," where Fray Luis and Darío are assigned lyric roles in Aleixandre's surrealist dramatization of love. Viewed in this situational context, the two poems act to strike up the tonic ideological and ancestral chord, which is subsequently played out in variations. Also noteworthy in Aleixandre's transformation of Rima 11 in "No busques, no" is the mutation of the model's circumstantial backdrop. Instead of the mental, daydream ambience from which the amorous chimeras of the rima hail, Aleixandre's poetic discourse arises from a post love-making scene, as suggested in the liminal verse, "Yo te he querido como nunca" [I have loved you as never before]. In any case, this change, like other instances of Aleixandre's reaction to Bécquer, is a sign that Aleixandre's poetic credo of love is formulated, to a great extent, against that of the forebear. The same dynamic is applicable to "Unidad en ella," in which Aleixandre reduplicates, rather than inverts, the mental ambit of Rima 11. In "Unidad en ella," a love poem studied in view of genre, Aleixandre elaborates the imaginary ambit of the rima as a phantasmagorical mental world wherein the invitation to the ethereal "tú" is tantamount to inviting non-love, that is, vital destruction.

In "Ven, ven tú," which likewise invokes Rima 11 via title, the outstanding means by which Aleixandre interprets the model is in the guise of deictics. Following are the first and penultimate of the poem's seven stanzas:

Allá donde el mar no golpea,
donde la tristeza sacude su melena de vidrio,
donde el aliento suavemente espirado
no es una mariposa de metal, sino un aire.

. . . .

Entonces este bosque, esta mota de sangre,
este pájaro que se escapa de un pecho,
este aliento que sale de unos labios entreabiertos,
esta pareja de mariposas que en algún momento va a amarse . . .
(*La destrucción* 142–43)

[Beyond, where the sea does not beat,
Where sadness shakes its mane of glass,
Where breath gently sighed
Is not a metal butterfly, but only an air.

. . . .

> Therefore this forest, this speck of blood,
> This bird that escapes from a breast,
> This breath that issues from lips open ajar,
> This pair of butterflies that at some moment is
>   going to make love. . . .]

Well over half of "Ven, ven tú" develops as a meditation on the first word, "allá," a directional sign pointing to Bécquer's choice of the intangible specter of dream. In the subsequent expansion on the nebulous "allá," Aleixandre qualifies the ancestor's amatory option. He does so by casting that ethereal longing as the sublimation of erotic instinct, a frequent plot motif throughout *La destrucción o el amor,* as "Unidad en ella" or "La selva y el mar" may have served to illustrate. In contrast, the remainder of "Ven, ven tú" is thickly inscribed with proximate deictics which, expressing an amorous and carnal "aquí," encapsulate the Aleixandrean reoption. The new amatory choice is dramatized as a vital epiphany that is spawned as the narrator realizes that amorous destiny cannot be summoned from the initially contemplated "allá," the fantastic Bécquerian region where love does not dwell.

It bears repeating that Aleixandre's most public advertisement of his Bécquerian kinship is the main title, *La destrucción o el amor.* Here, the "o," when taken as a disjunctive, iterates Bécquer's amorous choice, now casting it as an option between destruction and love. An escutcheon placed at the textual entrance to *La destrucción o el amor,* the title not only stands as an emblem of Aleixandre's Bécquerian lineage; it also encapsulates one of the book's seminal ordering principles, the Bécquer-inspired option. As discussed in chapter 4, all poems, whether they directly allude to Bécquer or not, either reduplicate the ancestor's amatory choice—and thereby poeticize the vital destruction of "desamor"—or they reverse it, thus portraying the realization or imminence of "amor." Together with other Bécquerian signs, the main title strongly suggests that a considerable portion of the poetic sense informing *La destrucción o el amor* lies in Aleixandre's relationship to Bécquer. Further investigation will confirm this impression.

Another appreciable sign of Aleixandre's lyric communion with Bécquer can be found in poems such as "Mina" or "Soy el destino." The self-defining-arcanum design on which these pieces are largely patterned points to Bécquer's Rima 5. This poem, it may be remembered, consists of the first-person narrative of the unfathomable "espíritu sin nombre" [spirit without name] who, as if articulating a riddle, enumerates a series of self-descriptions. While elaborating this veiled account of its own nature, the arcane voice concludes by identifying the poet as the vessel or privileged medium in whom that voice reverberates:

> Yo, en fin, soy ese espíritu,
> desconocida esencia,
> perfume misterioso
> de que es vaso el poeta.[3]
>
> [I, in sum, am that spirit,
> An unknown essence,
> A mysterious fragrance
> Of which the poet is the vessel.]

Aleixandre's internalization of this model is similar to his reception of Rima 11. In particular, there is a marked tendency on Aleixandre's part to invert the key elements and thematic sense of the intertext. The analysis of "Mina" in chapter 4 provided the occasion to see that Aleixandre's transformation of the precursor's arcane "espíritu" entails appreciable ontological re-engineering. Formerly a cosmic spirit, the ancestral mystery is assigned in Aleixandre to a somatic post within the carnal human. Here, the once ineffable spirit dwells in the guise of the id and, speaking in instinctual dialect, sagely clamors for erotic destiny: "Soy esa amenaza a los cielos con el puño cerrado" [I am that clench-fisted threat to the heavens]. Aleixandre frequently exploits the Bécquerian enigma as the basis for poeticizing his surrealist notion of love. The result is a series of amorous mystery poems, including "Mina," "La luz," "Quiero saber," "Eterno secreto," and "El frío." The chief poetic concern of such pieces is the mysterious nature of the human universe, specifically the id, the erotic arcanum and positive life-force dwelling therein. Evidence of Aleixandre's fecund reaction to these Bécquerian models is graphically illustrated in "Canción a una muchacha muerta," where the optative and enigma poems of the forebear are enmeshed and are two of the ingredients of the text's Bécquerian hybrid. "Canción a una muchacha muerta" [Song to a Dead Girl] will serve as the focal text for discerning with greater precision the role played by Bécquer in *La destrucción o el amor*.

To begin, a couple of general remarks regarding "Canción a una muchacha muerta." The first concerns the poem's place in *La destrucción o el amor*, which is in "Elegías y poemas elegíacos" [Elegies and Elegiac Poems], the only subtitled section of the book. "Canción a una muchacha muerta" shares this titular distinction with nine other poems: "A la muerta," "La luz," "Humana voz," "Tristeza o pájaro," "Plenitud," "Corazón negro," "Eterno secreto," "Lenta humedad," and "La ventana." Given Aleixandre's proclivity for the ode—the elegy's near kin—and his complex conceptual engagement with amorous death, this generic subtitle is by no means randomly produced. More importantly, and because the pieces contained in "Elegías y poemas elegíacos" do not necessarily look like the elegies of tradition, the subtitle serves as a most useful generic signal. Among other things, these surrealist elegies, like many traditional relatives, develop as meditations on death whose primary aim is to illuminate, in the course of that meditation, some aspect of life.[4] As elsewhere in *La destrucción o el amor*, the death, or life, contemplated by Aleixandre in "Canción a una muchacha muerta" is synonymous with "el amor," the human concern to which the poet's lyric energies are most passionately dedicated.[5] More will be said regarding genre as discussion progresses.

The second preliminary observation involves the ancestral profile of "Canción a una muchacha muerta." Although a relatively svelte piece, this elegy's genealogical composure is quite complex. In addition to Bécquer, who acts as the seminal forebear therein, Fray Luis and Darío are also present and, as in "La selva y el mar," play out key roles in the dramatization of Aleixandre's amorous thematics. The present analysis of the text will begin by discerning the Bécquerian intertexts; afterwards, those of Darío and Fray Luis will be considered. The place of Bécquer in this ancestral company proves to be most illuminating toward defining the seminal role allotted the Romantic in *La destrucción o el amor*. Below, "Canción a una muchacha muerta" [Song to a Dead Girl]:

> Dime, dime el secreto de tu corazón virgen,
> dime el secreto de tu cuerpo bajo tierra,
> quiero saber por qué ahora eres un agua,
> esas orillas frescas donde unos pies desnudos se bañan
>   con espuma.
>
> Dime por qué sobre tu pelo suelto,   5
> sobre tu dulce hierba acariciada,
> cae, resbala, acaricia, se va
> un sol ardiente o reposado que te toca
> como un viento que lleva sólo un pájaro o mano.
>
> Dime por qué tu corazón como una selva diminuta   10
> espera bajo tierra los imposible pájaros,

esa canción total que por encima de los ojos
hacen los sueños cuando pasan sin ruido.

Oh tú, canción que a un cuerpo muerto o vivo,
que a un ser hermoso que bajo el suelo duerme,   15
cantas color de piedra, color de beso o labio,
cantas como si el nácar durmiera o respirara.

Esa cintura, ese débil volumen de un pecho triste,
ese rizo voluble que ignora el viento,
esos ojos por donde sólo boga el silencio,   20
esos dientes que son de marfil resguardado,
ese aire que no mueve unas hojas no verdes.

¡Oh tú, cielo riente que pasas como nube;
oh pájaro feliz que sobre un hombro ríes;
fuente que, chorro fresco, te enredas con la luna;   25
césped blando que pisan unos pies adorados!
                    (*La destrucción* 165–66)

[Tell me, tell me the secret of your virginal heart,
Tell me the secret of your body under the earth,
I want to know why you are now a water,
Those cool shores where naked feet bathe in foam.

Tell me why, above your loose hair,   5
Above your sweet caressed grass,
The ardent or gentle sun that touches you
Falls, slips away, caresses, trails off
Like a wind that carries only a bird or hand.

Tell me why your heart like a minute jungle   10
Waits underground for the impossible birds,
That all-encompassing song that, above the eyes,
Is made by dreams when they noiselessly slip away.

Oh, you, song who to a body dead or living,
Who to a beautiful being that sleeps underground,   15
Sings in the color of stone, the color of kiss or lip,
Sings as if nacre slept or breathed.

That waist, that weak volume of a sad breast,
That vacillating curl that knows not the wind,
Those eyes on which only silence glides,   20
Those teeth of reinforced ivory,
That air that does not move non-verdant leaves.

Oh blissful sky, you who passes over like a cloud;
Oh happy bird that above a shoulder laughs;
Font whose cool stream entwines itself around the moon;   25
Soft carpet of grass upon which beloved feet tread!]

At first sight, Aleixandre's poem hardly seems related to Bécquer. The titular phrase, "muchacha muerta"—especially the plain and colloquial flavor of "muchacha"—strikes the ear as most un-Bécquerian. The same divergence may also be observed in the exuberant apostrophizing of the closure, which is so distant in tone from the ancestor, whose poems are often punctuated with a sense of uncertainty and even doom, not with the overflow of powerful, celebratory emotion. Despite this appearance, Bécquerian intertexts make up the formal and semantic nucleus of "Canción a una muchacha muerta." In the title and the first three stanzas, there are several indications that a significant portion of Aleixandre's "canción" is a remodulation of Rimas 5 and 11.

The most prominent sign of Bécquer is contained within the title, which reflects Aleixandre's penchant for titular allusion to this forebear. Like "A ti, viva," "Canción a una muchacha muerta" is a paraphrase of the optative fragment, "a ti," of Rima 11. In the present case, the components of "a ti" serve as the basis for lyric expansion, an expansion whose phrasing is markedly elegiac. The optative "a" is misread to produce the dedicatory "canción a"; following suit, Bécquer's "ti" is metamorphosed into the eminently concrete "muchacha muerta." The same transformation may be seen in the elegiac "A la muerta," which, in identical manner, develops as a meditation on the Bécquerian "tú." For her part, the titular "muchacha" acts as the focal subject on whose vital remains and internal conflict the poet meditates throughout. The poetic logic for generically reframing the ancestral model as an elegy obeys thematic and intertextual imperatives that will be examined in relation to Fray Luis. In any case, Aleixandre's transumption of Rima 11 both here and elsewhere makes it quite clear that this rima resounds with remarkable force in Aleixandre's lyric consciousness.

The most important additional sign of Bécquer is the phrase, "el secreto," which is encased in the opening verses. Immediately following the title, which alludes to Rima 11, "el secreto" lexically recalls Rima 5, specifically Bécquer's speaking protagonist, the arcane "espíritu sin nombre." The proximity of "el secreto" and the "a ti" paraphrase intimates that Aleixandre's "canción" develops as a variation on more than one Bécquerian piece. As for the lyric rationale for hybridizing Rima 5 and Rima 11, this may be appreciated by attending to the "tú," whose Bécquerian personality has been substantially re-engineered in order to express the ideological concerns of the younger poet. The most visible change is worked on the ethereal nature of Bécquer's "tú," who is—as the elegist insists—a "cuerpo." For its part, the "secreto"—the cosmic "espíritu" of Rima 5—finds itself relocated, having been installed in the cardio-amatory recesses of the carnal "tú." This precise geometaphoric locale is suggested in the first stanza by the phrases "el secreto de tu corazón" and "el secreto de tu cuerpo." On the basis of this metaphorical information, and from previous experience with *La destrucción o el amor*, it may be surmised that the arcane entity of Rima 5 is now made to pose as the id, that mysterious voice of erotic destiny who acts as narrator in "Mina" or "Soy el destino." The intergenerational signals thus far recovered strongly indicate that a large ontological portion of Aleixandre's "muerta" is determined by Bécquerian genealogy. Specifically, the "tú" and "espíritu sin nombre" of the ancestor's rimas are combined and refigured, a transumptive alchemy whose product is the arcane cadaver of love. The hybrid entity is addressed accordingly: "Dime, dime el secreto de tu corazón virgen, / dime el secreto de tu cuerpo bajo tierra." Apparently lacking in the hybrid, however, is the outstanding ancestral trait of vocality, one of the features of the speaking arcanum that Aleixandre so ingeniously exploited in producing "Mina" or "Soy el destino." The lyric motive for muting the arcane voice, actually for transforming it, may be discerned by attending to the plot of "Canción a una muchacha muerta."

Although the "yo"-"tú" relation and the situational nucleus is much clearer than that of "La selva y el mar" or "Sin luz," "Canción a una muchacha muerta" is also a psycho-narration that recounts an inner sexual conflict wherein powerful erotic urges vie with the repressive sway of the superego. In the present example, the elegist, who acts as an omniscient narrator, mediates the bulk of the internal drama played out within the addressed "tú" in stanzas 1–3. The inner perspective of the narrative is suggested both by "el secreto," which is held within the recesses of the focal "muchacha," and by the textual emphasis on interiority, in particular the insistence on the subcorporeal interment of the heart. The psychic quandary in which the focal "tú" finds herself has a most Bécquerian ring to it: she is faced with a choice, a choice between ideal love and erotic instinct. This vital option is textually embroidered into phrases such as "pájaro o mano," "cuerpo muerto o vivo." The phrases, which are Aleixandrean variants of "¿destrucción o amor?," "¿muerte o vida?," serve to figure an amorous "to be or not to be" dilemma like that played out in "Sin luz." In the present case, the psychosexual conflict within the focalizer is temporarily resolved by opting for "muerte," that is, by withdrawing into amorous fantasy. As in "Sin luz" or "La selva y el mar," the anti-vital alternative is metaphorically feathered as the flight of aloof, inaccessible birds, "imposibles pájaros." By means of this fantastic elopement, the instinctually threatened "tú" manages to remain air-borne, out of conscious earshot of the cardiac "selva diminuta," that is, above the roar of the erotic upheaval below. The ornithological figuration of the psychic denouement clearly evokes Darío who, in the aforementioned pieces, is similarly conscripted to figure the superego. Returning to the matter at hand, Aleixandre's "tú" is "muerta" both because she has succumbed to a vital paralysis or amorous nonlife and because, in having done so, she is as erotically nonexistent—and, in effect, as ethereal—as her sister, the "tú" chosen by Bécquer in Rima 11. The persistently directed "dime" indicates that, for his part, Aleixandre's elegist feels perplexed in the face of this vital rigor mortis. But the same cajoling, which also entails an effort to make the corpse speak, implies that the elegist perceives a hope and a remedy for the condition of the "muerta." The hope of instinctual resurrection lies in "el secreto," the vocal force of the id that the elegist inveighs the "tú" to utter and, thus, to liberate from its present entombment.

In terms of the poem's psychosexual plot, the muffling of the potentially eloquent arcanum reflects the superego's suppression of the id, the consequence of which is the mortuary silence of the focal character. But again, as the elegist's coaxing indicates, this story seems to have a hopeful catch to it. That catch lies in the carnal ontology of the "tú," in whom the speaking "secreto" of desire—quite to the contrary of the ornithological superego—is an innate component. Although apparently muffled, that voice, like the libidinous roar of the selvatic id in "La selva y el mar," is an ever-present reality waiting to manifest itself. The carnal immanence of the arcane voice is sketched out, and its eventual victory over repression is presaged, in the figurative elaboration of stanzas 1–3. Here, the ever-increasing sway of the libidinous voice is transmitted in a crescendo pattern; the climax itself is chronicled in stanza 4, where the id makes its full-blown figurative appearance as "canción." However, throughout stanzas 1–3, the voice of the libidinous arcanum, because it is entombed within the amorously defunct "tú," speaks "sotto voce," by way of connotation. The first instance of the erotic murmur may be heard in verse 1, where the sound of the acoustic "secreto" issues from the "corazón virgen." The erotic broadcast is a rather weak one, given that its source—the pulsing heart—is doubly entered, being ensconced in the thorax of the already entombed "muerta." Albeit faint, the throbbing of the telltale id does not die out, which is indicated by the maritime image of verse 4, "esas orillas frescas." Here, the voice of the arcane id, though rather faint, is emitted by association, by way of the low surf sound produced by the ebb and flow of waves lapping at the "orillas." The embryonic seashore scene, with the hushed seasong and vacillating waves that it connotes, comprises a symbolic miniature encapsulating the internal crisis of the focal "tú," whose balking at the sound of amorous destiny—the internal cardiac sea—brings about her vital demise. Picking up heat and greater acoustic force, the cardio-maritime voice of desire is metamorphosed, in verses 8–9, into a solar "viento" whose hot blustering, we may imagine, passionately beckons the moribund "tú" to life. Held aloft on the winds of this erotic gale, the optative "pájaro o mano" reiterates in iconic form the vital dilemma of ethereal vs. tangible love at the heart of the poetic anecdote. With respect to the psychonarration itself, the erotic tempest figures the ever-increasing sway of the id over the focal "tú," whose sexual pangs then trigger the superego's sublimation of eros and the focalizer's flight into fantasy.

In stanza 3, the arcane voice makes its second cardiac appearance and is now refigured in selvatic accent. The potentially deafening roar of love produced by the coronary jungle is, as "selva diminuta" intimates, a necessarily diminished sound, a consequence of the focalizer's aerial escape from erotic reality on the superego-impelled wings of the "imposibles pájaros." It is to the unnatural strains of this impossible amatory species, rather than to the libidinous voice of the heart, that the focalizer has futilely lent her ear, thus bringing about the unhappy psychic predicament. The unfortunate amatory/acoustic state of the "tú" is succinctly articulated in verse 18, where the narrator refers to her as "ese débil volumen de un pecho triste." The vital entombment of the "muchacha" is summarized in the imagery of verses 11–13. Here she is cast as a maiden who, as she gazes into the ether of fantasy, listens to "esa canción total," the illusory song of love produced by the winged superego. Without acoustic, that is, without amatory substance, that song of "sueños" passes with sepulchral silence, "sin ruido." The nonacoustic "canción" is "total" not only because it has apparently succeeded in silencing the voice of the arcane id within the Bécquerian "tú" but also because it is an ominous prelude to the absolute silence of the flesh, whose decease and irrevocable loss of amorous opportunity is inevitable. This amorous "tempus fugit" warning is transmitted by the elegist's repeated admonition, "dime," and, in stanza 3, by "espera" and "pasan" which, in close textual proximity, lexically evoke the time-honored topos of fleeting time.[6] The elegist reiterates the temporal moral in the closure, the section to which attention will presently be given, after a brief review of the intertextual information that has been gleaned from the first three stanzas of "Canción a una muchacha muerta."

Ancestral data indicate that "Canción a una muchacha muerta" is produced to a significant degree as the transumption of Rimas 5 and 11 which, in hybrid form, serve as the basis for poeticizing the "tú," the primary human subject addressed by Aleixandre. The ethereal quality of each model is reversed so that, under Aleixandre's tutelage, the mysterious "tú" becomes a "cuerpo," a sphinx-like cadaver in whose carnal recesses resounds the cardiac, rather than cosmic, voice of the libidinous enigma. The optative plot, in which the focalizer unhappily invites impossible love over instinct, is closely patterned on the story of choice played out in Rima 11. As seen so far, Aleixandre's figurative elaboration of this instinctual head vs. heart story seems to develop on the basis of a structural acoustic metaphor related to Rima 5. In particular, the id is cast as an arcane voice that has been temporarily drowned out by the "canción total," the silent dirge of the superego. However, and this is where Aleixandre radically differs from Bécquer, there exists amorous hope. In Aleixandre, that hope lies in the sonorous resurrection of the focalizer's amorous instinct: the voice of the id is a connate force whose strength gathers in an inexorable crescendo of libidinous volume. Above all else, the compilation of ancestral data in stanzas 1–3 affords compelling evidence that the primary intertextual concern of Aleixandre's "canción" is Bécquer, specifically his impossible quest for love in the ethereal unknown. The closure—most notably stanzas 4 and 6—confirms this impression and further corroborates the Bécquerian genealogy of "Canción a una muchacha muerta."

The closure appears to diverge radically from the preceding text. The poet, suddenly turning away from the "muchacha," now refocuses his lyric energies on the "canción," which now refers, in greatly expanded form, to the voice of the arcane id. The abruptness of the narrative turn obeys a generic logic associated with Fray Luis. As for the metaphoric explosion of the speaking enigma into "canción," this change obeys two sorts of lyric imperatives. The first is local and is related to the immediately preceding text. The expansion of the libidinous voice is produced antithetically, by contrast with the devastatingly mute "canción total" of the superego. The second imperative is intertextual and is dictated by Bécquerian genealogy. In view of the first three stanzas, it appears that the sudden vocal expansion comes about as a sort of acoustic restoration whereby the lately muffled "secreto" is now returned to the full-volume glory of its Bécquerian past in Rima 5. This impression is reinforced by the previously gathered Rima 5 signals and by the vocal figuration associated with it, which in tandem prepare the way for the full-volume "canción." But there are lyric features that, seen from the vantage of the closure, point to the intervention of an overriding Bécquerian intertext, Rima 1. Below, the text of Rima 1, which will be reviewed before proceeding:

> Yo sé un himno gigante y extraño
> que anuncia en la noche del alma una aurora,
> y estas páginas son de ese himno,
> cadencias que el aire dilata en las sombras.
>
> Yo quisiera escribirlo, del hombre
> domando el rebelde, mezquino idioma,
> con palabras que fuesen a un tiempo
> suspiros y risas, colores y notas.
>
> Pero en vano es luchar; que no hay cifra
> capaz de encerrarlo, y apenas, ¡oh hermosa!,
> si, teniendo en mis manos las tuyas,
> pudiera al oído cantártelo a solas.[7]
>
> [I know a strange and immense hymn
> That in the night of the soul announces a dawn,
> And these pages are cadences
> Of that hymn that the air disperses among the shadows.
>
> Would that I could write that hymn, about how
> Man tames stubborn and unruly language
> With words that were at once
> Sighs and laughter, colors and notes.
>
> But this is a vain struggle; there is no cipher
> Capable of containing that hymn, and barely,
> Oh beautiful one, would I be able sing it into your ear,
> Even if, alone with you, I were to hold your hands in mine.]

Bécquer boldly launches his poem by making the hopeful claim that he knows an ineffable cosmic hymn. The spiritual sense of "himno" suggests the transcendent and awesome nature of the poet's acoustic knowledge. The emotional and thematic impact of the rima is deftly achieved by decreasing, in rapid succession, the high tone of the liminal assertion. This operation is carried out by way of the descending acoustic pattern of the subsequent stanzas. Bécquer's

striking credo-like affirmation—"yo sé un himno gigante y extraño"—
becomes, in stanza 2, the wishful enunciation of a lyric quest, a quest
to translate the ineffable strains of the cosmic hymn into language.
The endeavor, which the poet couches in epic terms as an effort to
subjugate the "rebelde, mezquino idioma," is explicitly qualified, in
the first verse of stanza 3, as a futile or lost battle. The impossibility
of Bécquer's poetic task, indeed the undermining of his initial affirmation, becomes acutely clear in the final verses. Here, the poetic
voice—and thus the redemptive "himno" of which the voice is ide-
ally a "cadencia"—is effectively reduced to a whisper, a lyric under-
tone that is barely possible to utter, even in the ear of the absent but
yearned-for "tú." The diminuendo development of the text—its ever-
narrowing referential and acoustic range—eloquently serves to express a sense of hopelessness; it also enunciates a vital and artistic
anti-credo whereby Bécquer comes to negate his own ability to realize the poetic goal that he initially appeared to promise. The sense
of resignation and futility permeating the closure might seem to ob-
viate further lyric efforts on Bécquer's part. But it is the Bécquerian
anti-credo itself that defines the "razón de ser" and the thematic direction of the poet's work. In particular, Rima 1 defines Bécquer's
poetry as a poetry of search in which the poet endeavors, albeit
hopelessly, to attain an ideal, be it spiritual, artistic, or amorous. Bécquer's poems, including Rimas 5 and 11, lyrically chronicle the
poet's quest for these ideals and, when considered on the whole,
create the impression that *El libro de los gorriones* is a poetic autobiography in which Bécquer relates his unequal struggle to attain the
intuited but elusive destiny of which he is keenly aware. The pathos
inherent in this story of destiny-sought-but-unfulfilled is at the heart
of Aleixandre's response to Bécquer. Referring to Bécquer as the
prototype of the Romantic poet, Aleixandre says, "El amante román-
tico, nacido para la armonía inmortal, comprueba su efectivo
destierro y alucinadamente sueña . . . [los románticos son] vanos
anheladores de un destino encendido"[8] [The Romantic lover, born
for immortal harmony, experiences what is effectively his exile and
suffers hallucinatory dreams . . . (the Romantics are) vain seekers of
a luminous destiny].

An additional aspect of Rima 1 that in "Canción a una muchacha
muerta" has direct bearing on Aleixandre's response to Bécquer lies
in the Luisinian genealogy of this piece. As mentioned previously,
Bécquer is himself in intertextual dialogue with Fray Luis. Perhaps
the most limpid example of this lyric kinship is Rima 8, in which
Bécquer maintains a relatively open, and sustained, response to
"Noche serena."[9] In Rima 1, though in a less overt manner, Bécquer

replies to Fray Luis's "A Francisco Salinas." The most accessible signals of the poem's Luisinian genealogy are emitted by two textual features: the first is the musical theme itself, wherein the spiritual "himno gigante y extraño" evokes the Augustinian's deific "música de las esferas"; the second is "noche del alma." This phrase, while it makes reference to the Mystic tradition in general, recalls Fray Luis's story of spiritual metamorphosis wherein the Mystic "noche del alma" is figured as the happy oblivion of the soul. Thanks to Salinas's divinely inspired music, the soul achieves ecstatic union in the love of God. Symptomatic of Bécquer's misprision of the Mystic forebear, the previously happy night of the soul now becomes an emblem of the younger poet's spiritual crisis, a crisis wherein darkness figures the throes of doubt and anxiety in which the poet finds himself. The most compelling intertextual trace of Fray Luis is contained in Bécquer's liminal verses, "Yo sé un himno gigante y extraño / que anuncia en la noche del alma una aurora." Here, Bécquer reiterates, in capsule form, the ideological mission of the Luisinian ode, which is to express a firm faith in and a direct knowledge of the universe, a universe whose divinely modulated strains luminously reverberate both in the collective human soul and in the lyric voice of Fray Luis himself. Against the Luisinian horizon, the thematic contours of Rima 1 become especially sharp. Not only does this horizon allow one to see that Bécquer's anti-credo is formulated on the basis of Fray Luis's act of religious and poetic faith; it also intimates that Bécquer's doubt-ridden quest is impelled by a yearning for a medieval, Luisinian world in which the ideal and the real, rather than mutually exclusive goals, are inseparable aspects of a spiritual and artistic reality.[10] This dialogue of affirmation and doubt, which is inherited by Aleixandre, determines to a great extent both his reaction to and his pairing of these ancestors in "Canción a una muchacha muerta" and throughout *La destrucción o el amor*. Analysis now returns to Aleixandre's absorption of Rima 1 in that poem.

In "Canción a una muchacha muerta," the key sign of Rima 1 is to be found in the word "canción" itself, a figure for the id whose high-volume acoustic character iterates, though in secular accent, the "himno" showcased in the liminal verse of Rima 1. The second signal of the rima lies in the overall figurative structuration of Aleixandre's "canción." Most notably, this song, which develops on an acoustic crescendo pattern—from the muffled voice of the interred id to its full-blown sonic metamorphosis as "canción"—is the mirror image of the diminuendo paradigm of Rima 1. In overview, the Aleixandrean poem, in perfect symmetry, concludes where Bécquer's text began, on a most hopeful and high-sounding note. As is

Aleixandre's wont, his response to the ancestor entails a radical ontological and thematic re-engineering. To wit, Bécquer's titanic "himno," to which the gifted Romantic is intuitively privy, is retroped by Aleixandre as the pan-carnal song of the id that sings in the recesses of all flesh. The universal and collective dimensions of Aleixandre's libidinous hymn are stipulated by way of deictics, which undergo an appreciable shift from the definite markers of stanzas 1–3—for example, "el secreto de tu corazón" or "ahora"—to the ambiguous and catholic ones of stanza 4—"un cuerpo muerto o vivo," "un hombro." As "un cuerpo muerto o vivo" underscores, the universal range of the arcanum includes both the amorously deceased, such as the Bécquerian "muerta," and the erotically living. The eminently concrete nature of the libidinous hymn-of-all-flesh is emphasized, in stanza 4, by two means: via the acoustic hyperbole, "canción que cantas," which personifies the libidinous hymn; and by "color de piedra" and "color de beso o labio," synesthetic adverbials that, modifying "cantas," act to solidify the vocal id.

The most impressive, indeed the most revealing, metamorphosis of Bécquer's "himno gigante y extraño" is contained in the final strophe where, recast as the panerotic song of the id, that hymn becomes the central landscape element in a song-filled Eden of love. Here, in a joyous "amor omnia vincit" finale, the libidinous hymn appears under several acoustic guises: as a laughing sky and bird, and as a gurgling fountain. The most elaborate of these guises is the id-as-fountain: jetting from the instinctual-paradise-regained, the amorous stream is retroped as an aqueous tendril tenderly wrapping itself around the moon; the moon, irrigated by the life-giving waters of the font of instinct, becomes, in the last verse, a celestial "césped," an eminently tangible and vital feature of the titanic garden of love.[11] In general, this far-flung image of amorous-destiny-regained strikingly illustrates the positive force of instinctual love, namely its power to vanquish the sort of death-in-life exemplified by the Bécquerian "tú," to whose amorous remains this image ultimately makes reference, despite the discursive and metaphorical twists and turns of the poem. More particularly, the impressive metaphoric finale is most revealing of the nature of Aleixandre's response to Bécquer. First, the particular transformation of the "himno"—from an elusive and angst-producing music into the happy song of amorous destiny achieved—indicates that Aleixandre's stance toward Bécquer is, above all, a highly positive one. Second, Aleixandre's systematic reversal of Bécquer, here and elsewhere, not only markedly redirects the thematics of the model but, in doing so, suggests that Aleixandre's poetry constitutes a retort, whereby the younger poet effectively puts forth a solution to the elder's vital and poetic quest. The solution lies in Aleixandre's affirmation that the mystery of life lies in love, whose "cadencias" issue not from the cosmos but from within the flesh. Third, Aleixandre's reply entails an effort to revive, through lyric proxy, an admired but ill-fated ancestor. This effort is graphically brought to bear in the figuration of the moon, a Romantic emblem of absent or forlorn love that, in the closure of the markedly Bécquerian environment, becomes a sign of Bécquer himself. Aleixandre's lyric endeavor to revive Bécquer is specified by way of the amatory font, whose life-giving stream affectionately irrigates the ancestral moon, that is, infuses the forebear with new poetic life. These facets of Aleixandre's response to Bécquer, in particular the lyric rationale behind them, become sharper as the complete ancestral horizon comes into view. Before further consideration of that horizon, a brief review of the Bécquerian features of Aleixandre's poem is in order.

Having recovered Rima 1 confirms the complex Bécquerian genealogy of "Canción a una muchacha muerta" and indicates the appreciable degree to which Aleixandre's poem is ordered on the basis of that rima. The structural acoustic metaphor of Rima 1, now inverted in the new poem, is at the conceptual basis for elaborating the inner story of amorous destiny and serves as the frame into which the other Bécquerian intertexts are incorporated. Played out within the psychosomatic recesses of the Bécquerian "tú," that Rima 1–based story traces the crescendo of the libidinous "canción," an instinctual hymn that innately sounds not from the ether but from the "carne." The ultimate triumph, indeed, the apotheosis of the erotic hymn, is made all the sweeter by chronicling, in the stanza 1–3 interim, the sonic vicissitudes of the id within the "muerta." Although the Bécquerian focalizer senses the instinctual "canción" of the id, she opts to heed the deathly silent "canción" of the superego, thereby muffling the song of eros by withdrawing into amorous fantasy. The result, which there has been ample opportunity to appreciate, is the temporary muting of the sonorous id and the concurrent amatory silence of the "muerta." It is to the Daríoesque superego, and its nefarious sway over the focalizer, that attention will now be given.

While Aleixandre incorporates the Bécquerian intertexts into "Canción a una muchacha muerta" in order to construct the innate psychosomatic components of the focal character, he absorbs Darío in assembling the superego, that artificially acquired and love-inhibiting element of the psyche. Darío's antagonistic role is suggested in stanza 3 by the metaphorical raiment and action of the

superego. As in "La selva y el mar" or "Sin luz," this psychic entity
appears in ornithological garb, as the "imposibles pájaros" on whose
wings the focalizer takes fantastic flight. Coherent with the structural acoustic metaphor of the text, the winged superego is further
troped as the "canción total," a mute bird song that vanquishes, at
least temporarily, the libidinous voice of the id. The Daríoesque anecdote of amatory withdrawal is iterated in greater detail in stanza 5,
a sort of parenthesis in which the elegist, in closing, presents a
final view of the "muerta" in her superego-ridden state. Here, the
amorously defunct "tú" is sketched out via a string of physical references that include, in order, waist, breast, hair, eyes, and mouth.
Overall, the portrait of the "cuerpo" is lifeless and fragmented, an
effect that is textually enhanced through the litany-like iteration of
the "ese" demonstrative formula and by the elision of a main verb.
The Daríoesque character of the mortuary scene is made patent in
a lexical pastiche, including "triste," "boga," and "marfil" and, in the
last verse, "ese aire que no mueve unas hojas no verdes." The latter,
a rather open quote of the title, "Era un aire suave . . . ," would seem
to point the present superego image in the direction of that poem,
which recounts a sensual evasion of love. But the female principal of
that poem, the laughing and seductive Eulalia, has little relation to
the present superego victim, the deathly silent "muchacha." The
Darío model in whose likeness she is sketched is the princess of
"Sonatina" (Prosas profanas). This personage, it may be recalled, is
afflicted with a particular amorous malady: having withdrawn into a
fantasy world, she peers into the blue ether as she hopelessly awaits
the arrival of her illusory prince. But for her wistful sighs, the princess,
like Aleixandre's "muerta," is frozen in a melancholy silence. Below
is the first stanza of Darío's memorable poem:

> La princesa está triste . . . ¿qué tendrá la princesa?
> Los suspiros se escapan de su boca de fresa,
> que ha perdido la risa, que ha perdido el color.
> La princesa está pálida en su silla de oro,
> está mudo el teclado de su clave sonoro;
> y en un vaso olvidada se desmaya una flor.[12]

> [The princess is sad . . . What could be wrong with the princess?
> Sighs escape from her strawberry lips,
> Which have lost their laughter, which have lost their color.
> The princess is pallid in her golden chair,
> Silent are the keys of her sonorous clavichord;
> And fainting in a vase is a forgotten flower.]

Notwithstanding the plot motif of escape-into-amorous-fantasy, the feature that seals the kinship between Aleixandre's "muerta" and Darío's princess is the elaborate musical metaphor shared by the two texts. In the fifth verse of "Sonatina," the mouth of the dejected and silence-stricken princess is described as the silent keys of a clavichord. Here, the metaphorical "teclado" makes specific reference to her ivory-white teeth which, when she is happy, we may imagine, produce a laughter-filled "aire suave" [gentle air], as would befit the royal station and elegance of the princess. Aleixandre, in portraying the superego-ridden "muerta" of his poem, recasts the ancestral metaphor by exploiting its metonymic character. The royal "teclado" of Darío's princess is reiterated as "dientes de marfil resguardado," an appreciably harsh and morbid figure for the mouth of the amorously deceased. The addition of "resguardado" economically explains the silence of the "tú": under the nefarious sway of the superego she—as previously her Modernista counterpart—is a silent sound box. Because she is artificially girded in Daríoesque "marfil," she has become insensible to the primeval song of instinctual love. Aleixandre's pejorative and complex reelaboration of Darío's elegant acoustic metaphor is not limited to the buccal description of the "muerta" but serves as the basis for elaborating the entire funerary portrait in stanza 5.

In the first verse, the curvaceous form of "cintura," together with the pectoral sound box image, "débil volumen de un pecho triste," makes the amorous cadaver a curved musical instrument, a sort of Daríoesque "clave." The negative accent of "débil volumen" indicates that the only sound emitted is a wistful sighing, like the sighs that escape from the "teclado" of the sad princess. In the second verse, "rizo," while it ostensibly refers to the hair of the dead girl, has both a musical and a psychological sense. The musical sense of "rizo" is activated by "voluble," which, as a pun on the immediately preceding "volumen," brings an acoustic association to the ringlet. As meaning "voluted," the adjective would seem to be a hyperbolic description of the already spiral-shaped curl. But the combination of the geometric character and the musical association of "voluble" makes the "rizo" a sprung string or broken chord, an appropriate hair description for a nonfunctioning, that is, silent clavichord of flesh. The psychological sense of "rizo" is stipulated by "ignora," a cognitive verb that casts the lock as a metonym for the mind of the focalizer. In this mental environment, "voluble" takes on its additional meaning as "wavering," thus embroidering into the verse the pre-death quandary of the "tú" who, having opted for superego escape, now ignores the "viento," the hot blustering of the id. In verse 20, where the eyes of the defunct girl are described, Daríoesque acoustics come to bear on the text by way of "boga el silencio." "Bogar," a verb frequently paired with the swan in Darío, conjures up the sacred bird of Modernism, whose enigmatic silence is broken only in death. In "Blasón" (*Prosas profanas*), for example, "el olímpico cisne de nieve . . . / boga y boga en el lago sonoro / donde el sueño a los tristes espera"[13] [the Olympic swan of snow glides and glides across the sonorous lake where dreams await those who are sad]. In Aleixandre, the swan does not glide on a "lago sonoro," but across the forgetful waters of the focalizer's frozen eyes. A graphic image of the amorously devastating effects of the superego—in particular, of absorbing the azure artifice of ideal love—the mortuary image of Darío's winged icon also calls attention to Aleixandre's censuring response to Darío. The double referentiality implicit in this image is patently enunciated in the last verse of the Darío/superego section, where "ese aire" simultaneously alludes to the "muchacha muerta" and to the renowned Darío poem, "Era un aire suave. . . ." With respect to the "muchacha," "ese aire," which issues from her ivory teeth, is a figure for the last gasping sigh of the unfortunate superego-ridden focalizer; her "aire" does not move even dead leaves—"unas hojas no verdes"—because it is insubstantial, a weak "aire suave" or—as the particular intertextuality of the mortuary portrait would indicate—a "sonatina." As referring to "Era un aire suave . . . ," the "aire" of the closing verse acts as an interpoetic metonym whereby Aleixandre calls attention to Darío's Modernismo, and to his own response to the Nicaraguan precursor. In this context, the "aire" of the last verse acts to figure Darío's exquisitely refined poetry as an insubstantial song of love, an ivory-encrusted "aire." That song does not move "unas hojas no verdes," that is, it does not sing life from its inorganic "hojas no verdes," from its swan-white and elegantly sterile "páginas blancas," white pages.

While the superego example iterates Aleixandre's negative stance toward Darío, it also indicates, within the Bécquerian ambit of "Canción a una muchacha muerta," that the text recounts an ancestral event much like the one staged in "La selva y el mar." On the local level, Darío carries out the role of superego, that acquired psychic element whose repressive sway over the focal character is elaborated as a "sonatina"- or "aire"-like spell. The false music of the Daríoesque superego vanquishes the id, but only temporarily. For his part, Bécquer is drafted by Aleixandre to figure the body and the id, the innate elements of the focal "muchacha," a carnal vessel in whom the natural strains of the libidinous "himno gigante y extraño" resound.

The psychosomatic conflict is resolved as the Bécquer-inspired song of eros, having gathered in ever-increasing volume, triumphs over the superego music of Darío. On the ancestral level, Aleixandre's "canción" is an encounter between Bécquer and Darío in which Aleixandre, in the process of formulating his own amorous theme, juxtaposes and defines the poetics of the two forebears. The action of the Darío-related superego qualifies Darío's exquisitely wrought poetry as a poetry of escape that encapsulates a faux ideal of love. Seen against Darío, Bécquer incarnates a poetry of search, a quest for love that, though impelled by nature, is fatally misguided by the sort of ideal notion of love that is represented by the poetry of Darío, a poetry that, in lyric anachronism, has been internalized by the Bécquerian "tú." Although Bécquer's search may be misdirected— and in this Bécquer is strikingly different from Darío—it is a lyric quest that embodies universal, rather than aristocratic and private, amorous aspirations. The universal character of Bécquer's "poética" is made patent in the celebratory stanzas of the closure, where Aleixandre refigures the ancestral hymn as the pancarnal song of love.

As they have so far presented themselves, intertextual signs reveal that "Canción a una muchacha muerta" is a sort of poetic rebus similar to "La selva y el mar." In the latter poem, the vast selvatic wilderness acts as the poetic vehicle for a coextensive psychosomatic and ancestral event; the ancestry is indicated via title where "selva" and "mar" make metonymic reference to Darío and Fray Luis. In the present case, the body of the defunct "tú" serves as the metaphorical stage for the same kind of double event. Here, the ambiguous "canción" of the title, while it refers to the voice of eros and the related psychosomatic story, also alludes to the "canciones" of Darío and Bécquer, which Aleixandre has internalized in order to enunciate his amatory and ancestral theme. The titular addition of the apostrophic "a" serves to signal Fray Luis, whose odic "canción" also comes into play. One might think that the intervention of a third poet would further complicate an already complex poem. But the Luisinian intertext is the ingredient that imbues Aleixandre's text with its full formal and thematic coherence. In particular, it is in light of Fray Luis that the significance of Bécquer is thrown into vivid relief.

As throughout *La destrucción o el amor*, the signals of Fray Luis in "Canción a una muchacha muerta" are emitted via genre, conceptual play, and figuration. The generic link is titularly advertised by the apostrophic "a," which announces the odic character of the poem, a feature that is closely aligned with the Luisinian side of

Aleixandre's lyric personality. The text's generic modulation as elegy, the close relative of the ode, is tied to the Bécquerian "muerta," the contemplative point of departure. In tandem with the "a," the music-related "canción" of the title orients the text in the specific direction of "A Francisco Salinas," the forebear's ode on music and the seminal Luisinian model absorbed throughout the *La destrucción o el amor.* This genealogy is reinforced by the death-in-life portrayal of the focal "muchacha," a conceptual play that evokes the central "morir es vivir" conceit of the ode. Also present is the Luisinian destiny cluster of music, light, circle, and sea, which is recombined with figures of Bécquerian origin in poeticizing the id. The pairing of these two precursors is at the semantic core of Aleixandre's poem, as will be seen presently. Fray Luis's music symbol is manifest in the structural acoustic metaphor and appears in most graphic form in the closure where, heralded by the Luisinian apostrophe, "¡Oh!," the libidinous "himno gigante" is effectively retroped as the music of the carnal spheres. The Augustinian's maritime symbol is embroidered into verse 4, where it serves to figure desire as the amorous destiny that faces the vacillating "muchacha." The emblems of circle and light are actualized in combined form—as the sun—in the solar id figuration of verse 8. Like the maritime image of the id, the solar symbol casts the libidinous entity as an emblem of amorous destiny, a destiny that, but for mistaken choice, is within the grasp of the Bécquerian focalizer. Seen together, these signals not only point to the particular Luisinian model but also suggest that Fray Luis is thoroughly integrated into Aleixandre's poem, an absorption pattern applicable to *La destrucción o el amor* on the whole. In the present case, the model is incorporated into "Canción a una muchacha muerta" to serve as a figurative and generic frame in which the psychoancestral happening takes on its full formal and thematic significance. To be considered first is the figurative mission assigned to Fray Luis in Aleixandre's poem.

The most compelling evidence of the Augustinian's metaphorical role may be perceived by attending to the complete figurative plot of "Canción a una muchacha muerta." Spanning the text, that plot is the elegiac story of death and resurrection in which Aleixandre narrates the instinctual demise and rebirth of the Bécquerian "tú." Closely following Fray Luis's spiritual exemplum—wherein the "alma" is metaphorically garbed as a maiden—the virginal "muchacha" is initially defunct, an unhappy state brought about by heeding an artificial and discordant "aire," a music that has misdirected her from love, her innate destiny. In contrast, the redemption of the female personage is realized by the strains of a natural melody, the original "canción" or "música extremada" that promises to deliver the moribund protagonist to amorous glory. The symmetry between the figurative anecdotes not only provides a graphic sign of the Augustinian's organizational role in Aleixandre but is key to the metaphorical and thematic strategy followed by Aleixandre in poeticizing the psychoancestral event of his poem. Aleixandre's metaphorical strategy entails two sorts of lyric processes: the first, and most appreciable, is paradigmatic substitution, the second, ancestral recombination. The process of substitution applies to both Darío and Bécquer. The "sonatina" of the Nicaraguan is made to replace the false worldly music of the Luisinian ode and, similarly, is cast in the role of acoustic adversary as the "canción total" of the superego. Likewise, the Bécquerian "tú" takes the place of the Augustinian's once floundering "alma" and, like her, is rescued from a life-threatening dilemma by a redemptive music. In Aleixandre, that music is the "himno gigante" of the id, the amatory spirit of the focalizer and the acoustic counterpart of Fray Luis's redemptive "son divino" [divine sound]. In view of this process of substitution, Aleixandre's psycho-narration is a Freudian era restaging of Fray Luis's story of spiritual deliverance, a transformation in which the "canciones" of Darío and Bécquer are assigned opposing psychoacoustic roles. With respect to the resuscitation of Bécquer, which is dramatically figured in the last stanza, the Luisinian plot of deliverance allows us to discern that, in tandem with an organizational role, Fray Luis is allotted an auxiliary part in "Canción a una muchacha muerta." Indeed, it is through the proxy of Luisinian figuration that Aleixandre reverses the death-in-life dilemma of the Bécquerian "tú." Fray Luis's restorative part is iterated in Aleixandre's second metaphorical strategy, ancestral recombination

Ancestral recombination is a process germane to Fray Luis and Bécquer and entails the splicing of genealogical material. Local instances of ancestral recombination are visible in the aforementioned id figurations, wherein the libidinous "himno gigante y extraño" indwelling in the Bécquerian "tú" is retroped in the metaphorical raiment of Fray Luis's destiny cluster. The most spectacular product of this metaphorical hybrid is the singing "canción" of the closure, the triumphant music of the carnal spheres. As in the case of paradigmatic substitution, the net outcome of ancestral recombination is the amorous revival of the libidinous "alma" of the Bécquerian "tú," a victory of life over death achieved by splicing Bécquerian figures with those of Fray Luis. The local instances of Aleixandre's Bécquer-Fray Luis recombination are themselves signs of a large-scale retroping that, as previously recovered intertextual signals indicate, involves two family poems, Fray Luis's ode and Rima 1, the controlling Bécquerian intertext absorbed in "Canción a una muchacha muerta." It bears recalling that Bécquer's rima is born as an angst-ridden response to Fray Luis's music-based act of faith. The result is an anti-credo whereby, in acoustic diminuendo, Bécquer articulates his futile quest to recuperate the "himno gigante y extraño," the universal and divine music so clearly perceived by Fray Luis some three centuries earlier. The Luisinian horizon of "Canción a una muchacha muerta"—in particular, Fray Luis's restorative role therein—allows us to see that Aleixandre's figurative inversion of Rima 1—from a diminuendo to a crescendo pattern—is realized by recasting that poem under the aegis of its Renaissance relative, an eminently positive poem that, in odic fashion, develops in an ever-increasing referential and thematic direction. In view of this grand-scale recombination, "Canción a una muchacha muerta," in addition to recounting the psychoancestral conflict played out within the Bécquerian "tú," also constitutes an attempt on Aleixandre's part to assuage, through the meliorative agency of Fray Luis, the bitterness of Bécquer's unequal and misdirected quest, a search for an amorous and poetic destiny in the ethereal realm of the destabilized ideal. The auxiliary function of Fray Luis in this particular response to Bécquer is latent in the main title—*La destrucción o el amor*—which simultaneously poses the Bécquerian query—¿destrucción o amor?—and answers it in Fray Luis's positive affirmation—destrucción = amor. Aleixandre's compassionate transumption of Bécquer, indeed the full sense and poetic emotion latent in his reaction to the Romantic, takes on vivid relief against the generic horizon of the text. Like the overriding figurative design, the generic profile of "Canción a una muchacha muerta" is directly related to the Luisinian ode.

The generic function of the Luisinian intertext is stipulated in title and closure, where the apostrophes, "Canción a" and "Oh," place Aleixandre's poem under the aegis of the ancestral ode. It is within this generic environment that the complex psychoancestral event assumes its primary lyric purpose, which is to stand—like the love lyric contained in the Luisinian frame of "No busques, no"—as an exemplum expressive of Aleixandre's ideological and poetic concerns. The exemplary sense of the psychosexual and ancestral dimensions of that story will be treated separately.

In the exemplary ambit of the ode, the Bécquerian "tú"—and the instinctual struggle she incarnates—is invoked by the elegist to serve as a human prototype, an inter-human status that, as other Aleixandrean poems have substantiated, is one of the salient traits of Aleixandre's human subject throughout *La destrucción o el amor*. In

the present case, the collective personality of the focalizer is stipulated by her generic description and anonymity, and by way of the
previously cited shift in deictics, from the apparently particular "este
cuerpo" to the catholic "un cuerpo." In the course of the poem, the
focal "tú" is further reduced to one essential component, to "canción," that is, to the id, which is celebrated by the poet in the closure. A synecdoche for the "tú," and an emblem of the amorous
human, the libidinous "canción" ultimately figures that ingredient
of human ontology that transcends time, place, and gender. With
respect to the feminine identity of the "muchacha"—a relatively
rare specificity in *La destrucción o el amor*—this is overdetermined by
the particular ancestral confluence in "Canción a una muchacha
muerta." That is, the prototype is part "princesa" and part "tú"; and,
perhaps more than anything else, she is an "alma" who, like her
Luisinian counterpart, is a representation of humanity's innate
amorous spirit. The elegiac modulation of the ode further defines
the thematic function of the prototype. In memorializing the amorous
death and life of the "muchacha muerta," the poet displays her
mortal struggle as an edifying example for the living. The amorously
deceased "tú" embodies two particular aspects of human existence.
On one hand, she incarnates an amorous life cut short by heeding
the voice of the superego which, figured as the Daríoesque "sonatina," is the repressive force of civilization akin to the "milenaria
columna" of "Sin luz." This is illustrated in stanza 5, where the
elegist enunciates in Modernista accent the funerary portrait of
the "tú." On the other hand, and as the joyous closure indicates,
the focalizer also embodies hope, a hope that lies in the resurrection of the id, her innate amorous spirit. The latter is boldly brought
to bear in the elegist's apostrophic turn in stanza 4, where the in-
domitable song of instinctual love is enshrined by the apostrophic
"Oh." This discursive pattern of example and counter example
serves the poet as the materia prima of his elegiac lesson plan, the
aim of which is not only to warn of the nefarious effects of the
superego but, in celebrating the power of the id, to admonish
the "muchacha" and the reader alike to heed the voice of amorous
destiny. The poet puts forth this argument in verse 23—¡Oh tú, cielo
riente que pasas como nube"—wherein he articulates an amorous
"tempus fugit," a reminder that the opportunity to choose love is
fleeting. If it were to be asked, at this juncture, what Aleixandre's
poem does rather than what it narrates, the answer would be rather
simple: like the Luisinian hypotext and many other odic poems, it
invokes and poeticizes an exemplary personage whose attributes, in
this generic ambit, assume a transcendent significance. This schematic

description of "Canción a una muchacha muerta" is equally applicable to the ancestral level of the text, wherein Bécquer, while standing in the company of Aleixandre's forebears, becomes the subject in whom the new poet invests his lyric energies.

When read as referring to Bécquer, "Canción a una muchacha muerta" assumes a rather specific sort of lyric physiology and, like many other such poems—including Lorca's "Oda a Walt Whitman," Shelley's "Adonais: An Elegy on the Death of John Keats," or Auden's "In Memory of W.B. Yeats"—takes on two sorts of meanings. Before proceeding, allow a few brief remarks on those meanings. Such elegies are first of all a meditation on the life and work of an aesthetic model, an exemplary artist whom the elegist, in the course of his meditation, sets out to memorialize. In the Luisinian ambit of "Canción a una muchacha muerta," Bécquer—though through metonymic reference—acts as the counterpart of Salinas, the artistic prototype celebrated in the ode of the Augustinian. In *La destrucción o el amor,* "La dicha" belongs to the same odic subset and, although it is a scathing invective against Darío, is identical to "Canción a una muchacha muerta" in the indirect means by which it invokes its ancestry. "La dicha" provides concrete evidence that the qualities of the artistic other need not be exclusively positive ones. The second sort of meaning taken on in such elegies is self-definition. That is, the subject addressed by the elegist acts as an alter ego or vehicle through which the poet defines himself and his poetry. At work is a psychological dynamic roughly equivalent to Bloomian transumption, though such internalization is not necessarily hidden, nor motivated by anxiety. According to the qualities perceived in the model, the elegist may identify with that aesthetic other in a range of ways: for example, the model may embody what the poet is (Fray Luis-Salinas), aspires to be (Lorca-Whitman), rejects in part (Auden-Yeats), or totally (Aleixandre-Darío). In "Canción a una muchacha muerta," Aleixandre's concerted efforts to reverse Bécquer's misdirection suggest that Bécquer represents what Aleixandre could have been, if not for fortune and circumstance. For his part, Fray Luis—a transcendentalist—most nearly embodies what Aleixandre is as a poet while Darío, as in "La dicha," stands as Aleixandre's poetic antithesis.

As an ancestral elegy, the primary purpose of "Canción a una muchacha muerta" is to meditate on and memorialize the life and work of Bécquer. The story of this poet is communicated by way of the pastiche of Bécquerian intertexts absorbed within the poem. The rimas to which Aleixandre alludes outline that biography as a frustrated quest for an amorous and poetic ideal, a quest which is launched by mistaken choice. In the elegiac environment of the poem, Bécquer's story becomes a sort of allegory of the Romantic poet, an amorous Everyman who is set off the course of his natural destiny by notions of the ideal. The result of this vital disorientation is a sense of hopelessness and a loss of faith in the ability to achieve amorous and artistic destiny. The anxiety-producing search-for-destiny-obscured that Bécquer incarnates, and to which Aleixandre reacts, is compellingly articulated in Rima 66, where Bécquer, placing himself on the road of life, replies to the query of a fellow traveler:

> ¿De dónde vengo? . . . El más horrible y áspero
>   de los senderos busca.
> Las huellas de unos pies ensangrentados
>   sobre la roca dura;
> los despojos de un alma hecha jirones
>   en las zarzas agudas,
>   te dirán el camino
>   que conduce a mi cuna.
>
> ¿Adónde voy? El más sombrío y triste
>   de los páramos cruza:
> valle de eternas nieves y de eternas
>   melancólicas brumas.
> En donde esté una piedra solitaria
>   sin inscripción alguna,
>   donde habite el olvido,
>   allí estará mi tumba.[14]

> [Where do I come from? . . . Seek of all paths
>   The roughest and most dreadful.
> The traces of blood-covered steps
>   Over the hard rock;
> The shreds of a rended soul
>   On the sharp brambles
>   Will show you the way
>   That leads to my cradle.
>
> Where am I bound? Cross of all desolate moors
>   The darkest and most sad:
> The vale of eternal snows and of eternal
>   Melancholy mists.
> Where there is a solitary stone
>   With no inscription whatsoever,
>   Where oblivion dwells,
>   There will be my tomb.]

In "Canción a una muchacha muerta," Aleixandre's response to the vital and poetic dilemma incarnated by Bécquer involves a strong, and eminently compassionate, reply. Aleixandre's lyric endeavor is to rewrite the story of the ill-fated forbear, which he does by way of ancestral staging, by redramatizing the Bécquer allegory of destiny lost. Along the way, Bécquer is alternately hindered and helped: hindered by Darío, who acts as the agent of the faux ideal; and guided by Fray Luis, under whose sage tutelage the Romantic is ultimately led to his destiny. Thus seen, Aleixandre's rewriting of Bécquer in "Canción a una muchacha muerta" becomes a story of return-to-origins, which Aleixandre realizes by inverting, through Luisinian proxy, the form and outcome of the Bécquerian intertexts. In this lyric fiction, Aleixandre resolves the spiritual, artistic, and amorous crisis of the forebear. As articulated by plot, Aleixandre's solution is resounding and single-minded: human destiny is to be found in love, which is an instinctual Mystery clamoring for discovery, and release, from within the terraqueous vessel of the human, not in the ethereal sphere of the ideal. The most impressive feature of Aleixandre's redemptive fiction is the denouement, the resurrection of Bécquer. Symbolized by the singing and eminently concrete "canción" of the closure, Bécquer is poetically eternalized by Aleixandre in his own "canción." The new poet's memorialization of the forebear—an operation squarely in line with the elegy—serves to voice Aleixandre's admiration for Bécquer and stands as an emblem of the younger poet's compassionate identification with him. Thus understood, Aleixandre's title can feasibly be paraphrased as "Canción a una canción," "Canción a Bécquer," "A Bécquer," or, simply, "A ti." In its ultimate ancestral sense, "Canción a una muchacha muerta" is a reply and an epitaph, an inscription expressive of Aleixandre's esteem for Bécquer.[15]

What can be concluded from the ancestral information contained in "Canción a una muchacha muerta"? That is, does this example amplify or bring further coherence to the other things that La destrucción o el amor is? The strength of Aleixandre's response to Bécquer in this poem, together with other instances of the poet's transumption of Bécquer—the main title, subtitles, and the absorption of rimas throughout La destrucción o el amor—provides compelling evidence that one of the additional, and overarching, things that this surrealist book is is an eloquent and empathetic reply to Bécquer, who serves therein as the human and poetic model addressed by Aleixandre. In the context of Aleixandre's sustained response to Bécquer, we might reconsider several of the poems analyzed in the course of the present study. Like "Canción a una muchacha muerta," those pieces not only take on an increased poetic sense in reference to Bécquer but also produce an especially strong poetic emotion.

Appearing under different narrative guises, Bécquer is the inquisitive "tú" of "Mina," whose misdirected question regarding amorous knowledge triggers the curt "Calla. Calla." of the sage id; in "No busques, no" he is the model for the amorous prototype who, resigned to his melancholy quest for love in the ideal, is inveighed by the Luisinian odist to take note of his example of love achieved; Bécquer is also the amorous narrator of "Unidad en ella," whose invitation to the ideal produces phantasmagoria. Like all intertextual signals, whether open or covert, the many traces of Bécquer in *La destrucción o el amor* not only increase and deepen the sense of individual pieces but are also an essential key to the book's overall poetic logic and significance. Again viewed in reference to Bécquer, *La destrucción o el amor* is ultimately an attempt on Aleixandre's part to fathom, from the vantage of the Freudian era, the elusive Mystery that his Romantic forebear had so fervidly sought. In tandem with the other salient features of *La destrucción o el amor*—including its radical recasting of poetry's discursive structure, interpretive transumption of Fray Luis and Darío, and its poetization of the subconscious—the Bécquerian texture of this book strongly suggests that one of the ways in which the uniqueness of Aleixandre's surrealism may be appraised is by appealing to the literary and cultural ambit that nourished, and was transformed by, Aleixandre's fecund lyric imagination.

Conclusion

THE INTERTEXTUAL DATA GATHERED IN THE COURSE OF ANALYZING *La destrucción o el amor* suggest that an appreciable share of the poetic logic behind Aleixandre's surrealism lies in the poet's creative recasting of traditional materials. Such materials include narrative structure, genre, metaphor, and ancestral model poems. The net effect of Aleixandre's transumption of such sources is a highly original poetry whose strength and uniqueness would seem to make Aleixandre—as Cernuda observed—the founder of a new kind of poetry, a poetry whose enigmatic appearance has variously baffled, intrigued, and moved readers, including myself.

From among the intertextual information that has been accrued, perhaps it is Aleixandre's protracted response to Bécquer that most clearly defines the overriding sense of this complex and highly original book of love poetry. In particular, the urgency, firmness, and compassion that characterize Aleixandre's reaction to Bécquer strongly suggest that *La destrucción o el amor* is ultimately a lyric project undertaken by Aleixandre in order to assuage, indeed to resolve, the vital dilemma incarnated by his Romantic precursor. Acting as amorous archetype, Bécquer embodies an affective crisis spurred by a passionate though vain quest for love in the realm of the ideal, an impalpable ambit far removed from erotic reality, that is, from the vital sense of "el amor" advocated by Aleixandre. The consequence of this misguided search for love is affective segregation, a living death or vital "destrucción" bringing with it the loss of amorous destiny. However, and this is at the heart of the ideological mission of Aleixandre's lyric project, the tragic destiny that Bécquer represents is not sealed. Indeed, as poem after poem bears out, *La destrucción o el amor* is inscribed with a definite vital purpose, which is to serve as a surrealist "libro de buen amor" that, by way of lyric examples of ideal vs. instinctual love, is meant to move the reader to reject notions of an amorous ideal in favor of sensual and earth-bound love, that of "dos cuerpos amándose" [two bodies making love to each other]. Advertised in the main title, where one of the meanings of the ambiguous "o" is disjunctive, the amatory either/or put forth by Aleixandre is itself one of the principle signs of the poet's connection to

Bécquer who, in Rima 11, opts for the incorporeal "sueño de niebla y de luz" [dream of mist and light], the amorous being that inspires the Romantic's angst-ridden quest for love. In addition to Aleixandre's direct response to Bécquer, and to the amorous crisis embodied by this precursor, there are two other overarching intertextual features of *La destrucción o el amor* that are integral to the book's formal and thematic texture.

The first, and no doubt the less obvious one, entails Aleixandre's transumptive conscription of other lyric forebears, principally Fray Luis and Darío. While Bécquer, from among the members of this ancestral triad, is the model poet of most immediate concern to Aleixandre, Darío, and Fray Luis are assigned complementary roles that are played out in thematic counterpoint to Bécquer's. Cast in anachronistic allegory, Bécquer—an amorous Everyman—is hindered in his quest for love by the faux ideal of love incarnated by Darío; in contrast, the Romantic is steered toward the realization of his amorous fate by Fray Luis, who embodies a notion of love—albeit now in a non-divine sense—as an eminently attainable human destiny. In the course of this amorous allegory, all three ancestors—though more extensively so Bécquer and Fray Luis—avail Aleixandre of a considerable amount of poetic material, including metaphor, genre, syntax, and conceptual play. Aleixandre recombines and reinterprets this conglomeration of lyric building blocks in fashioning his highly original poetic world. But one example is the Luisinian ode, a thematically transcendent and public sort of lyric that becomes one of the poetic hallmarks of *La destrucción o el amor,* a book that, while it is passionately concerned with Aleixandre's lyric heritage, is equally engaged in addressing the collective human condition symbolized by Bécquer. Indeed, the ancestral allegory—and the intertextual constituents that produce it—is mirrored on the local level of the book by a coextensive and equally schematic psychosexual conflict, an erotic upheaval that takes place in the recesses of Aleixandre's amorous Everyman. In overview, this interior story consists of a plot in which the psychic forces of the id and superego vie for supremacy within the erotic underworld of Aleixandre's human archetype. This particular conception of the amorous conflict is directly related to Sigmund Freud. Together with Aleixandre's response to Bécquer and his other ancestors, the poet's interpretation of Freud's theory of the subconscious, a contemporary and scientific intertext, stands as one of the seminal ingredients informing *La destrucción o el amor.*

In contrast to the presence of Aleixandre's ancestry, the sway of the Freudian intertext in *La destrucción o el amor* is quite palpable, being immediately felt in the "automatism effect," the irrational and often baffling textual veneer designed to simulate the associative meanders and dreamlike world of the unconscious mind. This outstanding stylistic feature, which is most patent in the elastic syntax and in the irrational character of metaphors, is shared by *Pasión de la tierra* and *Espadas como labios,* the surrealist books preceding *La destrucción o el amor.* Under the aegis of Aleixandre's considerable lyric imagination, the integration of Freudian theory into poetry is the decisive revolutionary factor at work in Aleixandre's transumption of traditional lyric form and theme. There has been some opportunity to appreciate that Aleixandre's interpretation of Freud, in particular of the insight that human behavior is motivated by strong but unconscious instinctual forces, produces a poetry whose perspective is eminently psychic. Aleixandre, who himself alludes to Freud as "un psicólogo de vasta repercusion literaria" (*OC* 2:546) [a psychologist of vast literary repercussions], outlines, in uncompromisingly lyric language, the Freud-inspired inner world that he endeavors to simulate in his surrealism: "La pasión humana palpita en las paredes interiores de la carne, y el alma, con calidades vegetales, se siente azotada por el ventarrón, enraizada en el barro latiente, bajo un cielo aplastado, donde hay fulgores sanguíneos y a veces luces negras" (*OC* 2:527–28) [Human passion pulses in the inner fibers of the flesh, and the soul, with vegetable qualities and rooted in the throbbing clay, feels battered beneath a crushed sky where there are sanguine flashes and, at times, dark lights]. In *La destrucción o el amor,* Aleixandre's poetization of the intracarnal "pasión humana" not only brings with it the syntactical peculiarities and the arresting imagery that act to simulate the psychic perspective of the poems but also entails a highly innovative narrative recasting of some of the lyric's primordial materials. One of the salient examples of this transformation is Aleixandre's poetic landscape, which often evokes the bucolic setting of Golden Age eclogues or the vast cosmic vistas of Romanticism. Aleixandre refashions such geography in the contours of the subconscious. The landscape of poetic tradition now serves as a vehicle for the "barro latiente," for the terraqueous human who is mapped as a psychosexual wilderness. In many poems, including "La selva y el mar," the id, figured as an untamed libidinous species afoot within the selvatic fibers of the human, vies for instinctual supremacy against the repressive force of the superego. In Aleixandre, the superego is cast as the coercive power of civilization, an internalized set of social mores that acts to inhibit the realization of instinctual destiny, that is, love. Another concrete instance of Aleixandre's poetization of Freud's model of human ontology in

La destrucción o el amor is the personification of the id, an otherwise impalpable psychic entity that in poems such as "Mina" or "Soy el destino" is cast as the poetic narrator. Metamorphosed into the arcane voice of desire, the id sagely inveighs the human in whose carnal recesses it resounds to claim the instinctual destiny of love to which he or she was born. The speaking-enigma design, which is closely patterned on Bécquer's Rima 5, is symptomatic of the figurative part played by ancestor poets in Aleixandre's poetic rendering of Freud's psychological model. Indeed, the poetries of Fray Luis and Bécquer serve as materia prima for constructing the body and id, the innate components of Aleixandre's amorous Everyman; the antagonistic superego, on the other hand, is figured in Daríoesque raiment.

The instances cited above, as well as the many examples seen throughout this study of *La destrucción o el amor,* provide strong evidence that Aleixandre's adaptation of Freud supersedes scientific accuracy. From an intertextual perspective, such liberal and inaccurate transumption of a source, be it literary or scientific in origin, is to be expected, misprision being the normative dynamic at the heart of artistic creation. Notwithstanding such poetic imprecision, Aleixandre's personal reception of Freud, as well as being fundamental to the form and sense of a book such as *La destrucción o el amor,* is instrumental toward discerning Aleixandre's place in the greater artistic ambit of his time. In general, Aleixandre's poetization of the subconscious is the facet of his pre-Civil War poetry that squarely links the poet to surrealism, a movement whose seminal springboard and "patron saint" is Freud. In the first manifesto, André Breton—who has been called the "pope" of that ism—equates Freud's psychological theory with the discovery of the Mystery, in majuscule. The French poet goes on to observe that the exploration of the arcane inner world discovered by Freud is not only of interest to scholars but is the province of poets as well. The appeal—indeed, the fecundity—of Freudian theory is witnessed in the numerous attempts by writers and artists to explore and to give form to the unfathomable and formless Mystery lying in the depths of our psyche.

In the Spanish context, two outstanding examples are Dalí and García Lorca, whose own artistic incursions into the realm of the psyche produce works quite different in tone and sense from Aleixandre's. In *Poeta en Nueva York,* written in 1929–30, at approximately the same time as Aleixandre's *Pasión de la tierra,* Lorca transforms the cityscape of New York into the hallucinatory terrain of nightmare. Modern civilization, which is embodied by the American city, stands as an emblem of the superego that exerts its repressive force over instinct and over all other manifestations of the natural and innate. In "Nueva York: Oficina y denuncia," Lorca passionately voices his invective against civilization's crushing effects: "Yo denuncio la conjura / de estas desiertas oficinas / que no radian agonías, / que borran los programas de la selva"[1] [I denounce the conspiracy of these deserted offices that do not radiate deaths, that erase the programs of the jungle]. As for Dalí, any number of his paintings from the mid 1920s on are capital examples of surrealism and constitute Dalí's effort to give form to dark psychosexual conflicts. In such portraits of instinctual upheaval, there is a discernible tension between surfacing libidinous impulses and the inhibiting effects of inculturation. A striking instance of this libidinous turmoil is "The Lugubrious Game" (1929). One of the central images from among the painting's plentiful scatological and masturbatory elements is a female figure who, statuelike, stands on a pedestal inscribed with the words, "Gramme," "Centigramme," and "Milligrame." Placed at the foot of the pedestal is one of the bronze lions whose paw, resting on a cannon ball, guards the entrance to the Spanish Parliament. For her part, the statuelike figure holds out an engorged and tense right hand that points to an aerial orgasm replete with rather disturbing images of sexual fantasy; the left hand covers the face in shame. When added up, Dalí's imagery suggests a Freudian-era anecdote of neurosis in which the individual, assaulted by ego-threatening sexual fantasy, in effect becomes emotionally petrified by the internalized code of the rational, by the weights and measures of social law and order. While to a large extent *Pasión de la tierra* and *Espadas como labios* share the invective spirit infusing *Poeta en Nueva York* or Dalí's penchant for creating the perturbing imagery of neurosis, *La destrucción o el amor* stands out from among Aleixandre's surrealist works not only as the poet's most expressive and moving interpretation of Freud but also as his most personal (i.e., most inaccurate) and meliorative one. Notwithstanding the lyric experience accrued by Aleixandre by the time he wrote *La destrucción o el amor*—his fourth book—I would speculate, particularly in view of the passionate and sustained response to Bécquer that infuses this work—that the elegance and clear ideological thrust of *La destrucción o el amor* is directly related to the poet's now well-defined engagement with his ancestry. In particular, Aleixandre endeavors to fathom the spiritual and amorous arcanum that Bécquer had vainly sought to decipher. As Aleixandre's transumption of Freud suggests, the reply and the solution to the vital dilemma of his Romantic forebear was afforded Aleixandre by Freud's revolutionary discovery that the location of the Mystery is not in the celestial "allá," in the beyond, but in the psychic realm enshrouded in the palpable substance of flesh. In overview, Aleixandre's alchemistic fusing of Freud with Bécquer and with the other precursors makes *La destrucción o el amor* a book of discovery in which, in the cadences of the subconscious, the poet enunciates a lyric reply to the pre-established discourse on love and human destiny inherited from tradition. In abstract, Aleixandre's lyric of discovery follows, and transumptively reacts to, poetries of affirmation (Fray Luis), search (Bécquer), and escape (Darío). With respect to Aleixandre's long and fecund poetic trajectory, *La destrucción o el amor* is not only the poet's most refined expression of surrealism but stands as the work in which love's discovery is most ecstatically celebrated and to which, in following years, other of Aleixandre's books nostalgically respond.

Notes

INTRODUCTION

1. André Breton's words were originally a reply to Paul Valéry, who asked the surrealist what a poem should be. Qtd. in Michael Riffaterre, *Text Production,* trans. Terese Lyons (New York: Columbia University Press, 1983), 3.

2. Dámaso Alonso, "La poesía de Vicente Aleixandre," *Ensayos sobre poesía española* (Madrid: *Revista de Occidente,* 1944), 360; Luis Cernuda, "Aleixandre," *Crítica, ensayos y evocaciones* (Barcelona: Seix Barral, 1970), 221; Luis Antonio de Villena, Preliminary study and notes to *Pasión de la tierra* (Madrid: Narcea, 1977), 51. These and subsequent translations from the Spanish are my own, unless otherwise noted.

3. Although distinct from one another in their theoretical orientation, the following studies are examples of the trajectory format. Vicente Granados, *La poesía de Vicente Aleixandre* (Madrid: Cupa, 1977); Dario Puccini, *La palabra poética de Vicente Aleixandre* (Barcelona: Ariel, 1979); Lucie Personneaux, *Vicente Aleixandre ou une poésie du suspense: Recherches sur le réel et l'imaginaire* (Montpellier: Univesité Paul Valéry, 1980); Maya Schärer-Nussberger, *Vicente Aleixandre: Création et Poétique* (Boudry-Neuchatel, Switzerland: Baconniere, 1992).

4. Aleixandre explains his irrational aesthetic as stemming from his reading of Freud. Referring to *Pasión de la tierra,* the poet writes: "La ruptura que este libro significaba tomó la más libre de las formas: la del poema en prosa. Es poesía 'en estado naciente,' con un mínimo de elaboración. Hace tiempo que sé, aunque entonces no tuviera conciencia de ello, lo que este libro debe a la lectura de un psicólogo de vasta repercusión literaria (Freud), que yo acababa de realizar justamente por aquellos años" [The break that this book meant assumed the most free of all forms: that of the prose poem. It is poetry in 'nascent form,' with a minimum of elaboration. I have known for some time, though then I may not have been aware of it, what this book owes to my reading of a psychologist of vast literary repercussions (Freud). I had just finished that reading in those years]. *Obras completas* 2 vols. (Madrid: Aguilar, 1978), 2:546. Subsequent references to this collection are indicated parenthetically in the text and notes as *OC.*

5. Alfred Stern clearly explains the Freud-surrealism relationship. The critic points out that surrealism is based on a very loose and scientifically inaccurate interpretation of Freudian theory. Even if this were not the case, surrealist art, whether plastic or poetic, is of little or no value to psychoanalysis, which relies on personal interviews with the subject. Stern also notes that Freud himself gave little serious consideration to surrealist endeavors to explore the subconscious. "El surrealismo en la literatura," *Revista de letras* 21 (June 1974): 39–54. Nevertheless, Freud did show some interest in one surrealist youth, Salvador Dalí. Freud's reaction to Dalí's pilgrimage to Vienna may be found in *The Life and Work of Sigmund Freud* vol. 3, trans. Ernest Jones (New York: Basic Books, 1957), 235.

CHAPTER 1: AN INTERTEXTUAL TACK

1. Carlos Bousoño articulates his ideas on irrationalism and individualism in chapter 3, "Los elementos centrales de la poesía del siglo XX: Individualismo e irracionalismo," *La poesía de Vicente Aleixandre: Imagen, estilo y mundo poético* (Madrid: Insula, 1950).

2. Surrealism, whether in Aleixandre or in other writers, has been a subject of much debate among Hispanists. The polemic revolves around two questions, the definition of surrealism in general and the origins of this ism in Spanish literature and art. Paul Ilie, in *The Surrealist Mode in Spanish Literature* (Ann Arbor: University of Michigan Press, 1968), follows Bousoño's lead, asserting that the primary source of Spanish surrealism is not the French school but that it is born of a combination of the irrational tradition in Spanish art and the dissemination of Freud. C. B. Morris's *Surrealism and Spain: 1920–1936* (Cambridge, England: Cambridge University Press, 1971) exemplifies the opposing view. Morris provides scrupulously documented evidence for the Gallic importation of surrealism. For an overview of the surrealist polemic, see the introduction of Carlos Marcial de Onís, *El surrealismo y cuatro poetas de la Generación del 27* (Madrid: Porrúa, 1974). On repeated occasions, Aleixandre himself rejected the surrealist label. Like many others including Lorca, the poet objected to the term because he equated the ism with automatic writing, the surrealist technique proposed by Breton in the "First Surrealist Manifesto." Even in 1956, Aleixandre denies surrealism because, he writes, "no he creído en lo estrictamente onírico, la escritura 'automática,' ni en la consiguiente abolición de la conciencia artística" (*OC* 2:541) [I have never believed in the strictly oneiric, in 'automatic' writing, nor in the resulting erasure of artistic consciousness].

3. Carlos Bousoño's discussion of sources may be found in chapter 27, "Fuentes de la poesía aleixandrina," *La poesía de Vicente Aleixandre: Imagen, estilo y mundo poético,* 245–53.

4. Harold Bloom, *A Map of Misreading* (New York: Oxford University Press, 1975), 32.

5. The present synthesis of Bloom's theory is based on *The Anxiety of Influence: A Theory of Poetry* (New York: Oxford University Press, 1973) and *A Map of Misreading,* especially on the latter.

6. Bloom, *A Map of Misreading,* 18.

7. Ibid., 7.

8. Some critics would hesitate to call Fray Luis a "Mystic" because, it is argued, the Augustinian seems to have stopped short of achieving the culmination of the mystic experience, the obliteration of the self in God. See, for example, Dámaso Alonso, *Poesía española: Ensayo de métodos y límites estilísticos,* 5th ed. (Madrid: Gredos 1981), 170–92. Because I understand the ode, "A Francisco Salinas," to be a portrayal of that experience, I do not hesitate to use the term "Mystic" in reference to Fray Luis. I discuss that ode, and what I call the "Mystic conceit," in chapter 7.

9. Fray Luis de León, *Poesías,* ed. Francisco Garrote (Salamanca: Almar, 1978), 67.

10. Vicente Aleixandre, *Espadas como labios. La destrucción o el amor,* ed. José Luis Cano (Madrid: Castalia, 1986), 117. All citations from these books are from the Cano edition and appear parenthetically in text and notes as *La destrucción.* I have chosen this edition because in it are reproduced the punctuation and texts as they appeared originally, in 1935.

11. Fray Luis de León, *Poesías,* 88.

12. Gustavo Adolfo Bécquer, *Rimas, Leyendas y Narraciones* (México: Editorial Po-

rrúa, 1981), 8. The full text of Rima 11 may be found in the first pages of chapter 7, where the Bécquer-Aleixandre relation is studied in detail.

13. Ibid., 7.

14. Bloom, *A Map of Misreading*, 32.

15. William Wordsworth, "Ode: Intimations of Immortality from Recollections of Early Childhood," *The Poetical Works of William Wordsworth*, vol. 4, ed. E de Selincourt and Helen Darbishire (Oxford: Oxford University Press, 1947), 279.

16. *Historia del corazón* is not the only moment in Aleixandre's poetic trajectory in which one book makes reply to preceding works, especially to *La destrucción o el amor*, a particularly important ancestor book. The paradise lost to which *Mundo a solas* and *Sombra del paraíso* frequently allude is the erotic *locus amoenus* whose existence and recovery is chronicled in *La destrucción o el amor*, a book of Aleixandre's poetic youth.

17. Richard Dawkins, "Memes: The New Replicators," *The Selfish Gene* (Oxford: Oxford University Press, 1978), 203–15. For further discussion of Dawkins's theory as it applies to cultural and literary intertextuality, see Harold L. Boudreau, "Memes: Intertextuality's Minimal Replicators," in *Intertextual Pursuits: Literary Mediations in Modern Spanish Narrative*, ed. Jeanne Brownlow and John Kronik (Lewisburg, Pennsylvania: Bucknell University Press, 1998), 239–61.

18. George Lakoff and Mark Turner discuss the type of widely disseminated figure exemplified by the hombre/tierra meme. According to these authors, a large number of metaphorical expressions are instances of a reduced number of basic conceptual metaphors, analogies by which we conceptualize life. The human/earth metonym, which serves as a condensed formula facilitating our understanding of life and death and exists in a wide variety of variants, bears out the assertions of these critics. *More than Cool Reason: A Field Guide to the Poetic Metaphor* (Chicago: University of Chicago Press, 1989).

19. The original Latin and the English translation are cited from *Manual of Prayers*, ed. Clarence E. Woodman (New York: The Catholic Publication Society, 1888), 237.

20. Luis de Góngora, *Poems of Góngora*, ed. R. O. Jones (Cambridge: Cambridge University Press, 1966), 87.

21. Francisco de Quevedo, *Poesía varia*, ed. James O. Crosby (Madrid: Cátedra, 1982), 126.

22. Ibid., 255.

23. See the last four chapters of *Text Production*, where Riffaterre discusses surrealist texts. Of equal interest is his "Semantic Incompatibilities in Automatic Writing," in *About French Poetry from Dada to Tel Quel*, ed. Mary Ann Caws (Detroit: Wayne State Press, 1974), 223–41. In this article, Riffaterre's focus is the "automatism effect," which he identifies as one of the salient characteristics of the surrealist text.

CHAPTER 2: POETRY'S DISCURSIVE LOGIC

1. Riffaterre, "Semantic Incompatibilities in Automatic Writing," 224.

2. Citing poems of André Breton and Paul Eduard, Johnnie Gratton observes that there is a widespread critical tendency to focus almost exclusively on the imagery of surrealist poems. Gratton contends that the image-based tack "obeys an implicit, mythical protocol as to how surrealist poetry should be read and appreciated. And, in the absence of any question of an integrating context, it totally neglects a vital principle of literary structuring, according to which connotation derives above all

from the textual/intertextual axis. The logic of this overall critical set destines it to grasp the surrealist poem as little more than a sequence of concatenated images." "Poetics of the Surrealist Image," *Romantic Review* 69, no. 1–2 (January 1978): 110.

3. Jonathan Culler emphasizes the importance of speech acts in naturalizing poetry. From what Culler says, one may appreciate the correlation that exists between speech acts and genre: "one might say that our notion of the range of possible speech acts which a literary text might perform is the very basis of literary naturalization, because it provides us with a set of purposes which might determine the coherence of a particular text. Once a purpose is postulated (praise of a mistress, meditation on death, etc.) one has a focal point which governs the interpretation of metaphor, the organization of oppositions and the identification of relevant formal features." *Structuralist Poetics: Structuralism, Linguistics, and the Study of Literature* (Ithaca: Cornell University Press, 1975), 147.

4. Alastair Fowler develops the notion of "generic horizon" in *Kinds of Literature* (Cambridge, Mass.: Harvard University Press, 1982), 258–60.

5. I have reiterated one of Fowler's basic assertions as to the usefulness of genre, applying it to the entirety of poetry's narrative structure.

6. Fowler, *Kinds of Literature*, 256.

7. Ibid., 260, 250.

8. Pedro Salinas. *Poesías completas* (Barcelona: Barral Editores, 1971), 158.

9. The closing poem of *Seguro azar*, "Triunfo suyo," acts as the counterpart of "Fe mía." The triumph referred to in the title is that of chance, which Salinas personifies as a silent entity. In this piece, as in "Fe mía," the abstract "azar" is given iconic form. Here, chance is lyrically garbed in the trappings of the Beatific Vision from whose countenance now emanates not the divine light of salvation but the overwhelming light of silence: "—¡irresistible luz!—/ su rostro de sin remedio / eternidad, él, silencio" [—irresistible light!—his countenance of inevitable eternity, he, silence]. Ibid., 162.

10. Two critics who do pay heed to narrative aspects of poetry are Jonathan Culler and Michael Riffaterre. In "Semantic Incompatibilities in Automatic Writing," Riffaterre analyzes two Breton texts from *Poisson soluble* as conventional anecdotes whose predictable sequence only underscores the disparity of the irrational style in which these stories are narrated. For his part, Culler focuses on narrative discourse, in particular on the role and effects of apostrophe in poetry. "Apostrophe," *The Pursuit of Signs: Semiotics, Literature, Deconstruction* (Ithaca: Cornell University Press, 1981), 135–54. Also connected to narrative structure, and thus to poetic intelligibility, is the notion of persona, which Culler discusses with accustomed clarity in *Structuralist Poetics*, 131–60.

11. Gérard Genette, *Narrative Discourse: An Essay in Method*, trans. Jane E. Lewin (Ithaca: Cornell University Press, 1980). Genette elaborates the notion of narrative "mood" and "voice"—which are based on the grammatical categories of the same name—in chapters 4 and 5.

12. Genette's label for the structure of this prototype is "homodiegetic." That is, the narrator and the focal character are one and the same. Like that of the novel, the narratological repertoire of poetry is varied. For instance, there are poems—the eclogue comes to mind—organized as dialogue or quoted speech. In others, the narrator, though the vocal source of the poem, is not the focal character. Rather, this function is allotted to a human subject whose inner world becomes the poem's narrative material. This scheme, a highly innovative one, applies to much of the text of Lorca's "Preciosa y el aire" [Preciosa and the Air] *(Romancero gitano)*, where the image and action of the lascivious wind can be taken as the projection of Preciosa's

imagination, in particular, as her fear of her own awakening sexuality. Aleixandre employs this sort of interior narrative in poeticizing the preverbal world of an anonymous human subject. This mode of narrative presentation is discussed in detail in chapter 3. There are also narrative schemes in which the poetic speaker is in no way identifiable with the bard, being instead a non-human entity. One such example is Bécquer's Rima 5, where the cosmic enigma, the "espíritu sin nombre" [nameless spirit], enunciates an elaborate self-definition. Aleixandre's "Soy el destino," "Mina" and "El frío" (La destrucción o el amor) are organized on this same narrative design, which is examined in chapter 4.

13. Salinas, Poesías completas, 124–25.

14. A concrete example of this prototype is Carolina Coronado's "La luna es una ausencia" [The Moon is an Absence]. Aleixandre explicitly invokes Coronado in a poem of the same name, "La luna es una ausencia" (La destrucción 197), which he dedicates to the poet.

15. As for generic hybridization, there are abundant examples in Salinas. Salinas is especially fond of grafting epic elements onto his texts, as reflected in "Don de la materia." Indeed, Seguro azar opens and closes with an epic flavor. The liminal poem, "Cuartilla" [The Empty Page], casts Salinas's poetic endeavor as a military campaign in which the pen, now taking the place of the sword, is pitted in battle against chance. Referring to itself in the face of "el azar," the poem asks, "¿Vencer, quién vencerá? [Vanquish, who is likely to vanquish?]. The final poem of the book, "Triunfo suyo" [His Triumph], makes reply: "el azar" [chance]. The figuration of triumphant chance is particularly complex: "el azar" not only appears as a sort of Beatific Vision, as previously noted; this victor, who has an "imperial rostro" [imperial countenance], is also part triumphant monarch. Salinas's penchant for the epic often surfaces most unexpectedly, for example in the love poem, "Amor, amor, catástrofe" [Love, Love, Catastrophe] (La voz a ti debida), where the portrayed goal of the poem—the lovers' achieving their bare essence—is mapped as a crusade. Poesías completas, 107, 162, 248.

The aforementioned eight-syllable line in "Don de la materia" is itself a sign of the poem's mock epic character. This metric option links Salinas to poets such as Góngora and Quevedo, who frequently employ the "romance" [the ballad form] to parodic ends. See, for example, Góngora's "Leandro y Hero," Poems of Góngora, 104–7, or Quevedo's "Testamento de Don Quijote," Poesía varia, 445–51.

16. Bécquer, Rimas, Leyendas, y Narraciones, 3. Salinas, like Aleixandre and other Generation of '27 poets, is most conscious of Bécquer and responds to him in his own verse. A further example in Salinas is "Agua en la noche, serpiente indecisa" (Presagios), Poesías completas, 54. The poem's point of departure—the poet facing the enigma—its yo-tú structure, and development as a paradoxically elusive and imprecise definition, are signs of Bécquer's presence. Salinas inverts Bécquerian theme by staging the poem as a quest not for spiritual essence but for a cognitive one. Ironically, Salinas's goal proves just as impossible to realize as Bécquer's pursuit of the cosmic arcanum. Aleixandre's reaction to Bécquer is the subject of chapter 7.

17. Salinas, Poesías completas, 110.

18. José Ortega y Gasset, La deshumanización del arte y otros ensayos de estética (Madrid: Espasa-Calpe, 1987). See especially "Unas gotas de fenomenología," 57–61.

19. Garcilaso de la Vega, Obras, ed. T. Navarro Tomás (Madrid: Espasa-Calpe, 1948), 122.

20. Antonio Machado, Poesías completas (Madrid: Espasa-Calpe, 1982), 108–9.

21. Ibid., 329.

22. The etymology and function of prosopopeia is examined in depth by Paul de Man. De Man mildly chides Riffaterre for not having taken apostrophe, and thereby prosopopeia, into account in his theory of lyric semiosis. Referring to Riffaterre's analysis of a Victor Hugo poem, de Man asserts that, "description, if description there is, is embedded within a very different frame. The poem . . . is addressed to something or someone, staged as an address of one subject to another in a 'je-tu' situation which can hardly be called descriptive." "Hypogram and Inscription: Michael Riffaterre's Poetics of Reading," *Diacritics* 11, no. 4 (Winter 1981): 32. In response, Riffaterre adjusts his own reading of Hugo, showing how prosopopeia is tied to other figural elements of the poem. "Prosopopeia," *Yale French Studies* 69 (1985): 107–23.

23. Culler, "Apostrophe," 142.

24. Machado, *Poesías completas*, 275.

25. Culler, "Apostrophe," 152.

26. Culler cites major studies of the ode, including George N. Shuster's *The English Ode from Milton to Keats*, to show that apostrophe, despite its nuclear role in this genre, tends to be either ignored or summarily dismissed as an insignificant or merely conventional element of poetry. Ibid., 135–39.

27. Percy Bysshe Shelley, *The Complete Poetical Works of Percy Bysshe Shelley*, ed. Thomas Hutchinson (New York: Oxford University Press, 1956), 602.

CHAPTER 3: NARRATING THE SUBCONSCIOUS

1. Robert Hughes, *The Shock of the New* (New York: Knopf, 1981), 29.

2. Pedro Salinas, in reviewing *Espadas como labios*, spoke of the primary referent of Aleixandre's surrealist poetry in this way: "although, judging by titles ('El vals' [The Waltz], 'Toro' [Bull], 'Resaca' [Undertow], 'Forma sobre el mar' [Form upon the Sea]), some of the subjects treated seem to refer to external realities, they are always conceived of as independent psychological entities that are lyrically translated through perhaps a somewhat unhealthy, but deep and penetrating, sensibility." Qtd. in José Luis Cano, introduction to *Espadas como labios. La destrucción o el amor* (Madrid: Castalia, 1986), 22. Originally published in *Indice Literario* 1, no. 5 (December 1932).

3. This is not to say that "Sin luz" and other poems—"La selva y el mar" among them—have not been taken as referring to the natural world. In *La poesía de Vicente Aleixandre*, Carlos Bousoño praises Aleixandre's landscapes as "magnificent descriptions of nature." As previously noted, the poet's world has also been subject to psychoanalytic readings. "Sin luz," for example, is interpreted by Paul Ilie as a projection of Aleixandre's personal psychic turmoil. Ilie asserts that the crushed wing of the nightingale (penultimate stanza) means that Aleixandre's power of flight has been crippled, his song drowned in the subterranean waters of his mind. *The Surrealist Mode in Spanish Literature*, 46.

4. Among poems based on the poet-before-the-beloved scene are: "El amor no es relieve" *(Pasión de la tierra);* "Resaca," "El más bello amor," "Palabras," "Ida" *(Espadas como labios);* "La selva y el mar," "No busques, no," "Unidad en ella," "Soy el destino," "A ti, viva," "A la muerta," "Canción a una muchacha muerta" *(La destrucción o el amor);* "Humano ardor" *(Mundo a solas);* "Sierpe de amor" *(Sombra del paraíso);* "Tendidos, de noche" *(Historia del corazón).* Aleixandre's interpretation of the conventions of love poetry is discussed in chapter 5, which treats the role of genre in *La destrucción o el amor.*

5. Dorit Cohn, *Transparent Minds: Narrative Modes for Presenting Consciousness in Fiction* (Princeton: Princeton University Press, 1978).

6. Other poems from *La destrucción o el amor* that are also largely recuperable as narrated psychic events, or psycho-narrations, include "Noche sinfónica," "El mar ligero," "Tristeza o pájaro," "Verbena," and "El escarabajo." Of these, "Noche sinfónica" and "Verbena" are the least problematic, this due to the relatively clear visibility of their focal subjects. Like the much anthologized "El vals" *(Espadas como labios)*, the human referent of these pieces are fete-goers whose repressed sexuality acts as the narrative core. Another outstanding psycho-narration is the prose poem, "La muerte o antesala de consulta" *(Pasión de la tierra)*. Here, the narrative subject is a group of patients waiting their turn at a doctor's office.

7. The presence of Rubén Darío in the work of Aleixandre is a constant. One such example is "Fulguración del as" *(Pasión de la tierra)*, in which Darío's "Era un aire suave . . ." *(Prosas profanas)* is similarly fragmented and recast as one of the poem's miniatures. In the metapoem, "La dicha" *(La destrucción o el amor)*, "Era un aire suave . . ." acts as the poem's primary referent. "La dicha"—and Aleixandre's complex relation to Darío—is analyzed in further detail in chapter 5. In a later poem, "Entre dos oscuridades, un relámpago" [Between Two Darknesses, a Flash of Lightning] *(Historia del corazón)*, Aleixandre cites Darío's "Lo fatal" *(Cantos de vida y esperanza)* in the epigraph, "Y no saber adónde vamos, ni de dónde venimos" (*OC* 1:781) [And not to know where we are going, nor where we come from]. While Aleixandre's poem develops as a response to Darío, it also invokes Bécquer via title, which is paraphrastic of the first verse of Rima 69, "Al brillar de un relámpago nacemos" [In a flash of lightning are we born]. Having convened these ancestors, Aleixandre puts forth his own reply to the existential enigma they pose: "Sabemos adónde vamos y de dónde venimos. Entre dos oscuridades, un relámpago" [We know where we are bound and from where we have come. Between two darknesses, a flash of lightning]. The critic who has lent closest attention to the Aleixandre-Darío relationship in particular is José Luis Cano, who cites "Entre dos oscuridades, un relámpago" in "Tres poetas frente al misterio (Darío, Machado, Aleixandre)," *Cuadernos Americanos* 108, no. 1 (1960): 227–31. Two other notable examples of Aleixandre's long-standing poetic ties to Darío are "Conocimiento de Rubén Darío" *(Poemas de la consumación)* and "Tres retratos de Rubén Darío" *(Nuevos encuentros)*. The first piece is discussed by Ramón Espejo-Saavedra in "Conocimiento de Rubén Darío," *Tropos* 22, no. 1 (Spring 1996): 51–62. The critic points out that in this late poem Aleixandre feels a kinship with Darío and uses the elder's experience in order to explain his own view of life and poetry. In "Tres retratos de Rubén Darío," Aleixandre writes of his poetic initiation when, in the fall of 1917, Dámaso Alonso gave him the first edition of Darío's *El canto errante*. Aleixandre vividly recalls that, "Rubén Darío había sido para mí . . . el revelador de la poesía" [Rubén Darío had been for me the revealer of poetry] (*OC* 2:450).

8. In both the 1924 and 1928 manifestoes, André Breton cites Freud as the seminal influence on surrealism. In the 1924 manifesto, Breton describes Freud as the great vindicator of the irrational thanks to whose discoveries, "the human explorer will be able to carry his investigations much further, authorized as he will henceforth be not to confine himself solely to the most summary realities. . . . But it is worth noting that no means has been designated a priori for carrying out this undertaking, that until further notice it can be construed to be the province of poets as well as scholars, and that its success is not dependent upon the more or less capricious paths that will be followed." *Manifestoes of Surrealism*, trans. Richard Seaver and Helen R. Lane (Ann Arbor: University of Michigan Press, 1990), 10.

9. "Automatismo controlado" is coined by Luis Antonio de Villena in his discussion of Aleixandre's surrealism. Preliminary study to *Pasión de la tierra* (Madrid: Narcea, S. A., 1977).

10. Andrew Debicki lends special attention to "defamiliarization" as it applies to Aleixandre's poetry and focuses on how that technique affects reader reception. By way of illustration, Debicki cites "Toro" *(Espadas como labios)* and "En la plaza" *(Historia del corazón)*. "The Reader's Experience in Vicente Aleixandre's *Historia del corazón*," *The American Hispanist* 4:30–31 (1978): 12–16.

11. Santa Teresa de Jesús, "Véante mis ojos," in *An Anthology of Spanish Poetry*, vol. 1, ed. Arthur Terry (London: Pergamon Press, 1965), 65. The editor, Arthur Terry, notes that the four lines cited from Santa Teresa are an "a lo divino" gloss of the theme, "Véante mis ojos / y muérame yo luego, / dulce amor mío, / lo que yo más quiero" [May my eyes see you and may I thereupon die, my sweet love, which is what I most desire]. Terry quotes the theme from *Cancionero* of Montemayor (1554), *Biblioteca de autores españoles*, vol. 1 (Madrid: 1930).

12. I owe the "beber en los ojos del amado" connection to Vicente Cabrera, *Tres poetas a la luz de la metáfora: Salinas, Aleixandre y Guillén* (Madrid: Gredos, 1975), 155–59.

13. Anthony Leo Geist takes a different tack to the matter of Aleixandre's abstraction of the human. For Geist, this strategy involves a systematic deconstruction and decentering of the subject. The critic notes that Aleixandre's subject is the "tú" of love poetry who appears in undifferentiated form. "'Esas fronteras deshechas': Sexuality, Textuality, and Ideology in Vicente Aleixandre's *Espadas como labios*," in *The Surrealist Adventure in Spain*, ed. C. Brian Morris (Ottowa: Dovehouse Editions, 1991), 181–90.

14. Two examples of the "caza de amor" in Golden Age poetry are Gil Vicente's "Halcón que se atreve," in Arthur Terry, *An Anthology of Spanish Poetry*, 16, and "Tras de un amoroso lance," of San Juan de la Cruz, *Obras escogidas*, ed. Ignacio B. Anzoátegui (Madrid: Espasa-Calpe, 1974), 35. The refrain of San Juan's poem is "le di a la caza alcance" [I reached my quarry]. The Saint usurps the hawking imagery of secular poetry in order to express his firm belief in God's accessibility and to emphasize the positive character of death, which unites one in divine love.

15. Góngora, *Poems of Góngora*, 40.

16. At least one other fragment of "Las águilas" points to Gongorine intertextuality. The reference to the eagles as "arpas furiosas" (last strophe) recalls "Soledad Primera," wherein song birds are described as "Pintadas aves—cítaras de pluma—/ coronaban la bárbara capilla" [Painted birds—zithers of plume—crowned the rustic chapel] ("Soledad Primera," 556–57). Ibid., 55. "Las águilas" is not the only, nor the earliest, example of Aleixandre's reworking of Góngora. In "Toro" *(Espadas como labios)*, eros appears in the form of a celestial bull whose power is unleashed in heavenly orgasm, an "abandono asombroso del bulto que deshace / sus fuerzas casi cósmicas como leche de estrellas" *(La destrucción 65)* [astonishing abandon of the body that unleashes its nearly cosmic force like stellar cream"]. As in "Las águilas," the Gongorine genealogy of "Toro" is also advertised lexically, by way of "mentir," of the first verse, "Esa mentira o casta."

CHAPTER 4: THE VOICE OF DESIRE

1. Other examples of this sort of dramatically voiced introit are "No busques, no," and "Soy el destino," which begin in almost identical fashion: the first with "Yo te

he querido como nunca" [I have loved you as never before], the second with the affirmative "Sí, te he querido como nunca" (*La destrucción* 120, 191) [Yes, I have loved you as never before]. In these cases, title and first verse not only call attention to voice but also suggest that the texts arise from a post-lovemaking situation. Another instance of note is "Ven siempre, ven" [Come Always, Come]. The first verse—"No te acerques. Tu frente, tu ardiente frente, tu encendida frente" (*La destrucción*, 134) [Do not come near. Your brow, your ardent brow, your burning brow]—seems to contradict the titular imperative. In tandem, however, the title and the opening verse encapsulate the vacillating invitation-to-love on which the text develops.

2. There are a number of enigma poems in *La destrucción o el amor*. Several, such as "Soy el destino" and "El frío," are cast on the self-defining-arcanum design of Rima 5 that makes up the first part of "Mina." Several others—"Quiero saber," "La luz," "Canción a una muchacha muerta"—develop in a complementary fashion, as the questioning of the poetic persona, that is, like the off-stage query that sets "Mina" into motion. For example, "Quiero saber" begins with, "Dime pronto el secreto de tu existencia" [Tell me soon the secret of your existence] and "Canción a una muchacha muerta" with, "Dime, dime el secreto de tu corazón virgen" [Tell me, tell me the secret of your virginal heart] (*La destrucción* 153, 165). Enigma poems express Aleixandre's concern with knowledge, specifically with the sort of knowledge that should be sought. Promoted therein is carnal knowledge, the direct savoring of love, the polar opposite of intellectualized or ideal constructions of love. Guillermo Carnero discusses the question of knowledge in the later poetry of Aleixandre in "'Conocer' y 'saber' en *Poemas de la consumación* y *Diálogos del conocimiento*," *Cuadernos Hispanoamericanos* 276 (June 1973): 571–79.

3. Bécquer, *Rimas, Leyendas y Narraciones*, 5–6.

4. Confusing poetic structure with reality can dramatically alter the reading of a poem. This is graphically illustrated by Michel Gauthier's analysis of "Soy el destino," a piece narratively akin to "Mina." Gauthier, following a psychoanalytic tack, takes the poem as referring to the authorial mind. I single out Gauthier's study because it is a keenly sensitive and stimulating reading of Aleixandre marred by overlooking essentials, namely the identity of narrator and the circumstantial fiction out of which the poem arises. "Vicente Aleixandre, narcisse écartelé," *Les Langues Néo-Latines* 176 (March–April 1966): 84–104. For his part, Leopoldo de Luis suggests the possible dangers involved in relating too closely Aleixandre's poetry to his person. The critic observes that in 1935, when Aleixandre was in full health after a prolonged illness, he was to write his most pessimistic work, *Mundo a solas*. *Vida y obra de Vicente Aleixandre* (Madrid: Espasa-Calpe, 1978), 133.

5. Duque de Rivas, *Don Alvaro o la fuerza del sino,* ed. Alberto Sánchez (Madrid: Cátedra, 1982).

6. There are many instances of the lexical pun in *La destrucción o el amor*. Among them, the identical play on "luna"-"espejo" [moon-mirror] in "Corazón en suspenso" [Suspended Heart], a poem whose ostensible point of departure is the contemplation of the moon. Here, the generation of "espejo" from "luna" is central to the complex figurative amalgam related to the celestial orb. Exploiting the ambiguity of "luna," the poet variously describes the heart-moon as "colgada" [hung], "suspendida sin hilo" [suspended without wire], "sin un alma o cristal / contra lo que doblar un rayo bello" [without a soul or glass against which to reflect a beautiful beam], and as "espectro" [spectrum or specter], *La destrucción* 155. This particular figuration serves to express the Aleixandrean theme of the artificial, of false reflections of amorous reality. Another example of the lexical pun may be seen in "Cobra" in which the poet's play on the word "niña," which means both "girl" and

ocular "pupil," produces seemingly random imagery, as the fourth stanza may serve to illustrate:

Niñas como lagunas,
ojos como esperanzas,
desnudos como hojas
cobra pasa lasciva mirando a su otro cielo.

(*La destrucción* 202)

[Pupils like lakes,
Eyes like expectations,
Bare like leaves,
The cobra lasciviously passes looking at its other heaven.]

The girl-pupil pun is also exploited in "La dicha," which is analyzed in chapter 5.

7. Among the vast majority of Aleixandre critics, the ambiguous "o" [or] of the title is interpreted as a conjunctive, whereby destruction and love become paradoxically equivalent. This interpretation, like that of so many other aspects of Aleixandre's poetry, was established by Carlos Bousoño. Bousoño insists that the "o" works as a conjunction of equivalence and analyzes Aleixandre's texts accordingly. The critic also points out that the "o" is most frequently employed in *La destrucción o el amor*, followed by *Espadas como labios*, and is relatively scarce elsewhere. See chapter 16, "La conjunción identificativa 'o,'" *La poesía de Vicente Aleixandre*, 163–70. To my knowledge, only Lucie Personneaux and Céline Garcia have considered other meanings of the "o." Although Personneaux briefly entertains the disjunctive sense of the grammar word, she nonetheless cites its conjunctive meaning as the most frequent, and significant, in Aleixandre. *Vicente Aleixandre ou une poésie du suspens: Recherches sur le réel et l'imaginaire*, 42–43. For her part, Garcia, referring to "Instante" *(Espadas como labios)*, suggests that the "o" has a visual, iconographic dimension. Unfortunately, Garcia does not pursue this insight. "L'Espace Scénique dans L'Oeuvre de Vicente Aleixandre," *Iris* (1989): 86–87.

8. The information on the title comes by way of Leopoldo de Luis who, in *Vida y obra de Vicente Aleixandre*, mentions other such title changes, including that of *Pasión de la tierra*, originally *Hombre de tierra*, and that of *Mundo a solas*, originally *Destino del hombre*. Gustavo Correa also emphasizes the semantic function of Aleixandre's titles, and points to the close relation between main titles and individual poems. Among other things, the critic notes the thematic change heralded by *Historia del corazón*, which differs from the titular pattern of previous books. "Los títulos de los libros de poesía de Vicente Aleixandre," in *Vicente Aleixandre: A Critical Appraisal*, ed. Santiago Daydí-Tolson (Ypsilanti: Bilingual Press, 1979), 86–93.

9. Overtly vocal titles, apart from those found in *La destrucción o el amor*, are quite rare in Aleixandre. I am aware of these examples: "Madre, madre" *(Espadas como labios);* "Cantad, pájaros" *(Nacimiento último);* "Otra no amo," "Ten esperanza" *(Historia del corazón)*.

10. Aleixandre characterizes the mission of his poetry as both universal and pragmatic. The poet relays this ideal in two aphorisms: "Servir: la única libertad de la poesía" [To serve: poetry's only freedom]; "Hay muchos modos de tener conciencia de un destino común. Uno de ellos es la poesía" [There are many means of being aware of a common destiny. One of them is poetry]. See Aleixandre's aphorisms, "Poesía, moral, público," *OC* 2:656–66.

11. Breton, *Manifestoes of Surrealism*, 10.

12. Rodrigo Fernández Carvajal observes that each of Aleixandre's books is con-

structed according to a specific and determined concept of time. "El tiempo en la poesía de Vicente Aleixandre," *Corcel* 5–6 (1944): 41–43.

CHAPTER 5: LA RAZÓN DE LA SINRAZÓN: THE LOGIC OF GENRE

1. I am heartened to find that I am not alone in this reading. The acute Aleixandrean critic, Vicente Cabrera, also interprets the poem as a description of love achieved, adding that it is through "ella," the beloved, that unity or fusion with the world is realized. *Tres poetas a la luz de la metáfora: Salinas, Aleixandre y Guillén* (Madrid: Gredos, 1975), 153. To the same critic I am indebted for his insight that the poem is built on Romantic commonplaces. Ibid., 152–55.

2. An example of the flower-on-the-edge-of-the-abyss may be seen in Bécquer's Rima 22. The ostensible intention of this poem, like that of the introductory verses of "Unidad en ella," is to express the igneous danger of beauty. Here is the short piece in its entirety:

¿Cómo vive esa rosa que has prendido
    junto a tu corazón?
Nunca hasta ahora contemplé en la tierra
    sobre el volcán la flor.

[How survives that rose that you have placed
    Close to your heart?
Never until now have I seen on Earth
    The flower on the edge of the volcano.]

Rimas, Leyendas y Narraciones, 22. Michael Riffaterre alerted me to the flower-on-the-edge-of-the-abyss hypogram, which he cites in his discussion of descriptive systems in *Semiotics of Poetry* (Bloomington: Indiana University Press, 1984), 41.

3. San Juan, in "Llama de amor viva," expresses the love/destruction conceit in this way: "Matando, muerte en vida la has trocado" [By killing, death into life have you transformed]. *Obras escogidas*, 28.

4. The verb "querer" is titularly highlighted in two poems in *La destrucción o el amor*, "Quiero saber" and "Quiero pisar." In these pieces, the verb carries out the exact function that it has in "Unidad en ella." That is, "quiero" frames each of the narrations as a wish or daydream wherein the narrator directs himself to a yearned-for but ephemeral "tú." In these pieces the figuration of that "tú" is most hallucinatory and suggests, as in "Unidad en ella," that idle wishing born of sexual repression produces phantasmagoria. The imagery of these poems is comparable to many early paintings of Salvador Dalí, who frequently portrays troubling psychosexual conflicts.

5. Bécquer, *Rimas, Leyendas y Narraciones*, 10.

6. The "unidad" of "Unidad en ella," in that it means both "unity" and "solitary oneness," is an instance of syllepsis, a sort of punning whereby a word simultaneously contains opposite and seemingly incompatible meanings. Syllepsis is very much a part of the main title of *La destrucción o el amor*, where the "o" is at once a conjunctive and a disjunctive. Michael Riffaterre, who analyzes syllepsis in Derrida, asserts that this rhetorical figure, in and of itself, constitutes a sign of literariness and, in particular, creates literary "undecidability." "Syllepsis," *Critical Inquiry* 6 (Summer 1980): 625–38.

7. An instance of Death-as-Woman may be found in Rubén Darío's allegorical "La página blanca" [The White Page]. Here, "Ella" (la Muerte) brings up the rear of Darío's lyric caravan as it passes across the desert of the white page. Wrapped in dark clothes, She is "la Reina invencible, la bella inviolada" [the invincible Queen, the inviolate beauty]. *Prosas profanas y otros poemas*, 136.

8. San Juan, *Obras escogidas*, 28.

9. Fray Luis de León, *Poesías*, 88.

10. "Se querían," one of the final poems in *La destrucción o el amor*, is also an ode and, along with "No busques, no," is one of the few poems in which a past tense is a prominent textual feature. The love story expressed by way of the string of imperfect tenses throughout is summarized in the last words, "Se querían, sabedlo" [They loved each other, know this] (*La destrucción* 221). The apostrophe acts to contextualize the amatory anecdote as an exemplum, thereby relaying the didactic intention of the poem. Although *La destrucción o el amor* is the most intensely odic of all Aleixandrean books, examples of this lyric kind are to be found elsewhere. For example: "Fulguración del as" (*Espadas como labios*), "Al amor" (*Mundo a solas*), "Al hombre," "Al cielo" and "Primavera en la tierra" (*Sombra del paraíso*), "En la plaza" (*Historia del corazón*), "A mi perro" (*Retratos con nombre*).

11. The other metapoems, that is, poems whose major thematic thrust is the question of poetry, and art in general, are "El desnudo," "Humana voz," "Cuerpo de piedra" and "Aurora insumisa." The two studies that lend closest attention to metapoetry in Aleixandre are Vicente Cabrera's *Tres poetas a la luz de la metáfora: Salinas, Aleixandre y Guillén* and Jonathan Mayhew's "'Límites y espejo': Linguistic Self-Consciousness in the Poetry of Vicente Aleixandre," *Modern Language Notes* 105:2 (March 1990): 303–15. These studies cite no examples from *La destrucción o el amor*, an omission I attribute to the fact that this book, unlike most others, does not overtly signal metapoetry at the textual outset. For example, *Espadas como labios* opens with the Lord Byron epigraph—"What is a poet? What is he worth? What does he do? He is a babbler."—and is followed by the self-defining "Mi voz." Aleixandre's practice of placing explicit metapoems in the liminal position of his books is repeated in *Sombra del paraíso* ("El poeta"), *Nacimiento último* ("Palabras"), *En un vasto dominio* ("¿Para quién escribo?"), and *Poemas de la consumación* ("Las palabras del poeta").

12. John Keats, *The Complete Poetical Works and Letters of John Keats*, ed. Horace E. Scudder (Cambridge, Mass.: The Riverside Press, 1899), 135.

13. The question of life versus art is a constant in Aleixandre, as previous discussion may have served to suggest. Two of the most spectacular instances of this theme may be found in "Soy el destino" (*La destrucción o el amor*) and "El poeta" (*Sombra del paraíso*). In the latter, Aleixandre recommends that his very book be cast aside in favor of the direct experience of life.

14. Darío, *Prosas profanas y otros poems*, 89.

15. Ibid., 91.

16. The complement to the complex and negative Venus description of "La dicha" is "Hija de la mar" [Daughter of the Sea], a poem whose Venus is a living and anonymous "muchacha," a "naturaleza viva" antithetical to the statuary goddess of Darío's art.

17. Aleixandre's representation of Darío's poetry as a beautiful and desirable woman has a precedent in Darío himself who, as in "Mía" and "Dice Mía," figures his poetry as his beloved. *Prosas profanas y otros poems*, 113–15. It is worth noting that Darío's female personification of his poetry was taken up as well by Juan Ramón Jiménez, the mentor of Aleixandre's poetic generation. In the well-known "Vino,

primero, pura" [At first, she was pure] (*Eternidades*, 1916–17), Juan Ramón describes the development of his poetry as an on-going love affair, at different junctures of which his lyric beloved appeared in various stylistic attire, including that of Modernismo. *Libros de poesía* (Madrid: Aguilar, 1957), 577.

18. Darío, *Prosas profanas y otros poemas*, 91.

19. Aleixandre's complex reaction to Darío is reflected in a letter written to Carlos Bousoño: "Rubén Darío fue el primer gran poeta que tuve entre las manos, y aunque no me influyó en mis primeros poemas, le debo más de lo que parece. La familiaridad en el verso con su materia verbal, el número y el ritmo, ese fluidísimo conocimiento que ha de estar en la sangre del poeta, creo que a él se lo debo más que a nadie. Sin embargo, la estricta sensibilidad modernista me fue ajena siempre, y aunque en 1918 leí a los poetas de esa escuela pasada, yo los admiraba, pero no me influían" [Rubén Darío was the first great poet that I read and, although he did not influence my first poems, I owe to him more than it seems. His familiarity with the verbal material of poetry, with meter and rhyme, that fluid knowledge that must be in the poet's blood, I believe I owe all of this to him more than to anybody else. Nonetheless, the strictly Modernista sensibility was always distant from me and, even though in 1918 I read the poets of that school, I admired them but they had no influence on me]. Bousoño, *La poesía de Vicente Aleixandre*, 9.

20. Bloom, *A Map of Misreading*, chapter 8.

21. Santiago Daydí-Tolson, in speaking of *La destrucción o el amor*, sharply enunciates the relation between Aleixandre's art and his ideological concerns: "Aleixandre has conceived a metaphorical world, a pure literary construction, to make visible his own interpretative vision of man in nature." "Vicente Aleixandre: A New Voice of Tradition," in *Vicente Aleixandre: A Critical Appraisal*, ed. Santiago Daydí-Tolson (Ipsilanti: Bilingual Press, 1981), 13. The same volume in which Daydí-Tolson's article appears—*Vicente Aleixandre: A Critical Appraisal*—contains a number of other fine articles and an excellent bibliography.

CHAPTER 6: LUZ NO USADA

1. There are numerous examples of Aleixandre's consciousness of, and admiration for, other poets, both ancestors and contemporaries. In addition to already cited instances, others include: "A Fray Luis de León" and "A don Luis de Góngora" *(Nacimiento último);* "Gustavo Adolfo Bécquer, en dos tiempos," "Tres retratos de Rubén Darío" *(Nuevos encuentros);* "Noche mía," subtitled "Homenaje a San Juan de la Cruz" *(Poemas varios).*

Alice Poust, in analyzing Aleixandre's comments on literature, underlines that Aleixandre's understanding of poetry entails a "unity of sense." That is, the poet sees his own work, as well as that of other poets, as part of the greater tradition. "Phenomenological Hermeneutics and Vicente Aleixandre's Self-Reading," *Revista de Estudios Hispánicos* 26:3 (October 1992): 327–43.

2. Bloom, *A Map of Misreading*, 198.

3. Ibid., 32.

4. In "Love and Honour in the 'Novelas Sentimentales' of Diego de San Pedro and Juan de Flores," Pamela Waley underlines the conventionality of the conceptual play on death-life in the secular tradition of the Renaissance. Referring to the *Tractado de amores* of Diego de San Pedro, the critic observes that "the inspiration, the ideas, the motives and the expression . . . , as well as the conception of love that dominates it, derive principally from the same sources as the poetry of the cancioneros. Verse

is used in various ways in the story itself, as devices on shields, as inscriptions, as a song, and poems are interpolated in the work. What Gil y Gaya calls the leit-motif of the novel is the poetic commonplace *muero porque no muero*; it is written over the door of Arnalte's house in the wilderness, it is embroidered on his cloak, he uses it himself to describe his way of life." *Bulletin of Hispanic Studies* 43–44 (1966–67): 253.

5. The example comes by way of Dámaso Alonso, who lucidly discusses the "a lo divino" transformation of secular literature in the Spanish tradition and the place of San Juan and Santa Teresa therein. *Poesía española: Ensayo de métodos y límites estilísticos*, 217–56.

6. Fray Luis de León, *Poesías*, 68–69.

7. Dámaso Alonso, "La poesía de Vicente Aleixandre," in *Ensayos sobre poesía española*, 368. The most complete study on Aleixandre's relation to the Mystics is Vicente Gaos's "Fray Luis de León, 'fuente' de Aleixandre," in *Temas y problemas de la literatura española* (Madrid: Guadarrama, 1959), 341–59. Gaos, who concentrates on stylistic similarities between Aleixandre and Fray Luis, remarks that of all poetic sources including Góngora, Fray Luis is the closest and most extensive one in Aleixandre. Carlos Bousoño refutes Gaos's thesis and, citing Aleixandre's Luisinian paraphrase, "Allá por las remotas / luces o aceros aún no usados," asserts that this allusion is cosmetic. *La poesía de Vicente Aleixandre*, 250. For his part, Louis Bourne goes to some length to show that Aleixandre could not be considered a Mystic in the proper sense since he does not espouse a belief in God or in any other divinity. "The Spiritualization of Matter in the Poetry of Vicente Aleixandre," *Revista de Letras* 22 (June 1974): 166–89.

8. Fray Luis, *Poesías*, 67.

9. To my knowledge, this apostrophic verse, despite its anomalous character in the poem's narrative pattern, has never been singled out by readers of Aleixandre. This omission would reinforce Jonathan Culler's assertion, in "Apostrophe," that apostrophe is generally "embarrassing" to readers, who therefore tend to ignore or overlook this rhetorical figure in their analyses. Be that as it may, the apostrophic "Oh" of the present example, like the vocal incursion of "Pero . . ." in "Sin luz," carries out an important structural role.

10. Darío, *Prosas profanas y otros poemas*, 89.

11. The genesis of Aleixandre's delicate focalizer is not exclusively Daríoesque. The swooning, as well as the chromatic detail of the eyes—the mauve "ojeras violáceas"—recall the Belle Epoch world satirized by Aleixandre in pieces such as "La muerte o antesala de consulta" *(Pasión de la tierra)*, "El vals," "Salón" *(Espadas como labios)*, or in "Bomba en la ópera" *(En un vasto dominio)*. In contrast to "La selva y el mar," in these pieces Aleixandre's portraiture of this demi-monde is quite explicit. The world of the salon is tuxedoed and tightly corseted, being populated by bourgeois who step to the tune of the waltz rather than to the voice of destiny, the "sordo rumor" of instinct. E. C. Graf lends close and sensitive attention to Aleixandre's sardonic and conceptually complex treatment of the Belle Epoch world in "May I Have This Dance?: Unveiling Vicente Aleixandre's 'El vals,'" *Romanic Review* 85 (March 1994): 313–26.

12. Darío, *Prosas profanas y otros poemas*, 151–52.

13. Ibid., 154.

14. Fray Luis, *Poesías*, 67–69.

15. The collective sense of "A Francisco Salinas," as well as the generic profile of this Luisinian ode, is discussed in greater detail in Daniel Murphy, "'Oda a Francisco Salinas,' Fray Luis de León's Celestial Air," *Bulletin of Hispanic Studies* 74 (1997): 159–78.

16. The philosophical basis for Fray Luis's ascendant pattern and for the Pythagorean system employed in the ode is thoroughly discussed by Dámaso Alonso in *Poesía española*, 170–88. Alonso interprets the ode as an account of the poet's spiritual trajectory, precisely as a kind of frustrated circle in which the Fray Luis returns, still yearning for Mystic ecstasy, to earth, the point from which he began.

17. The inset referred to occupies stanzas 13 and 14 of "Vida retirada," *Poesías*, 63–64. Here, the wind-swept and endangered ship of fools acts as a counter example to the simplicity of country life, where gentle breezes make the mind forget the clatter of the court. In "Descanso después de la tempestad," the shipwreck allegory is a most visible textual feature, but it is not used as agilely as in "Vida retirada" or in "A Francisco Salinas."

18. A non-Aleixandrean example of the serpent-under-the-rose metaphor may be seen in the Góngora sonnet, "La dulce boca que a gustar convida." Góngora advises lovers to be wary of the sweet mouth that offers a taste of its pearl-distilled nectar because, he warns, under rosy lips lurks venomous love like a serpent hidden among flowers. *Poemas de Góngora*, 88. Aleixandre incorporates the libidinous serpent into several poems, including "Cobra" *(La destrucción o el amor)*, "Sierpe de amor," and "Como serpiente" *(Historia del corazón)*. José Angel Valente analyzes the symbolic function of this poetic creature in Aleixandre, connecting it with dream and myth. "El poder de la serpiente," *Las palabras de la tribu* (Madrid: Siglo XXI de España, 1971), 170–84.

The mouth/rose analogy, with the accompanying thorn-beneath-the-rose expansion is most likely behind the title, *Espadas como labios*, the book immediately preceding *La destrucción o el amor*. The titular conversion involves two lyric operations, both common in Aleixandre's surrealist period. The first is syntactic inversion, whereby the usual tenor (lips) and vehicle (roses) order is reversed. Even without further elaboration, the resulting "roses like lips" metaphor is most arresting. In addition to this defamiliarization, the rosaceous and buccal thorn is hyperbolically expanded into swords. The net impact is that the traditional amatory metaphor is radically refigured, and now powerfully advertises the annihilating power of love. I am not the first to ponder the mysteries of the title of *Espadas como labios*. Dario Puccini, for instance, proposes that the title is derived from the popular saying, "tener una lengua como una espada" [to have a tongue like a sword]. According to Puccini, the title encapsulates Aleixandre's conception of poetry as a sort of weapon wielded by the poet in a poetic campaign for life and love. *La palabra poética de Vicente Aleixandre* (Barcelona: Ariel, 1979), 57.

19. One may find an intertextual relative of the stunning rose figuration of "Soy el destino" in "Paradiso" of Dante's *Divine Comedy*. In the final cantos, Dante's vision of Paradise is that of a gyrating celestial rose, a sonorous and effulgent sphere whose center, occupied by Divine Love, is encircled by layers of petals, themselves inhabited by the generations of the redeemed. I thank H. L. Boudreau for alerting me to this connection.

20. Aleixandre's poetization of Fray Luis is not limited to *La destrucción o el amor*. The amorous destiny cluster composed of the Luisinian symbols functions as a most productive hypogram throughout subsequent books. In fact, the functioning of the cluster effects a sort of poetic causality in Aleixandre's poetic world. Where there is light, there more than likely will be sea, circle, or music, often in variant forms and hybridized with other figures. In the opening stanzas of "El poeta," the liminal poem of *Sombra del paraíso*, Aleixandre describes his poetry as a selvatic song in which "de repente una gota fresquísima de rocío/ brilla sobre una rosa" (*OC* 483) [suddenly the coolest bead of dew shines on a rose].

21. Fray Luis, *Poesías*, 88.

22. In *La destrucción o el amor,* the circular antithesis of the Luisinian sphere is the moon, an orb of Romantic origin. An emblem of absent or ideal love, the moon often acts to figure the superego. The point of departure of several poems is the contemplation of this atmospheric circle: "Corazón en suspenso," "Corazón negro," "Eterno secreto," and "La luna es una ausencia."

23. The iconographic character of the title, *La destrucción o el amor,* is reinforced in the 1935 Signo edition by the publisher's logo. A happy visual coincidence, the logo is a "rosa de los vientos," a round compass, and is centered just below Aleixandre's "o"-embroidered title. A reproduction of the original title page may be found in *La destrucción,* 113.

CHAPTER 7: ANSIA PERPETUA

1. Despite this citational clarity, I am aware of only a few instances in which the direct relation between Aleixandre and Bécquer has been pointed out. In a footnote, Vicente Granados observes that "Ven, ven tú" directly quotes Rima 11. Although Granados does not pursue the relation between poems, he affirms that "Bécquer's influence on Aleixandre is not limited to a few details, but is much deeper" (*La poesía de Vicente Aleixandre* [Madrid: Cupa, 1977], 256). A second example comes from the anthology of poetry annotated for classroom use by Adrián García Montoro and Sergio A. Gigol. In the "Ejercicio" accompanying "Ven, ven tú," students are asked to compare Aleixandre's poem to Bécquer's Rima 11 (*En torno al poema: De Bécquer a Miguel Hernández* [New York: Harcourt, Brace and World, 1969], 141). The most extensive and revealing study of the Aleixandre-Bécquer relation is José Luis Cano's "La fusión con la naturaleza en Bécquer y Aleixandre," *Revista de Filología Española* 52 (1969): 227–31. Cano not only cites extra-poetic instances in which Aleixandre articulated his affinity with Bécquer—"En la vida del poeta: el amor y la poesía," "Gustavo Adolfo Bécquer, en dos tiempos," and a letter to Carlos Bousoño—but also asserts that the "yo soy" formula in Aleixandre is an explicit link to Bécquer. Among other examples, Cano cites "Memoria," "Nacimiento último," and "Acaba" *(Espadas como labios),* and "Soy el destino," "Nube feliz," and "El frío" *(La destrucción o el amor).* While Cano observes that both poets are moved by the same yearning for fusion with nature, he notes that while, "in Aleixandre that powerful urge is at times a pleasurable and joyful eagerness, in Bécquer it is usually a desire for annihilation, for withdrawal from the pain that the amorous wound leaves like a scar" (Ibid., 647).

Unlike the particular Aleixandre-Bécquer connection, the poet's general affinity with Romanticism has been frequently noted. One of the first critics to comment on this relationship is Dámaso Alonso, who emphatically insists that the Aleixandre of *La destrucción o el amor,* "Is, of course (we had already glimpsed this in *Espadas como labios),* a Romantic poet." *Poetas españoles contemporáneos* (Madrid: Gredos, 1952), 278.

2. Bécquer, *Rimas, Leyendas y Narraciones,* 8.

3. Ibid., 6.

4. In the Spanish tradition, perhaps the most celebrated elegy is Jorge Manrique's "Coplas por la muerte de su padre." While memorializing the exemplariness of his father's life, Manrique brings to bear in his elegiac meditation the all-encompassing themes of the transitory nature of worldly existence and the eternity of the life

to come. This move toward transcendence, which is so integral to the elegy and ode, is an outstanding thematic feature of *La destrucción o el amor.*

5. For Ricardo Gullón, "Canción a una muchacha muerta"—like "En el fondo del pozo" *(Espadas como labios)*—is based on "the conception of the world-beyond-death." This poem, he adds, "shows the buried girl lying in wait for life, listening to the rhythm of nature (and perhaps taking part in it), sensitive to the beauty of the world, in a permanently frustrated vigil." "Itinerario poético de Vicente Aleixandre," *Papeles de Son Armadans* 11, no. 32–33 (1958): 207, 218. Alejandro Amusco sets out to demonstrate the rational character of "Canción a una muchacha muerta" and interprets the titular "canción" as the song of Nature. The critic adds that this poem exemplifies that, "In Aleixandre, death is a 'glorious' form of life. For that very reason, when a being becomes part of Nature, the latter, moved by an elemental joy, 'sings' the blissful union into which flows everything that dies." "Lectura de un poema de Aleixandre," *Cuadernos Hispanoamericanos* 313 (July 1976): 174. Amusco, who closely studies the meter of "Canción a una muchacha muerta," notes that the verses are predominantly alexandrines.

6. The amorous "tempus fugit" theme is repeated in variations throughout *La destrucción o el amor.* Among the many examples is "Nube feliz" wherein the id, in the guise of a passing cloud, inveighs the sleeping "tú" to awake. The nebulous id reminds the addressee that the opportunity for love must be seized: "escapo con el viento, . . . / como el agua feliz que desciende cantando" (*La destrucción* 214) [I fly away on the wind, like the happy water that sings as it descends].

7. Bécquer, *Rimas, Leyendas y Narraciones,* 3.

8. Quoted from "En la vida del poeta: El amor y la poesía," the speech given by Aleixandre on the occasion of his investiture into the Real Academia de la Lengua in 1949. To illustrate Bécquer's frustrated quest for amorous destiny, Aleixandre cites Rima 11. *OC* 2:414.

9. In addition to their common point of departure—the contemplation of the night sky—the connection between Rima 8 and "Noche serena" is reinforced in several ways. Among them, Bécquer's close paraphrase of the liminal verses of the ode and even the form of his stanzas, which at a glance look like Fray Luis's "liras." In Bécquer's reply to the Augustinian, the elder poet's stable and defined firmament becomes an enigma hidden in the golden mists of twilight. Enshrouded in a "gasa de polvo / dorado e inquieto" [gauze of restless, golden dust], Bécquer's firmament intimates that mortal death, rather than eternal bliss in divine love, awaits the poet. *Rimas, Leyendas y Narraciones,* 7.

10. Carlos Bousoño analyzes Rima 1 in view of "símbolos," which he defines as "words or phrases that produce in us emotions that come not from what the poet says, from the symbolizer, but from unconscious associations that that symbolizer unleashes in the reader's sensibility." Thus, Bousoño asserts that it is possible to feel, without being able to rationalize on first reading, the symbols of Rima 1. The critic succinctly voices the questions raised by those symbols: "what is that 'himno' that the poet apparently knows?; why does he qualify it as 'gigante' and as 'extraño'?; why does it announce 'en la noche del alma una aurora'?" "La actualidad de Bécquer," *Boletín de la Real Academia Española* 67, no. 240 (January–April 1987): 31.

11. This powerful and far-flung image, in particular its ever-metamorphosing nature, finds a surrealist counterpart in García Lorca's "Llanto por Ignacio Sánchez Mejías." In the subsection, "La sangre derramada," the dead bullfighter's blood is likewise troped in a mixed aqueous-acoustic metaphor. That blood is like a "long, dark, sad tongue" that sings as it flows to the Guadalquivir river (*Obras completas,*

2 vols. [Madrid: Aguilar, 1980], 1:555). The majestic breadth of Lorca's poem, as well as its masterly blend of surreal and inherited poetic diction, makes it a capital example of the fusion of traditional and avant-garde art in modern Spanish literature. Aleixandre's "Soy el destino" is another such example of this kind of masterly fusion.

12. Darío, *Prosas profanas y otros poemas*, 97.

13. Ibid., 100.

14. Bécquer, *Rimas, Leyendas y Narraciones*, 26.

15. A most moving example of Aleixandre's stance toward Bécquer is "Paisaje" (*La destrucción o el amor*), a pastoral elegy in which Aleixandre's memorialization of Bécquer is perhaps more easily detected than in "Canción a una muchacha muerta." The tragic precursor is invoked via a series of lyric and affective epithets that encapsulate the artistic and human qualities that spur Aleixandre's sustained reaction to him. The series includes "voz" [voice], "ternura humana"[human tenderness], "signo" [sign], "trueno rumoroso que rueda" [rumbling thunder that rolls], "espuma fugitiva" [fleeting foam], "nube" [cloud], "corazón" [heart], "pájaro" [bird], and "dedo que escribe" [finger that writes] (*La destrucción* 146–47). Although Aleixandre makes the most direct and sustained response to Bécquer in *La destrucción o el amor*, his feelings for the earlier poet are nonetheless long-lived, as may be seen in the elegiac "El escuchador (Gustavo Adolfo Bécquer)" (*Retratos con nombre*), written some thirty years after *La destrucción o el amor*.

CONCLUSION

1. García Lorca, *Obras completas*, 1:519.

Bibliography

Abad Nebot, Francisco. "El mito como saber y como forma literaria." *Cuadernos Hispanoamericanos* 352–54 (1979): 297–314.

Abrams, M. H., ed. *English Romantic Poets.* Oxford: Oxford University Press, 1975.

Alberti, Rafael. *Sobre los ángeles. Yo era un tonto y lo que he visto me ha hecho dos tontos.* Edited by C. B. Morris. Madrid: Cátedra, 1992.

Aleixandre, Vicente. *Poesía superrealista.* Barcelona: Barral Editoriales, 1971.

———. *Obras completas.* 2 vols. Madrid: Aguilar, 1978.

———. *Espadas como labios. La destrucción o el amor.* Edited by José Luis Cano. Madrid: Castalia, 1986.

Alonso, Dámaso. "La poesía de Vicente Aleixandre." In *Ensayos sobre poesía española.* Madrid: *Revista de Occidente,* 1944, 351–93.

———. *Poetas españoles contemporáneos.* Madrid: Gredos, 1952.

———. *Poesía española: Ensayo de métodos y límites estilísticos.* 5th edition. Madrid: Gredos, 1981.

Amusco, Alejandro. "Lectura de un poema de Aleixandre." *Cuadernos Hispanoamericanos* 313 (July 1976): 167–79.

Antokoletz, María Adela. "Apuntes para un estudio del amor exultante en el poema 'Triunfo del amor.'" *Cuadernos Hispanoamericanos* 352–54 (1979): 496–98.

Arbeleche, Jorge. "Una poética del amor." *Cuadernos Hispanoamericanos* 352–54. (1979): 244–61.

Auden, W. H. *The Collected Poetry of W. H. Auden.* New York: Random House, 1945.

Balakian, Anna. *Literary Origins of Surrealism: A New Mysticism in French Poetry.* New York: New York University Press, 1965.

———. "Metaphor and Metamorphosis in André Breton's Poetics." *French Studies* 19, no. 1 (1965): 34–41.

———. "Dada-Surrealism: Fundamental Differences." In *From Surrealism to the Absurd.* Edited by Wolodymyr T. Zyal, 13–30. Lubbock: Texas Tech Press, 1970.

———. *André Breton: Magus of Surrealism.* New York: Oxford University Press, 1971.

———. *Surrealism: The Road to the Absolute.* London: Unwin Books, 1972.

———. "Latin American Poets and the Surrealist Heritage." In *Surrealismo/surrealismos latinoamericano y español.* Edited by Peter G. Earle and Ricardo Gullón, 11–19. Philadelphia: University of Pennsylvania Press, 1977.

Beaujour, Michel. "Text without a Theory, Theory without a Text." In *French Poetry from Dada to Tel Quel.* Edited by Mary Ann Caws, 285–92. Detroit: Wayne State Press, 1974.

Bécquer, Gustavo Adolfo. *Rimas, Leyendas y Narraciones.* México: Editorial Porrúa, 1981.

245

Berroa, Rei. "Presencia y sentido de la fauna en Aleixandre." *Cuadernos Hispanoamericanos* 352–54 (1979): 434–50.

Bloom, Harold. *The Anxiety of Influence: A Theory of Poetry.* New York: Oxford University Press, 1973.

———. *A Map of Misreading.* New York: Oxford University Press, 1975.

———. *Agon: Towards a Theory of Revisionism.* New York: Oxford University Press, 1982.

Bodini, Vittorio. *Los poetas surrealistas españoles.* Translated by Carlos Manzano. Barcelona: Tusquets, 1963.

Boudreau, Harold L. "Memes: Intertextuality's Minimal Replicators." In *Intertextual Pursuits: Literary Mediations in Modern Spanish Narrative.* Edited by Jeanne Brownlow and John Kronik, 239–61. Lewisburg, Pennsylvania: Bucknell University Press, 1998.

Bourne, Louis M. "The Spiritualization of Matter in the Poetry of Vicente Aleixandre." *Revista de Letras* 22 (June 1974): 166–89.

———. Introduction. *The Crackling Sun: Selected Poems of Vicente Aleixandre.* Madrid: Sociedad General Española de Librería, 1981.

Bousoño, Carlos. *La poesía de Vicente Aleixandre: Imagen, estilo y mundo poético.* Madrid: Insula, 1950.

———. *Teoría de la expresión poética.* 5th edition. Madrid: Gredos, 1970.

———. "The Greatness of Aleixandre's Poetry." Translated by Louis M. Bourne. *Revista de Letras* 22 (June 1974): 190–99.

———. *Superrealismo poético y simbolización.* Madrid: Gredos, 1977.

———. "La actualidad de Bécquer." *Boletín de la Real Academia Española* 67, no. 240 (January–April 1987): 29–36.

Breton, André. *Manifeste du surréalisme. Poisson soluble.* Paris: Kra, 1929.

———. *Manifestoes of Surrealism.* Translated by Richard Seaver and Helen R. Lane. Ann Arbor: University of Michigan Press, 1990.

Brihuega, Jaime, ed. *Manifiestos, proclamas, panfletos y textos doctrinales: Las vanguardias artísticas en España. 1910–1931.* Madrid: Cátedra, 1982.

Cabrera, Vicente. *Tres poetas a la luz de la metáfora: Salinas, Aleixandre y Guillén.* Madrid: Gredos, 1975.

———, and Harriet Boyer, eds. *Critical Views on Vicente Aleixandre's Poetry.* Lincoln, Nebraska: Society of Spanish and Spanish-American Studies, 1979.

Campanella, Hortensia. "El tema de la fraternidad en *Historia del corazón.*" *Cuadernos Hispanoamericanos* 352–54 (1979): 451–56.

Campos, Rene A. "El apóstrofe lírico en la poesía de Vicente Aleixandre." *Journal of Contemporary Spanish Studies: Twentieth Century* 7, no. 1 (Spring 1979): 23–32.

Cano, José Luis. "Tres poetas frente al misterio." *Cuadernos Americanos* 108, no. 1 (1960): 227–31.

———. "La fusión con la naturaleza en Bécquer y Aleixandre." *Revista de Filología Española* 52 (1969): 641–49.

———. "La poesía de Vicente Aleixandre." In *La poesía de la Generación de 1927.* Madrid: Guardarrama, 1970, 126–88.

———. *Vicente Aleixandre: El escritor y la crítica.* Madrid: Taurus, 1977.

———, ed. *Los cuadernos de Velintonia.* Barcelona: Seix Barral, 1986.

———. Introduction. *Espadas como labios. La destrucción o el amor,* by Vicente Aleixandre. Madrid: Aguilar, 1986.

Carnero, Guillermo. "'Conocer' y 'saber' en *Poemas de la consumación y Diálogos del conocimiento.*" *Cuadernos Hispanoamericanos* 276 (June 1973): 571–79.

Caws, Mary Ann. *The Poetry of Dada and Surrealism: Aragon, Breton, Tzara, Eluard and Desnos.* Princeton: Princeton University Press, 1970.

Cernuda, Luis. *La realidad y el deseo.* México: Fondo de Cultura Económica, 1964.

———. *Crítica, ensayos, evocaciones.* Barcelona: Seix Barral, 1970.

Charry Lara, Fernando. *Cuatro poetas del siglo veinte: Aleixandre, Rilke, Machado, Valéry.* Bogotá: Universidad Nacional, 1947.

Cohn, Dorrit. *Transparent Minds: Narrative Modes for Presenting Consciousness in Fiction.* Princeton: Princeton University Press, 1978.

Colinas, Antonio. *Conocer a Vicente Aleixandre y su obra.* Barcelona: Dopesa, 1977.

———. *Aleixandre.* Barcelona: Editorial Barcanova, 1982.

Comincioli, Jacques. "Surrealismo existencial en Vicente Aleixandre." *Revista de Letras* 22 (junio 1974): 200–209.

Corbalán, Pedro. *Poesía surrealista en España.* Madrid: Ediciones del Centro, 1974.

Coronado, Carolina. *Poesías.* Edited by Noël Valis. Madrid: Castalia, 1991.

Correa, Gustavo. "Conciencia poética y clarividencia." *Cuadernos Hispanoamericanos* 352–54 (1979): 41–74.

———. "Los títulos de los libros de poesía de Vicente Aleixandre." In *Vicente Aleixandre: A Critical Appraisal.* Edited by Santiago Daydí-Tolson, 86–93. Ypsilanti: Bilingual Press, 1981.

Cruz, San Juan de la. *Obras escogidas.* Edited by Ignacio B. Anzoátegui. Madrid: Espasa-Calpe, 1974.

Culler, Jonathan. *Structuralist Poetics: Structuralism, Linguistics, and the Study of Literature.* Ithaca: Cornell University Press, 1975.

———. "Apostrophe." In *The Pursuit of Signs: Semiotics, Literature, Deconstruction.* Ithaca: Cornell University Press, 1981, 135–54.

———. *Framing the Sign: Criticism and Its Institutions.* Norman: University of Oklahoma Press, 1988.

Curran, Stuart. *Poetic Form and British Romanticism.* Oxford: Oxford University Press, 1986.

Dante Alighiere. *La divina commedia.* Milan: Hoepli University, 1911.

Darío, Rubén. *Cantos de vida y esperanza.* Madrid: Espasa-Calpe, 1967.

———. *Azul. . . .* Madrid: Espasa-Calpe, S.A., 1968.

———. *Prosas profanas y otros poemas.* Edited by Ignacio M. Zuleta. Madrid: Editorial Castalia, S.A., 1987.

Dawkins, Richard. "Memes: The New Replicators." In *The Selfish Gene.* Oxford: Oxford University Press, 1978, 203–15.

Daydí-Tolson, Santiago. "Vicente Aleixandre: A New Voice of Tradition." In *Vicente Aleixandre: A Critical Appraisal.* Edited by Santiago Daydí-Tolson, 1–34. Ipsilanti: Bilingual Press, 1981.

Debicki, Andrew P. "The Reader's Experience in Vicente Aleixandre's *Historia del corazón.*" *The American Hispanist* 4:30–31 (1978): 12–16.

Díaz-Plaja, Fernando, ed. *Antología del romanticismo español.* Madrid: *Revista de Occidente,* 1959.

Dufour, Gérard. "A propos du Surrealisme de *La destrucción o el amor." Revista de Letras* 22 (junio 1974): 242–46.

Durán, Manuel. *El superrealismo en la poesía española contemporánea.* México: Universidad Nacional Autónoma, Facultad de Filosofía y Letras, 1950.

Earle, Peter G., and Germán Gullón, eds. *Surrealismo/surrealismos. Latinoamérica y España.* Philadelphia: Univeristy of Pennsylvania, 1977.

Espejo-Saavedra, Ramón. "Conocimiento de Rubén Darío." *Tropos* 22, no. 1 (Spring 1996): 51–62.

Fernández Carvajal, Rodrigo. "El tiempo en la poesía de Vicente Aleixandre." *Corcel* 5–6 (1944): 41–43.

Ferrán, Jaime. "Vicente Aleixandre o el conocimiento total." *Cuadernos Hispanoamericanos* 352–54 (1979): 157–66.

Ferreres, Rafael. "Los sonetos retratos." *Cuadernos Hispanoamericanos* 352–54 (1979): 474–81.

Forrest-Thomson, Veronica. *Poetic Artifice.* New York: St. Martin's Press, 1978.

Fowler, Alastair. *Kinds of Literature.* Cambridge, Mass.: Harvard University Press, 1982.

Freud, Sigmund. *The Basic Writings of Sigmund Freud.* Translated by A. A. Brill. New York: Randon House, 1938.

———. *The Life and Work of Sigmund Freud.* Vol. 3. Translated by Ernest Jones. New York: Basic Books, 1957.

Friedrich, Hugo. *Estructura de la lírica moderna.* Translated by Joan Petit. Barcelona: Seix Barral, 1974.

Galilea, Hernán. *La poesía superrealista de Vicente Aleixandre.* Santiago, Chile: Editorial Universitaria, 1972.

Gaos, Vicente. "Fray Luis de León, 'fuente' de Aleixandre." In *Temas y problemas de literature española.* Madrid: Guadarrama, 1959, 341–59.

Garcia, Céline. "L'espace scénique dans l'oeuvre de Vicente Aleixandre." *Iris* (1989): 73–103.

García Lorca, Federico. *Obras completas.* 2 vols. Madrid: Aguilar, 1980.

García Montoro, Adrián, and Sergio A. Rigol. *En torno al poema: De Bécquer a Hernández.* New York: Harcourt, Brace and World, 1969.

Garrison, David. "Rhetorical Strategy in the Surrealist Poetry of Vicente Aleixandre." *The University of Denver Quarterly* 15, no. 3 (1980): 21–26.

Gauthier, Michel. "Vicente Aleixandre, Narcisse écartelé." *Les Langues Néo-Latines* 176 (March–April 1966): 84–104.

Geist, Anthony Leo. *La poética de la Generación del 27 y las revistas literarias: De la vanguardia al compromiso (1918–1936).* Madrid: Guadarrama, 1980.

———. "'Esas fronteras deshechas': Sexuality, Textuality, and Ideology in Vicente Aleixandre's *Espadas como labios."* In *The Surrealist Adventure in Spain.* Edited by C. Brian Morris, 181–90. Ottowa: Dovehouse Editions, 1991.

Genette, Gérard. *Narrative Discourse: An Essay in Method.* Translated by Jane E. Lewin. Ithaca: Cornell University Press, 1980.

Góngora, Luis de. *Poems of Góngora.* Edited by R. O. Jones. Cambridge: Cambridge University Press, 1966.

González, Angel. Prologue. *El grupo poético de 1927.* Madrid: Taurus, 1986.

González Muela, Joaquín and Juan Manuel Rozas. *La generación poética de 1927.* Madrid: Editorial Alcalá, 1974.

Graf, E. C. "May I Have This Dance?: Unveiling Vicente Aleixandre's 'El vals.'" *Romanic Review* 85 (March 1994): 313–26.

Granados, Vicente. *La poesía de Vicente Aleixandre.* Madrid: Cupa, 1977.

———. "Olvidar es morir (Análisis de 'El enterrado')." *Cuadernos Hispanoamericanos* 352–54 (1979): 515–33.

Gratton, Johnnie. "Poetics of the Surrealist Image." *Romanic Review* 69, no. 1–2 (Jan. 1978): 103–14.

Gullón, Ricardo. "Itinerario poético de Vicente Aleixandre." *Papeles de Son Armadans* 11, no. 32–33 (1958): 195–234.

Harter, Hugh A. "El concepto del amar en *La destrucción o el amor* de Vicente Aleixandre." *Hispanófila* 32 (1968): 23–32.

Harvey, Sally. "Pastoral in *Sombra del paraíso.*" *Bulletin of Hispanic Studies* 68, no. 2 (1986): 125–36.

Hedges, Inez. "Surrealist Metaphor: Frame Theory and Componential Analysis." *Poetics Today* 4 no. 2 (1983): 275–95.

Hernstein Smith, Barbara. *Poetic Closure: A Study of How Poems End.* Chicago: University of Chicago Press, 1968.

Hughes, Robert. *The Shock of the New.* New York: Knopf, 1981.

Ilie, Paul. *The Surrealist Mode in Spanish Literature.* Ann Arbor: University of Michigan Press, 1968.

———. "The Term 'Surrealism' and its Philological Imperative." *Romanic Review* 69, no. 1–2 (January 1978): 90–102.

Jiménez, José Olivio. "Una aventura hacia el conocimiento." *Cuadernos Hispanoamericanos* 352–54 (1979): 11–40.

Jiménez, Juan Ramón. *Libros de poesía.* Madrid: Aguilar, 1957.

Jiménez Fajardo, Salvador. *Vicente Aleixandre.* Madrid: Júcar, 1981.

Keats, John. *The Complete Poetical Works and Letters of John Keats.* Edited by Horace E. Scudder. Cambridge, Mass.: The Riverside Press, 1899.

Krieger, Murray. *Ekphrasis.* Baltimore: The Johns Hopkins University Press, 1992.

Lakoff, George and Mark Turner. *More than Cool Reason: A Field Guide to Poetic Metaphor.* Chicago: University of Chicago Press, 1989.

Lapesa, Rafael. "La evolución poética de Vicente Aleixandre." In *Homenaje a José Manuel Blecua,* 307–23. Madrid: Gredos, 1983.

León, Fray Luis de. *Poesías.* Edited by Francisco Garrote. Salamanca: Almar, 1978.

Lovejoy, Arthur O. "On the Discrimination of Romanticism." In *English Romantic Poets.* 2d ed. Edited by M. H. Abrams, 3–24. New York: Oxford University Press, 1968.

Luis, Leopoldo de. *Vida y obra de Vicente Aleixandre.* Madrid: Espasa-Calpe, 1978.

———. "Función moral de la poesía (Una página inédita)." *Cuadernos Hispanoamericanos* 352–54 (1979): 113–22.

Machado, Antonio. *Poesías completas.* Madrid: Espasa-Calpe, 1982.

Man, Paul de. "Hypogram and Inscription: Michael Riffaterre's Poetics of Reading." *Diacritics* 11, no. 4 (Winter 81): 17–35.

————. *The Resistance to Theory.* Minneapolis: University of Minnesota Press, 1986.

Mandlove, Nancy B. "Ultraísmo and Tradition: Two Sonnets of Gerardo Diego." In *At Home and Beyond.* Edited by Salvador Jiménez Fajardo and John Wilcox, 69–76. Lincoln, Neb.: Society of Spanish and Spanish-American Studies, 1983.

Manrique, Jorge. *Poesía completa.* Edited by Vicente Beltrán. Barcelona: Planeta, 1988.

Mantero, Manuel. *La poesía del yo al nosotros.* Madrid: Guadarrama, 1972.

————. "La vida como relámpago de Bécquer en la poesía española de posguerra (Aleixandre, Hidalgo, Otero, García Nieto)." In *Studies in Eighteenth-Century Spanish Literature and Romanticism in Honor of John Clarkson Dowling.* Edited by Douglas Barnette and Linda Jane Barnette, 177–86. Newark, Del.: Juan de la Cuesta, 1985.

Mathews, J. H. *The Imagery of Surrealism.* Syracuse: Syracuse University Press, 1977.

Mayhew, Jonathan. "'Límites y espejo': Linguistic Self-Consciousness in the Poetry of Vicente Aleixandre." *Modern Language Notes* 105:2 (March 1990): 303–15.

Monegal, Antonio. "La 'poesía nueva' de 1929: Entre el álgebra de las metáforas y la revolución surrealista." *Anales de la Literatura Española Contemporánea* 16 (1991): 55–72.

Morelli, Gabrieli. *Linguaggio poetico del primo Aleixandre.* Milan: Ciralpino-Goliardica, 1972.

————. "La presencia del cuerpo humano en *Pasión de la tierra.*" Translated by Antonio Colinas. *Revista de Letras* 22 (junio 1974): 225–34.

Morgan, Thaïs. "The Space of Intertextuality." In *Intertextuality and Contemporary American Fiction.* Edited by Patrick O'Donnell and Robert Con Davis, 239–79. Baltimore: The Johns Hopkins University Press, 1989.

Morris, C. B. *Surrealism and Spain: 1920–1936.* Cambridge, England: Cambridge University Press, 1971.

Murphy, Daniel. "'Oda a Francisco Salinas,' Fray Luis de León's Celestial Air." *Bulletin of Hispanic Studies* 74 (1997): 159–78.

Nadeau, Maurice. *The History of Surrealism.* New York: Macmillan, 1965.

Neruda, Pablo. *Odas elementales.* 2d ed. Buenos Aires: Editorial Losada, 1967.

Nora Eugenio. "Aleixandre, renovador." *Corcel* 5–6 (1944): 95–96.

————. "Forma poética y cosmovisión en la poesía de Vicente Aleixandre." *Cuadernos Hispanoamericanos* 7 (enero de 1949): 115–21.

Novo Villaverde, Yolanda. *Vicente Aleixandre: Poeta surrealista.* Santiago, Spain: Unversidad de Santiago, 1980.

O'Donnell, Patrick and Robert Con Davis, eds. *Intextuality and Contemporary American Fiction.* Baltimore: Johns Hopkins University Press, 1989.

Onís, Carlos Marcial de. *El surrealismo y cuatro poetas de la Generación del 27.* Madrid: Porrúa, 1974.

Ortega y Gasset, José. *La deshumanización del arte y otros ensayos de estética.* Madrid: Espasa-Calpe, 1987.

Paraíso, Isabel. *El verso libre hispánico.* Madrid: Gredos, 1985.

Parisier Plottel, Jeanine and Hanna Charney, eds. *Intertextuality: New Perspectives in Criticism.* 2 vols. New York: New York Literary Forum, 1978.

Parker, Alexander A. *La filosofía del amor en la literatura española, 1480–1680.* Translated by Javier Franco. Madrid: Cátedra, 1986.

Pedemonte, Hugo Emilio. "La metáfora mítica." *Cuadernos Hispanoamericanos* 352–54 (1979): 315–24.

Pérez Firmat, Gustavo. "Apuntes para un modelo de la intertextualidad." *Romanic Review* 69, no. 1–2 (1978): 1–14.

Personneaux, Lucie. *Vicente Aleixandre ou une poésie du suspens: Recherches sur le réel et l'imaginaire.* Montpellier: Université Paul Valéry, 1980.

————. "El surrealismo en España; espejismos y escamoteo." In *Actas del VII Congreso Internacional de Hispanistas,* 447–54. Madrid: Istmo, 1986.

Poust, Alice. "Phenomenological Hermeneutics and Vicente Aleixandre's Self-Reading." *Revista de Estudios Hispánicos* 26, no. 3 (October 1992): 327–43.

————. "Vicente Aleixandre in the Crossfire: Classicism vs. Romanticism." *Hispania* 81, no. 2 (May 1998): 287–98.

Puccini, Dario. *La palabra poética de Vicente Aleixandre.* Barcelona: Ariel, 1979.

Quevedo, Francisco de. *Poesía varia.* Edited by James O. Crosby. Madrid: Cátedra, 1982.

Read, Herbert, ed. *Surrealism.* London: Faber and Faber, 1924.

Riffaterre, Michael. "The Self-sufficient Text." *Diacritics* 3, no. 3 (Fall 1973): 39–45.

————. "Semantic Incompatibilities in Automatic Writing." In *About French Poetry from Dada to Tel Quel.* Edited by Mary Ann Caws, 223–41. Detroit: Wayne State Press, 1974.

————. "The Referential Fallacy." *Columbia Review* 57 (1978): 21–35.

————. "Syllepsis." *Critical Inquiry* 6 (Summer 1980): 625–38.

————. *Text Production.* Translated by Terese Lyons. New York: Columbia University Press, 1983.

————. "Intertextual Representation: On Mimesis as Interpretive Discourse." *Critical Inquiry* 11 (1984): 141–62.

————. *Semiotics of Poetry.* Bloomington: Indiana University Press, 1984.

————. "Prosopopeia." *Yale French Studies* 69 (1985): 107–23.

————. "The Intertextual Unconscious." *Critical Inquiry* 13 (1987): 371–85.

Rivas, duque de [Angel de Saavedra]. *Don Alvaro o la fuerza del sino.* Edited by Alberto Sánchez. Madrid: Cátedra, 1982.

Rodgers, Timothy J. "Reader Cognition and the Dialectical Imagery in the Poetry of Gerardo Diego." In *At Home and Beyond.* Edited by Salvador Fajardo Jiménez and John Wilcox, 77–86. Lincoln, Neb.: Society of Spanish and Spanish-American Studies, 1983.

Rodríguez, Claudio. "Algunos comentarios sobre el tema de la fauna en la poesía de Vicente Aleixandre." *Insula* 33 (enero-febrero 1978): 374–75.

Rodríquez Padrón, Jorge. "Lectura en tres tiempos." *Cuadernos Hispanoamericanos* 352–54 (1979): 137–56.

Rodríguez Spiteri, Carlos. *Vicente Aleixandre.* Málaga: Librería El Guadalhorce, 1980.

Salinas, Pedro. "Vicente Aleixandre entre la destrucción y el amor." In *Literatura del Siglo XX.* Madrid: Alianza, 1970, 204–12.

————. *Poesías completas.* Barcelona: Barral Editories, 1971.

Schärer-Nussberger, Maya. *Vicente Aleixandre: Création et Poétique.* Boudry-Neuchatel, Switzerland: Baconniere, 1992.

Schwartz, Kessel. *Vicente Aleixandre.* New York: Twayne, 1970.

———. "The Isakower Phenomenon and the Dream Screen in the Early Poetry of Vicente Aleixandre." *Revista de Letras* 22 (junio 1974): 210–18.

Shelley, Percy Bysshe. *The Complete Poetical Works of Percy Bysshe Shelley.* Edited by Thomas Hutchinson. New York: Oxford University Press, 1956.

Shuster, George N. *The English Ode from Milton to Keats.* New York: Columbia University Press, 1940.

Silver, Philip. *"Et In Arcadio Ego": A Study of the Poetry of Luis Cernuda.* London: Tamesis, 1965.

———. "Vicente Aleixandre o el máximo grado de lo anteico." In *La casa de Anteo.* Madrid: Taurus, 1985, 148–56.

Stern, Alfred. "El surrealismo en la literatura." *Revista de Letras* 21 (junio 1974): 39–54.

Terry, Arthur. Introduction and notes. *An Anthology of Spanish Poetry: 1500–1580.* Vol. 1. London: Pergamon Press, 1965.

Valdés, Jorge H. "La aportación de Egloga, elegía, oda a la evolución poética de Luis Cernuda." In *At Home and Beyond.* Edited by Salvador Fajardo Jiménez and John Wilcox, 97–112. Lincoln, Neb.: Society of Spanish and Spanish-American Studies, 1983.

Valente José Angel. "El poder de la serpiente." In *Las palabras de la tribu.* Madrid: Siglo XXI de España, 1971, 170–84.

Valverde, José María. "De la disyunción a la negación en la poesía de Vicente Aleixandre (y de la sintaxis a la visión del mundo)." *Escorial* 32 (1945): 447–57.

Vega, Garcilaso de la. *Obras.* Edited by T. Navarro Tomás. Madrid: Espasa-Calpe, 1948.

Videla, Gloria. *El ultraísmo.* Madrid: Gredos, 1971.

Villena, Luis Antonio de. Preliminary study and notes. *Pasión de la tierra,* by Vicente Aleixandre. Madrid: Narcea, 1977.

Vivanco, Luis Felipe. "El espesor del mundo en la poesía de Vicente Aleixandre." In *Introducción a la poesía española contemporánea.* Madrid: Guadarrama, 1957, 339–87.

Volek, Emil. *Cuatro claves para la modernidad: Análisis semiótico de textos hispánicos.* Madrid: Gredos, 1984.

Waley, Pamela. "Love and Honour in the 'Novelas sentimentales' of Diego de San Pedro and Juan de Flores." *The Bulletin of Hispanic Studies* 43–44 (1966–67): 252–69.

Wimstatt, W. K. "The Structure of Romantic Nature Imagery." In *English Romantic Poets.* 2d ed. Edited by M. H. Abrams, 25–36. New York: Oxford University Press, 1968.

Woodman, Clarence E., ed. *Manual of Prayers.* New York: The Catholic Publication Society, 1888.

Wordsworth, William. *The Poetical Works of William Wordsworth,* vol. 4. Edited by E. de Selincourt and Helen Darbishire. Oxford: Oxford University Press, 1947.

Zardoya, Concha. *Poesía española contemporánea.* Madrid: Guadarrama, 1961.

———. "Vicente Aleixandre en 'La plaza pública.'" *Cuadernos Hispanoamericanos* 352–54 (1979): 470–73.

Index